WRITING ON THE WALL

WRITING ON THE WALL

Writing Education and Resistance to Isolationism

EDITED BY
DAVID S. MARTINS,
BROOKE R. SCHREIBER,
AND XIAOYE YOU

UTAH STATE UNIVERSITY PRESS
Logan

© 2023 by University Press of Colorado

Published by Utah State University Press
An imprint of University Press of Colorado
1624 Market Street, Suite 226
PMB 39883
Denver, Colorado 80202-1559

All rights reserved

 The University Press of Colorado is a proud member of the Association of University Presses.

The University Press of Colorado is a cooperative publishing enterprise supported, in part, by Adams State University, Colorado State University, Fort Lewis College, Metropolitan State University of Denver, University of Alaska Fairbanks, University of Colorado, University of Northern Colorado, University of Wyoming, Utah State University, and Western Colorado University.

ISBN: 978-1-64642-442-9 (hardcover)
ISBN: 978-1-64642-323-1 (paperback)
ISBN: 978-1-64642-324-8 (ebook)
https://doi.org/10.7330/9781646423248

Library of Congress Cataloging-in-Publication Data
Names: Martins, David S., editor. | Schreiber, Brooke R., 1981– editor. | You, Xiaoye, 1974– editor.
Title: Writing on the wall : writing education and resistance to isolationism / edited by David S. Martins, Brooke R. Schreiber, and Xiaoye You.
Description: Logan : Utah State University Press, [2022] | Includes bibliographical references and index.
Identifiers: LCCN 2022040103 (print) | LCCN 2022040104 (ebook) | ISBN 9781646424429 (hardcover) | ISBN 9781646423231 (paperback) | ISBN 9781646423248 (epub)
Subjects: LCSH: English language—Rhetoric—Study and teaching (Higher)—Social aspects. | English language—Rhetoric—Study and teaching (Higher)—Political aspects. | Isolationism—United States. | Multicultural education. | Transnationalism—Social aspects.
Classification: LCC PE1404 .W7289 2022 (print) | LCC PE1404 (ebook) | DDC 813/.6—dc23
LC record available at https://lccn.loc.gov/2022040103
LC ebook record available at https://lccn.loc.gov/2022040104

This publication was supported, in part, by the Rochester Institute of Technology, College of Liberal Arts Publication Cost Grant.

Cover photographs: border wall in Nogales, Sonora, Mexico, photo by Layli Maria Miron (*top*); writing by a detained immigrant on Angel Island, California, photo by Layli Maria Miron (*bottom left*); graffiti in Lisbon, Portugal, photo by Daniel Thiele/Unsplash.com (*center*); graffiti in Valparaiso, Chile, photo by Layli Maria Miron (*bottom center*); banners in Valparaiso, Chile (*bottom right*).

CONTENTS

Preface
    David S. Martins, Brooke R. Schreiber, Xiaoye You   vii

1. Writing Education across Borders, an Anti-isolationist Project
    David S. Martins   3

    PART I: NEGOTIATING LEGACIES: RACIST, COLONIAL, AND MATERIAL ANTECEDENTS

2. On the Semantic Borders of White Nationalism
    Keith Gilyard   19

3. Strangers in a Strange Land: "The Foreign Student" at US Universities after World War II
    Amy J. Wan   31

4. "To Supplant Ignorance Requires Instruction": Literacy as Transnational Racial Project in the Colonial Philippines
    Florianne Jimenez Perzan   49

5. Scaling Cosmopolitanism in the Age of Precarity
    Tony Scott   67

    PART II: RESISTING ETHNOLINGUISTIC STEREOTYPES: COMMUNITY-ENGAGED LITERACIES AND PEDAGOGIES

6. Writing to Mend Literate Fragmentation
    Rebecca Lorimer Leonard   89

7. Multilingualism beyond Walls: Undocumented Young Adults Subverting Writing Education
    Sara P. Alvarez   106

8. Public Pedagogy and Multimodal Learning on the US-Mexico Border
   Layli Maria Miron   129

   PART III: BUILDING TRANSNATIONAL CONNECTIONS: PARTNERSHIPS AND COSMOPOLITAN DISPOSITIONS

9. Combating Isolationism through COIL Virtual Exchange: Programmatic and Pedagogical Perspectives
   Olga Aksakalova and Tuli Chatterji   151

10. Fostering Cosmopolitanism: International Educational Partnerships in a Professional Communication Course
    Joleen Hanson   171

11. Smoothing the Path: Chinese-American Joint-Degree Programs as Resistance to Nationalism
    Brooke R. Schreiber and Brody Bluemel   193

    Afterword
    Kate Vieira   215

    Index   219
    About the Authors   229

PREFACE

David S. Martins, Brooke R. Schreiber, and Xiaoye You

It seems very strange that a conference devoted to addressing issues of teaching writing across borders would not have any international participants, but this was the case when the third conference on Writing Education across Borders (WEAB) was held in State College, Pennsylvania, United States, in fall 2019. Compared with the first and second iteration of this conference, the absence is even more noteworthy. When the first conference was held in State College in 2011, 20 percent of scholars came from Asia and Europe; at the second conference held in Guangzhou, China, in 2016, 10 percent came from North American and other Asian nations. The causes for the drop of the number of foreign scholars were primarily geopolitical: the "Muslim ban" made some foreign intellectuals wary about traveling to the United States, and the heightened political tensions between China and the United States discouraged Chinese scholars. The absence of foreign bodies in this space reminded us of the battle over US border walls, and the impact that battle was having on the bodies of people seeking to cross into the US. More importantly, this absence convinced us of the significance of teaching writing to resist walls.

The border walls are manifestations of a deep-seated isolationism in US history, one which profoundly affects higher education. However, the field of writing studies has not given sustained attention to this political ideology and its practice. At best, isolationism has been treated tangentially when the field discussed English monolingualism in the teaching of writing. As one of the reviewers of this collection rightly stated, "isolationism is arguably a paranoid expression of the monolingualism of American culture, which in turn is the stubborn legacy of white-supremacist British imperialism." Previous scholarship has revealed that monolingualism has been the vehicle of both isolationism and imperialism. Its presence can be seen in the colonial period (Kimball 2021), in the genocidal "education" of Indigenous peoples (Spack 2002; Webster 2010), in the xenophobic education of minoritized people and of immigrants (Dayton 2005), in ESL/EFL pedagogy developed during the nineteenth and twentieth centuries (You 2010), in the more contemporary emergence of English as an International Language (EIL) abroad and Defense Language Institute at home, and so on.

By focusing on isolationism, this collection highlights the historical connections among monolingualism, racism, and white nationalism, and introduces community- and classroom-based practices to resist isolationist thoughts and practices. Scholarship dealing with writing education across borders, also termed "transnational writing education," over the last decade has largely focused on theorizing and describing language practice in multilingual contexts, exploring the teaching of writing from a translingual perspective, and administering writing programs in neoliberal universities. This collection has drawn insights from ethnic studies to understand the colonial history of writing education within and outside the United States. Further, it showcases the opportunities writing educators have created in communities and classrooms where they have become leaders of border-crossers.

This collection of essays resulted from conversations that started at the third conference on Writing Education across Borders and continued during the summer of 2020, in the middle of the COVID-19 lockdowns. Therefore, this collection has addressed not only the building of border walls but also the additional traumas resulting from maintaining social distance. The contributors gathered online in the early days of the pandemic, where they discussed issues related to transnational writing education that the pandemic had heightened, resolved, or brought to light.

We want to thank the contributors, as well as those whose work was not included in this collection, for their participation in the conversations. The conference was made possible thanks to the generous sponsorship provided by the Department of English, the Migration Project, and the Center for Democratic Deliberation at Pennsylvania State University. Special thanks are due to Suresh Canagarajah, Cheryl Glenn, and Keith Gilyard for their expert guidance and support. Local representatives Ruiying Niu, Qirong Sun, Su Young Lee, and Layli Miron helped with the conference organization.

This collection would not be possible without the stewardship of Rachael Levay, editor-in-chief of the University Press of Colorado, Laura

Furney, assistant director and managing editor, and Daniel Pratt, production manager for Utah State University Press, and the constructive critique of the two anonymous reviewers. The RIT College of Liberal Arts, through its "Publication cost grant," contributed financial support for proofreading and indexing. Carolyn Elerding expertly edited each chapter. Thank you, all.

Finally, we would like to thank our families for their steadfast support over the years. As in everything, David thanks Jill, Will, and Eleanor, for giving him space to think new thoughts while still expecting coherent arguments, and is particularly appreciative for the opportunity to collaborate with such generous and compassionate coeditors. Brooke thanks her husband, Constantin Schreiber, and daughter, Maja, for listening, believing in her, and bringing her the joy that sustains academic work. Xiaoye wants to thank his wife, Hsiao-Hui Yang, and children, Joy Tianhuan You and Felix Tianle You, for their unfailing love and understanding.

REFERENCES

Dayton, Amy E. 2005. "Representations of Literacy: The Teaching of English and the Immigrant Experience in Early Twentieth-Century America." PhD diss., University of Arizona.

Kimball, Elizabeth. 2021. *Translingual Inheritance: Language Diversity in Early National Philadelphia*. Pittsburgh, PA: University of Pittsburgh Press.

Spack, Ruth. 2002. *America's Second Tongue: American Indian Education and the Ownership of English, 1860–1900*. Lincoln: University of Nebraska Press.

Webster, A. K. 2010. "'Still, She Didn't See What I Was Trying to Say': Toward a History of Framing Navajo English in Navajo Written Poetry." *World Englishes* 29 (1): 75–96.

You, Xiaoye. 2010. *Writing in the Devil's Tongue: A History of English Composition in China*. Carbondale: Southern Illinois University Press.

WRITING ON THE WALL

1
WRITING EDUCATION ACROSS BORDERS, AN ANTI-ISOLATIONIST PROJECT

David S. Martins

Around the globe, nationalist rhetorics and isolationist policies reemerged in early twenty-first-century mainstream politics. We see this in the European and US backlash against Syrian refugee migrants beginning in 2011, Viktor Orban's reelection as Hungary's prime minister in 2014, Narendra Modi's election as India's prime minister in May 2014, the UK Brexit referendum vote in June 2016, Donald Trump's election as the president of the United States in November 2016, and Jair Bolsonaro's election as Brazil's president in 2018. So-called populist politicians won elections throughout the world, and autocratic politicians consolidated power in China, Russia, and elsewhere. In the US, the 2016 presidential campaign rhetoric turned into administrative policies that resulted in, for example, bans on Muslims entering the US, family separations at the US-Mexico border, violent provocations by white supremacists, withdrawal from climate agreements, renegotiation or withdrawal from global trade agreements, and the extension of physical walls between the US and Mexico. The impact of such isolationist leaders and policies is also seen in higher education, as US-based transnational faculty and students have been caught up in immigration bans (Redden 2017), undocumented students have faced deportation (Plevin 2019), and future international student visas have been increasingly uncertain (Jung 2019). With each example, there are clear displays of xenophobia, cynicism, and distrust. The COVID-19 global pandemic added new fear, prompting the closing of borders, offices, restaurants and schools; sending workers and students online; and forcing millions of people to watch news reports of community members and loved ones suffering alone or in the care of health-care workers with their pictures pinned to their personal protective equipment. In the US, the murders of Ahmaud

Arbery, Breonna Taylor, and Tony McDade and the recorded murder of George Floyd in Minneapolis ignited these tensions and destroyed any false sense of unity across racial, class, or national differences. Even so, despite pandemic fears and in spite of significant military and police intimidation, demonstrators reflecting unity of purpose across racial differences put on protective masks to protest ongoing policy brutality of men, women, and children of color across the US and around the world.

How did we arrive at this moment in history? Journalists, historians, politicians, neighbors—all have theories. Of Donald Trump's election in the US, Matt Flegenheimer and Michael Barbaro (2016) of the *New York Times* posited "a decisive demonstration of power by a largely overlooked coalition of mostly blue-collar white and working-class voters who felt that the promise of the United States had slipped their grasp amid decades of globalization and multiculturalism" (para. 4). When people feel that their economic and social well-being is precarious, engagement with the broader world through globalization and multiculturalism becomes an easy scapegoat for voter distress, rather than offering benefit. In the US, Donald Trump's election signified that a part of the electorate, though not a majority, wanted "America First," or limits on US involvement abroad and a singular focus on national well-being.

Isolationism, as one way to describe such a singular focus, is typically a term used in relation to governmental foreign and economic policy. Discussions about isolationist policies usually reach a fever pitch around times of war and economic hardship. Recent examples in the US include the debate regarding intervention in Syria following the 2008 global recession, and the executive orders initiating a trade war with China in 2019. But an earlier example, again in the US, addressed whether or not the US should enter into World War II. High profile, celebrity spokespeople like Charles Lindbergh (1941a) made emphatic arguments against the US becoming involved in the war that was igniting in Europe: "I now oppose our entry into the war because I do not believe that our system of government in America can survive our participation or our way of life can survive our participation" (para. 9). The sense of vulnerability that Lindbergh expresses provides some clarity about the conditions that may lead to isolationist viewpoints and arguments. As a member of the "America First" Committee, Lindbergh's speeches resonate with the contemporary rhetoric of Trump's "Make America Great Again," where specific populations were identified as posing threats to the social, economic, and political success of "America." For Lindbergh it was "the British, the Jewish, and the Roosevelt Administration" (1941b); for Trump it was Mexicans, Muslims, and the media. The racism behind both men's positions cannot be denied. In his "Make America Great Again" rhetoric, Trump boasted about the superiority of white people and, by extension, the white United States. Given the history of racism in the US, those racist overtones should not be surprising.

Immigration and naturalization law in the US, for example, is wrapped up in the legacies of colonialism, slavery, and exceptionalism. In 1790, although the "founding fathers" had envisioned open immigration, the US Congress limited naturalization to "free white persons" only, a racial qualification that remained legitimated by law well into the mid-twentieth century (Smith 2002, para. 9). Until 1882, with the Chinese Exclusion Act, immigration law and nationality law were not explicitly coordinated and rarely referenced one another. Though primarily an immigration law, the Chinese Exclusion Act did include a section on citizenship, which stipulated that "hereafter no State court or court of the United States shall admit Chinese to citizenship; and all laws in conflict with this act are hereby repealed" (Smith 2002, para. 10). Conflating race and nationality is only one of the ways that this law and others like it have highlighted isolationist viewpoints and encouraged race-based interpretations of who belongs in the US and who can become a citizen.

In 1941, the rhetorical wall that the isolationist "America First" argument was meant to build crumbled when the Japanese bombed Pearl Harbor on December 7. Just two months later, however, new, more material fences were built when President Roosevelt signed an executive order on February 19, 1942, that allowed the Secretary of War to use the military to detain and forcibly relocate all persons of Japanese descent to inland internment camps. Thus, while isolationist policies may be vulnerable to events, isolationist ideologies are adaptable. Since the election of Joseph Biden as president of the US, for example, the "Big Lie" that the 2020 election was stolen, perpetuated by 147 US representatives such as Marjorie Taylor Greene and Kevin McCarthy and 8 US senators including Josh Hawley and Ted Cruz, has created new opportunities for isolationist beliefs to be codified in state laws. According to the Brennan Center for Justice (2021), as of April 1, 2021, state legislators had introduced "389 bills with restrictive provisions in 48 states." Largely understood as a response to effective voter registration and turnout efforts in communities of color, especially in Georgia where Democratic senate candidates Rev. Raphael Warnock and Jon Ossoff defeated two Republican incumbents and created an evenly split US Senate, these voter restrictions, denounced as "Jim Crow 2.0" (Ward 2021), are erecting unabashedly racist limits to voting in an attempt to further isolate people of color within their own country.

As history demonstrates, isolationism can be associated with xenophobia and nativism, reluctance to engage in other people's civic and communal affairs, cynicism and pessimism, and a strong sense of independence and self-reliance. Isolationism is historically associated with racism as well, reinforcing racial divisions and working to marginalize people of color within the US. Supported by such beliefs, isolationism creates rhetorical, psychological, and material walls, fences, and borders. Ideologies that tend to counter isolationism, however, are galvanized by idealism and desire for connection and growth, and they share a sense of interdependence and responsibility for others. Adopting such beliefs positions writing teachers to break down walls, dismantle fences, and reach across borders. Writing teachers commonly endeavor to create meaningful relationships with and to support the diverse students in our classes and colleagues who teach alongside us. Writing teachers dedicated to justice seek opportunities to cultivate cosmopolitan, antiracist attitudes that may substantively counter xenophobic ideologies and enable students, international and domestic, to work across national and political borders as well as social, racial, economic, religious, and linguistic ones.

In his work *On Tyranny: Twenty Lessons from the Twentieth Century*, Timothy Snyder (2017) offers instructive lessons learned from democratic opposition to fascism, Nazism, and communism:

> In fact, the precedent set by the Founders demands that we examine history to understand the deep sources of tyranny, and to consider the proper responses to it. Americans today are no wiser than the Europeans who saw democracy yield to fascism, Nazism, or communism in the twentieth century. Our one advantage is that we might learn from their experience. Now is a good time to do so. (13)

Snyder explains that both fascism in Europe and communism in the Soviet Union were responses to globalization in the twentieth century (12). The current responses to globalization come at a time when two anti-historical ways of considering the past threaten to produce complacency and cynicism: what Synder terms a "*politics of inevitability*, the sense that history could move only in one direction: toward liberal democracy" (118), and a "politics of eternity, [in which] the seduction by a mythicized past prevents us from thinking about possible futures" (123). While Snyder never addresses the dark history of racism in the US, a significant omission in his pocket-sized book, he advocates an appreciation of history that "allows us to see patterns and make judgments," to see "the structures within which we can seek freedom" (125). Referencing Polish poet Czesław Miłosz, Snyder encourages readers to "be responsible: not for everything, but for something" (125). Following such a view of history, this present collection offers chapters that identify patterns of interaction and create educational structures that foster both freedom and opportunities for us all to take responsibility for each other. The collection does not offer a singular ideological resistance to isolationism. Instead, the collection joins distinct threads of research, pedagogy, and ideological commitments together to resist isolationist tendencies in our work and create multiple paths for building connections across borders.

Based upon presentations given at the 2019 Writing Education across Borders Conference, the chapters in this collection reveal how writing teachers—often working directly with students who are immigrants, undocumented, first-generation, international, or students of color—strive to embody ideas that counter isolationism. Each chapter shares a profound hope in the promise of literacy education broadly conceived. They describe a range of literacies, pedagogies, relationships, and the practices that emphasize diversity. The essays foreground commitments to, for example, cosmopolitanism (You 2016, 2018); translingual education (Canagarajah 2013; Horner and Tetreault 2017; Bloom-Pojar 2018; Frost, Kiernan, and Malley 2020); critical engagement with transnationalism in curricula, teaching, research, and administration (Payne and Desser 2012; Thaiss et al. 2012; Martins 2015; Rose and Weiser 2018); and the design of globally networked learning environments (Starke-Meyerring and Wilson 2008; Tcherepashenets 2015; Rice and St. Amant 2018). Focused in this way, much of the work presented here highlights national and linguistic borders. But this collection is not focused solely on the experiences of students from other countries studying in the US. Chapters addressing community-based literacy initiatives as well as racist and colonial legacies, for example, also exemplify projects that are both antiracist (Inoue and Poe 2012; Inoue 2015; Hammond 2019; Perryman-Clark and Craig 2019) and decolonial (Ruiz 2016; Ruiz and Sánchez 2016; Garcia and Baca 2019). All of these approaches, as reflected in writing scholarship and pedagogy, have helped to bring connection, appreciation, recognition, and accountability into the lives of the people in our diverse communities, and provide a creative and enriching outlet to express and give meaning to experience. Although some essays focus more directly on the experience of isolationism than others, each acknowledges the challenges isolationist tendencies pose to the kind of literacy education proposed.

The title of the collection, *Writing on the Wall*, serves as a productive metaphor for the creative, direct action we believe writing education can engender. For us, *Writing on the Wall* is a way to build on studies of how people, ideas, and texts can cross borders, by calling attention to the borders themselves and then repurposing those walls—or finding ways around and past them. We take inspiration from such works of protest as those that have turned a national border fence into a site of play in the form of a transnational teeter-totter, a site of art in the form of murals depicting the very people shut out by the walls (see Kroth 2019), or a site of protest in the form of posters that adorn fences meant to limit dissent (see Cascone 2020). Our title invokes the many ways people have (literally) inscribed their refusal to accept the isolationist worldview that separates people from one another. We hope that the chapters in this collection strengthen existing efforts and inspire new programs, pedagogies, and research agendas that resist racism, linguistic discrimination, and isolationism. Simply stated, "writing on the wall" implies a reimagining of border spaces as sites of identity expression, belonging, relationship, and resistance.

Thus, with a desire to resist isolationism, and inspired by reimagined possibilities, this collection connects transnational writing education with the fight for racial justice in the US and around the world, a connection that prior studies have not always made or made explicitly. In this way, the collection extends existing research that grapples with the following questions: Historically, how have racist and colonial rhetorics impacted writing education? What impact do translingual, transnational, and cosmopolitan language ideologies have on student learning and student writing? What role can international educational partnerships play in pushing back against isolationist ideologies? To provide a range of responses to these questions, the collection is organized around three themes: (1) "Negotiating Legacies: Racist, Colonial, and Material Antecedents," (2) "Resisting Ethnolinguistic Stereotypes: Community-Engaged Literacies and Pedagogies," and (3) "Building Transnational Connections: Partnerships and Cosmopolitan Dispositions."

NEGOTIATING LEGACIES: RACIST, COLONIAL, AND MATERIAL ANTECEDENTS

The four chapters in part 1 highlight the racist, colonial, and material antecedents to contemporary assumptions and beliefs that continue to shape writing administration, curriculum, pedagogy, and assessment as well as student admissions. Each chapter shares a commitment to prioritizing issues of power—racial, colonial, economic, and political—in the analysis and consideration of writing and writing education.

Although writing scholars have often discussed the impact of race, we have not always explicitly named "white nationalism" and "white supremacy" as the underlying problem. Recent work, however, has been more direct. For example, James Rushing Daniel (2017) advocates for "a precariate approach" to writing pedagogy that would enable students to analyze critically emergent voices expressing "the white nationalism of the alt-right" (81). Laurie Gries and Phil Baratta (2019) develop a "racial politics of circulation" that deepens our understanding of "how whiteness, nationhood, and doxa intertwine to reinforce and amplify white supremacy" (417). Asao B. Inoue (2019), during his 2019 CCCC Chair's Address, challenged writing teachers to address "the conditions of white language supremacy, not just in our society and schools, but in our own minds, in our habits of mind, in our dispositions, our bodies, our habitus, in the discursive, bodily, and performative ways we use and judge language in the writing curriculum" (357). For his contribution to this collection, "On the Semantic Borders of White Nationalism," Keith Gilyard travels to Wakanda and beyond to trace the harmful implications of how white nationalism has been defined inaccurately as a parallel to Black nationalism. Gilyard draws lessons from critical race theory on how to create a pedagogy that enables students to do the rhetorical work of dismantling racist argumentation. The chapter, then, is Gilyard's effort to *historicize, contextualize, and problematize* the term "white nationalism" for writing teachers and students.

Teachers and researchers who have worked to historicize, contextualize, and problematize racial, colonial, and material legacies in writing education have long focused on the effects of specific pedagogical strategies on particular student populations in localized contexts. Research has focused on the role of ESL education in relation to national education projects (Ray 2013; Ullman 2010), the impact of writing education on students in colonial education systems (Jeyaraj 2009; Legg 2014) and refugee communities (MacDonald 2017), and also forms of resistance, made visible in writing, to ethnic incarceration (Shimabukuro 2011) and apartheid (Trabold 2006). For her chapter, "Strangers in a Strange Land: 'The Foreign Student' at US Universities after World War II," Amy J. Wan traces the rhetorical construction of "foreign" students in the post-WWII project of higher education, which aimed to cultivate American citizenship. Wan examines the logic behind recent public messages communicated to international students, by connecting contemporary examples of racialized judgments around language to a longer history of international students and anti-Asian sentiment in the United States. Wan argues that knowing how the mid-century expansion of higher education established many of the current administrative structures, as well as assumptions and beliefs about international students, will help writing administrators and teachers to dismantle the ideologies that continue to dominate institutional understanding of international students.

In "'To Supplant Ignorance Requires Instruction': Literacy as Transnational Racial Project in the Colonial Philippines," Florianne Jimenez Perzan addresses literacy education in English as a part of the American colonial occupation of the Philippines at the turn of the twentieth century, examining how a student writer negotiates discourses of American colonial policy, Filipino elite ideology, and the myth of literacy as social equalizer. Adding a transnational perspective to scholarship on race and literacy education, this chapter argues that literacy education in English is implicated in the formation of racial and class hierarchies.

In the final chapter of the first section, "Scaling Cosmopolitanism in the Age of Precarity," Tony Scott calls for a more robust scholarly focus on the professional mechanisms that sustain connections between scholarship and practices, and which have been steadily eroded by austerity economics as well. Scott presents a case study drawn from an ongoing qualitative research project on the uptake of research in rhetoric, composition and writing studies by faculty hired to teach first-year writing, and considers how cosmopolitanism, as part of an emergent disciplinary discourse, can be scaled across institutional sites and courses.

RESISTING ETHNOLINGUISTIC STEREOTYPES: COMMUNITY-ENGAGED LITERACIES AND PEDAGOGIES

Throughout this second section, the authors present research conducted beyond the classroom in order to understand the impact of literate activities in the lives of people negotiating multiple borders, languages, and identities. Questions concerning "translingualism" and "translanguaging" have been increasingly a focus of disciplinary interest. What started as a project to identify and then challenge monolingual ideologies of language prevalent in US education (see Horner and Trimbur 2002; Spack 2002; NeCamp 2014; Wan 2014), translingualism (see García 2009; Blackledge and Creese 2010; Horner et al. 2011; Canagarajah 2013; Jordan 2015; Frost, Kiernan, and Malley 2020) has taken on a transformational role in writing research, scholarship, and teaching. In the tradition of Deborah Brandt's literacy research (2001, 2014), the first two chapters in this section draw from interviews and analysis of artifacts from writers, to understand more clearly the experience and practice of literacy in people's lives.

Through her chapter "Writing to Mend Literate Fragmentation," Rebecca Lorimer Leonard describes a partnership between an undergraduate literacy studies course and a community language school, showing how the writing undertaken during that collaboration enhances multilingual writers' understandings of their own critical dispositions regarding cross-border language and literacy practices in nationalist times. Tracing students' writing about language and identity during the project, Lorimer Leonard details the ways that its nationalist political moment shapes writers' literate awareness, helping them reconnect with the literate selves that political or educational contexts seek to actively separate them from.

Analyzing the multilingual literacy practices of an undocumented South Korean student's advocacy work and poetry, Sara P. Alvarez demonstrates how multilingual writers explicitly contest monolithic views of language, nation, belonging, and academic writing, in "Multilingualism beyond Walls: Undocumented Young Adults Subverting Writing Education." Alvarez argues that the practices of racialized immigrant writers cultivate a multilingual language ideology that is more conscientious of how citizenship and immigration impacts people's literacies, highlighting the imperative to (re)think the role of writing as a set of practices shaping and impacting life—beyond the classroom setting—while also posing implications for writing education.

Scholars have also focused on the literacy practices located at the US-Mexico border (see also Meyers 2014; Ruecker 2015; Thatcher, Montoya, and Medina-Lopez 2015). In the third essay, Layli Maria Miron offers examples of public pedagogy and embodied learning in "Public Pedagogy and Multimodal Learning on the US-Mexico Border." Analyzing examples of multimodal public pedagogy (a comic book and an immersion program) used by an organization dedicated to the rights of undocumented immigrants, Miron highlights three strategies that encourage US audiences to rethink undocumented immigration: humanizing, accompanying, and complicating. These strategies, Miron demonstrates, can promote embodied learning and lead to new practices for college writing classrooms.

BUILDING TRANSNATIONAL CONNECTIONS: PARTNERSHIPS AND COSMOPOLITAN DISPOSITIONS

In the final section of the collection, Olga Aksakalova and Tuli Chatterji, Joleen Hanson, and Brooke Schreiber and Brody Bluemel provide strategies for designing, implementing, and responding to transnational partnerships that aim to cultivate a cosmopolitan disposition in students. As with other scholarship on globally networked learning (see, for example, Starke-Meyerring and Wilson 2008; Charry Roje and Martins 2015; Moore and Simon 2015; O'Brien and Alfanso 2015; Starke-Meyerring 2015), the three chapters of this section discuss the challenges to international collaboration, along with evidence of the high impact such partnerships can have on student learning.

In "Combating Isolationism through COIL Virtual Exchange: Programmatic and Pedagogical Perspectives," Olga Aksakalova and Tuli Chatterji examine how collaborative online international learning (COIL) and other transborder pedagogies can work to critique isolationist national policies beyond the US. The authors first detail the development of COIL at LaGuardia Community College as a subset of a movement towards global learning, considering practical strategies for professional development and logistical and technological support for faculty implementing COIL. They then provide a case study of a collaborative project in a world literatures course addressing the partition of India, illuminating the potential of this transnational pedagogy to counter xenophobic perceptions and rigid portrayals of state borders as firm entities separating homogenous, inherently antagonistic groups of people.

In her chapter "Fostering Cosmopolitanism: International Educational Partnerships in a Professional Communication Course," Joleen Hanson explores her experiences conducting transnational pedagogical activities as a member of a worldwide network of college instructors called the Trans-Atlantic and Pacific Project (TAPP), working with a local student population of primarily white, monolingual students with limited international experience. Hanson illustrates how, as they negotiate communication norms with international partners, students become aware of language conventions and choices and show evidence of developing cosmopolitan perspectives, ultimately coming to see themselves as simultaneously members of both local and global communities.

Based on surveys of administrators and institutional websites, "Smoothing the Path: Chinese-American Joint-Degree Programs as Resistance to Nationalism" considers what role Chinese-American joint-degree programs are playing in keeping educational pathways open for Chinese students in the US, and how that role can be bolstered by improving the practical implementation of the programs at the administrative level. Brooke R. Schreiber and Brody Bluemel argue that these programs can serve as a potential point of resistance to nationalist and anti-Chinese policies within the US, and to anti-American sentiment in China—but only if implemented with an eye towards ethics as well as thoughtful attention to a range of issues such as assessment, placement, curriculum equivalency, and cultural difference.

REFERENCES

Blackledge, Adrian, and Angela Creese. 2010. *Multilingualism: A Critical Perspective*. New York: Continuum.
Bloom-Pojar, Rachel. 2018. *Translanguaging outside the Academy: Negotiating Rhetoric and Healthcare in the Spanish Caribbean*. Writing and Rhetoric. Urbana, IL: Conference on College Composition and Communication and National Council of Teachers of English.
Brandt, Deborah. 2001. *Literacy in American Lives*. Cambridge, UK: Cambridge University Press.
Brandt, Deborah. 2014. *The Rise of Literacy: Redefining Mass Literacy*. Cambridge, UK: Cambridge University Press.
Brennan Center for Justice. 2021. "State Voting Bills Tracker 2021." Accessed May 7, 2021. https://www.brennancenter.org/our-work/research-reports/state-voting-bills-tracker-2021.
Canagarajah, Suresh. 2013. *Literacy as Translingual Practice: Between Communities and Classrooms*. New York: Routledge.
Cascone, Sarah. 2020. "Donald Trump Put a Fence around the White House to Keep Demonstrators Away. It Is Now Completely Covered in Protest Art." *ArtNet News*, June 9, 2020. Accessed May 10, 2020. https://news.artnet.com/art-world/activists-cover-white-house-fence-george-floyd-protest-art-1882389.
Charry Roje, Rebecca, and David S. Martins. 2015. "Between 'Pleasantville' and 'My Way or the Highway': Promoting Productive Discussion of Social Justice in a Globally Linked Learning Environment." In *Globalizing On-line: Telecollaboration, Internationalization, and Social Justice*, edited by Nataly Tcherepashenets, 151–73. Bern: Peter Lang.
Daniel, James Rushing. 2017. "Freshman Composition as a Precariat Enterprise." *College English* 80 (1): 63–85.
Flegenheimer, Matt, and Michael Barbaro. 2016. "Donald Trump Is Elected President in Stunning Repudiation of the Establishment." *New York Times*, November 9, 2016. Accessed June 3, 2020. https://www.nytimes.com/2016/11/09/us/politics/hillary-clinton-donald-trump-president.html.
Frost, Alanna, Julia Kiernan, and Suzanne Blum Malley. 2020. *Translingual Dispositions: Globalized Approaches to the Teaching of Writing*. Ft. Collins, CO: WAC Clearinghouse; Longmont: University Press of Colorado.
García, Ofelia. 2009. "Education, Multilingualism and Translanguaging in the 21st Century." In *Social Justice through Multilingual Education*, edited by Tove Skutnabb-Kangas et al., 143–58. Buffalo, NY: Multilingual Matters.
García, Romeo, and Damián Baca. 2019. *Rhetorics Elsewhere and Otherwise: Contested Modernities, Decolonial Visions*. Urbana, IL: National Council of Teachers of English.
Gries, Laurie, and Phil Baratta. 2019. "The Racial Politics of Circulation: Trumpicons and White Supremacist *Doxai*." *Rhetoric Review* 38 (4): 417–31.
Hall, Jonathan. 2014. "Multilinguality Is the Mainstream." In *Reworking English in Rhetoric and Composition: Global Interrogations, Local Interventions*, edited by Bruce Horner and Karen Kopelson, 31–48. Carbondale: Southern Illinois University Press.
Hammond, James W. 2019. "Making Our Invisible Racial Agendas Visible: Race Talk in Assessing Writing, 1994–2018." *Assessing Writing* 42 (1): 1–19.
Horner, Bruce, Min-Zhan Lu, Jacqueline Jones Royster, and John Trimbur. 2011. "Language Difference in Writing: Toward a Transligual Approach." *College English* 73 (3): 303–87.
Horner, Bruce, and Laura Tetreault. 2017. "Translation as (Global) Writing." *Composition Studies* 44 (1): 13–30.
Horner, Bruce, and John Trimbur. 2002. "English Only and U.S. College Composition." *College Composition and Communication* 53 (4): 269–300.

Inoue, Asao. 2015. *Antiracist Writing Assessment Ecologies: Teaching and Assessing Writing for a Socially Just Future*. Ft. Collins, CO: WAC Clearinghouse.

Inoue, Asao. 2019. "How Do We Language So People Stop Killing Each Other, or What Do We Do about White Language Supremacy?" *College Composition and Communication*, 71 (2): 352–69.

Inoue, Asao, and Mya Poe. 2012. *Race and Writing Assessment*. New York: Peter Lang.

Jeyaraj, Joseph. 2009. "Modernity and Empire: A Modest Analysis of Early Colonial Writing Practices." *College Composition and Commuinication* 60 (3): 468–92.

Jordan, Jay. 2015. "Material Translingual Ecologies." *College English* 77 (4): 364–82.

Jung, Carrie. 2019. "Advocates and Universities Say Student Visas Have Become 'Increasingly Uncertain.'" WBUR. Accessed May 10, 2020. https://www.wbur.org/edify/2019/08/27/college-student-visas.

Kroth, Maya. 2019. "10 Border Walls That Artists Have Turned into Powerful Protests." *Afar*, July 30, 2019. Accessed May 10, 2020. https://www.afar.com/magazine/10-border-walls-that-artists-have-turned-into-powerful-protests.

Legg, Emily. 2014. "Daughters of the Seminaries: Re-landscaping History through the Composition Courses at the Cherokee National Female Seminary." *College Composition and Communication* 66 (1): 67–90.

Lindbergh, Charles. 1941a. "Election Promises Should Be Kept. We Lack Leadership That Places America First." May 23, 1941. Accessed May 10, 2020. http://www.charleslindbergh.com/pdf/speech7.pdf accessed June 10, 2020.

Lindbergh, Charles. 1941b. September 11, 1941. Des Moines Speech. Accessed May 10, 2020. http://www.charleslindbergh.com/americanfirst/speech.asp Accessed June 10, 2020.

MacDonald, Michael T. 2017. "'My Little English': A Case Study of Decolonial Perspectives on Discourse in an After-School Program for Refugee Youth." *Community Literacy Journal* 11 (2): 16–29.

Martins, David S. 2015. *Transnational Writing Program Administration*. Logan: Utah State University Press.

Meyers, Susan V. 2014. *Del Otro Lado: Literacy and Migration across the U.S.-Mexico Border*. Carbondale: Southern Illinois University Press.

Moore, Alexandra Schultheis, and Sunka Simon. 2015. *Globally Networked Teaching in the Humanities: Theories and Practices*. Research in Higher Education. New York: Routledge.

NeCamp, Samantha. 2014. *Adult Literacy and American Identity: The Moonlight Schools and Americanization Programs*. Carbondale: Southern Illinois University Press.

O'Brien, Alyssa, and Christine Alfanso. 2015. "Tech Travels: Connecting Writing Classes across Continents." In *Transnational Writing Program Administration*, edited by David S. Martins, 48–71. Logan: Utah State University Press.

Payne, Darin, and Daphne Desser. 2012. *Teaching Writing in Globalization: Remapping Disciplinary Work*. New York: Lexington Books.

Perryman-Clark, Staci M., and Collin Lamont Craig. 2019. *Black Perspectives in Writing Program Administration: From the Margins to the Center*. Urbana, IL: National Council of Teachers of English.

Plevin, Rebecca. 2019. "'I Want to Learn': Like DACA, the Future Is in Limbo for These Undocumented COD Students." *Palm Springs Desert Sun*, September 5, 2019. Accessed June 3, 2020. https://www.desertsun.com/story/news/2019/09/05/undocumented-students-attend-college-two-years-after-trump-tried-end-daca/2123109001/.

Ray, Brian. 2013. "ESL Droids: Teacher Training and the Americanization Movement, 1919–1924." *Composition Studies* 41 (2): 15.

Redden, Elizabeth. 2017. "Stranded and Stuck." *Inside Higher Ed.* January 30, 2017. Accessed May 10, 2020. https://www.insidehighered.com/news/2017/01/30/students-and-scholars-are-stranded-after-trump-bars-travel-nationals-7-countries.

Rice, Rich, and Kirk St. Amant. 2018. *Thinking Globally, Composing Locally: Rethinking Online Writing in the Age of the Global Internet.* Logan: Utah State University Press.
Rose, Shirley K., and Irwin Weiser. 2018. *The Internationalization of US Writing Programs.* Logan: Utah State University Press.
Ruecker, Todd. 2015. *Transiciones: Pathways of Latinas and Latinos Writing in High School and College.* Logan: Utah State University Press.
Ruiz, Iris D. 2016. *Reclaiming Composition for Chicanos/as and Other Ethnic Minorities: A Critical History and Pedagogy.* New York: Palgrave.
Ruiz, Iris D., and Raúl Sánchez. 2016. *Decolonizing Rhetoric and Composition Studies: New Latinx Keywords for Theory and Pedagogy.* New York: Springer.
Shimabukuro, Mira. 2011. "'Me Inwardly, before I Dared': Japanese Americans Writing-to-Gaman." *College English* 73 (6): 648–71.
Smith, Marian L. 2002. "Race, Nationality, and Reality: INS Administration Racial Provisions in U.S. Immigration and Nationality Law Since 1898." *Prologue Magazine* 34 (2). Accessed May 7, 2021. https://www.archives.gov/publications/prologue/2002/summer/immigration-law-1.html.
Snyder, Timothy. 2017. *On Tyranny: Twenty Lessons from the Twentieth Century.* New York: Tim Duggan Books.
Spack, Ruth. 2002. *America's Second Tongue: American Indian Education and the Ownership of English, 1860–1900.* Lincoln: University of Nebraska Press.
Starke-Meyerring, Doreen. 2015. "From 'Educating the Other' to Cross-Boundary Knowledge-Making: Globally Networked Learning Environments as Critical Sites of Writing Program Administration." In *Transnational Writing Program Administration,* edited by David S. Martins, 307–31. Logan: Utah State University Press.
Starke-Meyerring, Doreen, and Melanie Wilson. 2008. *Designing Globally Networked Learning Environments.* Rotterdam: Sense Publishers.
Tcherepashenets, Nataly. 2015. *Globalizing On-line: Telecollaboration, Internationalization, and Social Justice.* Bern: Peter Lang.
Thaiss, Chris, Gerd Bräuer, Paula Carlino, and Lisa Ganobcsik-Williams. 2012. *Writing Programs Worldwide: Profiles of Academic Writing in Many Places.* Anderson, SC: Parlor Press; Ft. Collins, CO: WAC Clearinghouse.
Thatcher, Barry, Omar Montoya, and Kelly Medina-Lopez. 2015. "Global Writing Theory and Application on the US-Mexico Border." In *Transnational Writing Program Administration,* edited David Martins, 163–202. Logan: Utah State University Press.
Trabold, Bryan. 2006. "'Hiding Our Snickers': 'Weekly Mail' Journalists' Indirect Resistance in Apartheid South Africa." *College English* 68 (4): 382–406.
Ullman, Char. 2010. "The Connections among Immigration, Nation Building and Adult Education English as a Second Language Instruction in the United States." *Adult Learning* 21 (1–2): 4–8.
Wan, Amy J. 2014. *Producing Good Citizens: Literacy Training in Anxious Times.* Pittsburgh, PA: University of Pittsburgh Press.
Ward, Jason Morgan. 2021. "Georgia's Voter Law Is Called 'Jim Crow 2.0' for a Reason." *The New York Times,* March 31, 2021. Accessed April 3, 2021. https://www.nytimes.com/2021/03/31/opinion/georgia-voting-law.html.
You, Xiaoye. 2016. *Cosmopolitan English and Transliteracy.* Carbondale: Southern Illinois University Press.
You, Xiaoye. 2018. *Transnational Writing Education: Theory, History, and Practice.* New York: Routledge.

PART I

Negotiating Legacies

Racist, Colonial, and Material Antecedents

2
ON THE SEMANTIC BORDERS OF WHITE NATIONALISM

Keith Gilyard

I recall being at a university function at which a well-known scholar had concluded a lecture about the virtues of democracy as a form of social organization. During the question-and-answer period, a quite self-assured and oppositional student reminded the audience that the United States was a republic. He then asked the guest speaker whether, given this fact of history, we should all be Republicans and not Democrats. It wasn't really a question; it was intended as an expression of one-upmanship. It was a polite imperative: We *should* all be Republicans is what he meant. I cannot do justice here to the collective response. But imagine a flurry of WTF? text messages. "He goes to *this* school?" The moment obviously was bizarre. Amid the gasps and murmurs, the guest speaker responded well enough, trying to make it clear that a commitment to small-*d* democracy does not require membership in, or allegiance to, the Democratic Party. Nor does republicanism as a social formation rely conceptually on the existence of the Republican Party. The republic preceded the Republican Party by sixty-five years. While that exchange ensued, I was thinking, among other things, that there is always work for semanticists to perform. Insufficient concepts and language slippage manifest continually and in many ways. Unfortunately, the results are often not so humorous as that university gathering, which was at least a bit comedic to me.

I remember that event as I consider how white nationalism has become paramount among the myriad signs and symbols that must be deciphered by consumers of American political discourse. Of course, this population includes numerous students in writing classes along with their instructors. It is, therefore, appropriate that we collectively clarify the term, to take best advantage of certain teachable moments to stimulate the most fruitful deliberations—spoken and written—rather than foster what we see too much of on media broadcasts, that is, verbal firefights generating much heat but little light. Part of the problem is that people, quite naturally, play word games, often by creating false equivalents. If Black pride or Black nationalism can be respectable political discourse, they wonder, why not white pride or white nationalism? But similar to how the phrase *people of color* is not an exact translation of *colored people* because of different connotations, *white nationalism* does not translate as the direct and benign opposite of *Black nationalism*. Connotations and social contexts are part and parcel of definition. $3 \times 4 = 2 \times 6$ is a correct mathematical proposition, but the equation is not a model for determining social-linguist meaning. To ignore this fact is to court the nightmare that George Orwell (1946) suggested in "Politics and the English Language": specious ideas leading to specious language that ensures additional specious ideas, and so on. It is the very definition, as Donald Lazere (2009) indicated, of a vicious circle. But Lazere also pointed out that "perhaps a starting point for American students and citizens to break the vicious circles they are caught in is to develop the critical vocabulary and rhetorical concepts enabling them to understand ideas like vicious circle" (10). This is some of the work before us.

Perhaps productive talk about white nationalism can unfold in a way represented by the guest lecturer. This involves exploring the term and its ramifications as well as examination of its semantic borders. For example, on the semantic border of white nationalism sit various rights and diversity arguments, as well as racial and ethnic constructions, along with ruminations about cosmopolitanism, permanent racism, and rhetorical education. This terrain must be negotiated well to promote progressive conversation about such matters as, say, ethnic diversity. But the situation is indeed more urgent than a simple ideal of improved communication. As Adam Serwer (2019) noted in *The Atlantic*, white nationalism is a serious ideological threat to American democracy and can only be thwarted through the political processes—read: rhetorical processes—of the American people.

Most people are probably familiar with the overarching white-nationalist narrative, but allow me to lock in a streamlined American version. The United States was constitutionally established as a structural ethnostate, a formation punctuated by a law restricting naturalization to free white persons (the United States Naturalization Law of March 26, 1790). Procedural democracy took root, but substantive democracy and the most robust citizenship ideals were stillborn. Settler colonialism, Manifest Destiny, and chattel enslavement along with their oppressive aftermaths became dominant features of the political landscape for decades upon decades. Of course, numerous activists have struggled to make America more fully human, to borrow an education phrase from Paulo Freire (1970). The nation, say post-1965, *maybe* obtained a multicultural soul to match its multicultural appearance. Some tolerance of racism, sexism, and homophobia was still exhibited, but articulated expressions about valuing diversity became normative. The idea of a white ethnostate was considered fringe—except among discontents who felt aligned with the concept for various reasons, sometimes simple xenophobia or the perception of diminished economic opportunities. That fringe idea has entered the mainstream once again. MAGAMITES[1] have populated numerous rallies, rationalizing right-wing extremism and helping to solidify the scapegoating of immigrants and ethnic minorities. *Why can't we maintain a white majority? Why can't we all just be Norwegian? Or at least some kind of full-blooded European?*

The ever-perceptive James Baldwin (1998) noted forty years ago that white-supremacist logic calls either for the exploitation or disappearance of Black people, and that the actions of white supremacists against other ethnic minorities are also linked in their minds to a troubling Black presence. As he remarked, "they are really cursing the nigger, and the nigger had better know it" (801). White nationalism is the contemporary verbal expression of the white ethnostate ideal. But demographic projections do not favor it. Nor do powerfully emergent anti-oppressive voices. To linger with Baldwin a moment longer as he describes intergenerational Black struggle: "The irreducible miracle is that we have sustained each other a very long time, and come a long, long way together. We have come to the end of a language and are about the business of forging a new one. For we have survived, children, the very last white country the world will ever see" (807). Baldwin held out hope for what critical ethnicity makes plain and invites—that is, the exposure of whiteness as unfair social privilege and the rejection, enacted by more than a few, of white identity and the attached privileges. Yet, white nationalists struggle to maintain white-nationalist power or, put another way, white political dominance.

Fittingly, journalist Andrew Marantz (2019) uses a Baldwin quote as an epigraph in his recent book, *Antisocial*, citing Baldwin's 1962 observation in "As Much Truth as One Can Bear" that we cannot fix anything morally unless we face it. Marantz is concerned with the negative aspects of social media, including the shift that it has enabled from the widespread vertical dissemination of information to widespread horizontal dissemination (3). To be sure, Marantz recognizes that the gatekeeping function of traditional media was problematic, but he realizes that bypassing the gatekeepers has not ensured transition to a more productive information ecosystem (50). Instead, the bright promise of social media as a tool to contest abusive power and promote social justice has devolved into sharp divisions inside a chaotic world where we must reckon with the effects of alt-right shitposters and edgelords (5).[2]

Obviously, I agree with those who see white nationalism as largely an expression of fascist impulses. It would be hard not to concur given that some trolls circulate in cyberspace calling themselves *fashy*. However, I think, maybe being overly optimistic, that *impulses* is the operative word here. I share a belief with critic Christopher Vials (2014) that America is too steeped in liberal democracy, and perhaps possesses too strong a left-liberal alliance, to bow down completely to ultra-right-wing authoritarianism. On the other hand, I also share his belief that we need to remain vigilant in tracking expressions of fascism in contemporary American discourse. While he envisions no American Reich on the horizon, no Blackshirts and Brownshirts goose-stepping in the streets, Vials warns that we should always be on guard against fascism's "functional equivalents," a term he borrows from political scientist Robert O. Paxton (2005). Vials feels that the ability to identify and evaluate these political signs is a crucial task. I am guessing that this is in line with all our teaching goals.

We certainly can identify fascism's functional equivalents at work in the presidency and ongoing campaigns of Donald Trump, and we have time-honored models for contextualizing and evaluating them. For example, we saw the former president repeating rhetorical moves that Kenneth Burke (1939) analyzed more than eighty years ago regarding Adolf Hitler's political ascent. *Common enemy, inborn dignity, scapegoating,* and *symbolic rebirth* are among the tropes that Burke analyzed. In Trump's pronouncements, the common enemy is the dark and migrating hordes supposedly threatening American civilization and that have, according to him, already led to significant decay. These hordes are contrasted to those who possess inborn dignity, those who are examples of the preferred archetype. These hordes are scapegoated and made the cause of all social ills, an argument made by use of selected worst-case scenarios. These hordes are described as a major obstacle to a symbolic rebirth. One can easily map these tropes onto cries for a border wall, ruminations about the good people among tiki-torchers, the display of racist stereotypes, and the expressed imperative to "make the country great again." These are fascist impulses. These are the pronouncements that also mark white-nationalist discourse in the United States.

A debate currently unfolds about whether Trump can accurately be labeled a white nationalist. I decline to referee that one. I'll just say that he definitely has some feathers like them, be walking like them, be in the water with them, and be quack-quacking like them. It reminds me of a scene from the recent film *BlacKKKlansman* (Lee 2018), in which a white police officer explains to a rather credulous African-American colleague that white supremacists sometimes tone down their vulgar racism because they have designs on elected office, including the highest in the land. The younger officer responds, "America would never elect somebody like David Duke president of the United States of America." His coworker replies, "Coming from a Black man that's pretty naïve. Why don't you wake up?"

The main point is not name-calling—or simply name-calling. The aim is to understand the political discourse of white nationalism to have specific antecedents, traces, and reverberations that can be, as my colleague Bernard Bell (2005) is fond of saying, historicized, contextualized, and problematized. This is proper work for any language classroom. The goal is not to push a political perspective but to uncover political perspective *per se* and demonstrate to students the importance of grappling with politics, as part of any liberal arts curriculum. To paraphrase Lazere, we have to keep students aware of the fact that while they might not be interested in politics, politics is interested in them (2009, 4).

As indicated, part of the work is explaining what white nationalism is *not*. It is not, to reiterate, the opposite of Black nationalism, which is a cluster of ideologies that recognizes the efficacy of organizing economically, culturally, or politically along lines of Black identity. As W. E. B. Du Bois ([1897] 2004) raised the question in "The Conservation of Races," "Does my black blood place upon me any more obligation to assert my nationality than German, or Irish, or Italian would?" (1093). Of course, I am sure that the good Dr. Du Bois also knew that such nationality could be pressed upon him, which is why he guarded his home with a shotgun during the 1906 race riot in Atlanta. At any rate, ideologies of Black nationalism have arisen *in response* to protracted encounters with white supremacism. In other words, an existential grasp of the long suffering of Black people under the weight of a prevailing white power structure has formed the basis for proposals such as migration to Africa, the creation of a Black nation-state in the US South, the establishment of control by African Americans of all institutions that operate in Black communities, the connection of African-American political aspirations to the worldwide community of Africans and African descendants, and the emphasis on Black cultural celebrations. For the formation of white nationalism to be a direct analogue to any form of Black nationalism, whites would have had to develop the position as a reaction to a Black-supremacist hegemony, something that has never unfolded in the United States. White nationalism does not stem from the exploitation of whites by Blacks. Therefore, given different origins and imperatives, along with numerous historical permutations, white nationalism and Black nationalism are hardly mirror discourses overall, though the narrowest articulations of both, namely racial separatism, have been in such alignment. That is why George Lincoln Rockwell could be hosted by Elijah Muhammad and, in turn, be a supporter.[3] However, a revolutionary Black nationalism—that is, an implied leftist politics—entails not the sentiments of binary thinkers but the vision of adequate measures of Black power and self-determination within a far more equitable multiethnic or pluralist national experiment. White nationalism, to the contrary, is the yearning for a firm, everlasting, white ethnostate. It wants no part of redistributive justice.

I am sure that proponents are clear about this among themselves, but they try all manner of arguments in attempts to make headway among the broader public. They feign innocence when they ask what is wrong with ethnic or racial groups wanting to stay among their own. I say, partly tongue in cheek, maybe nothing—and that they should have thought of that four or five hundred years ago before their conquests of Black, Brown, Yellow, and Red territories. They somewhat cleverly, reminiscent of Rockwell, monitor Black social developments for rhetorical linkages. They even embrace the movie *Black Panther*. Kevin Litman-Navarro (2018) has reported on the claim that King T'Challa, because he has been isolationist, antiglobalist, and in favor of racial homogeneity, espouses central tenets of which white nationalists approve. Among numerous social media entries in this vein, a meme circulated under the title "Black Panther is Alt-Right." It featured a checklist of nine alt-right platform points supposedly illustrated by the movie, namely that it is anti-immigration, isolationist, pro-wall, anti-diversity, ethnonationalist, anti-refugee, antidemocratic, and traditionalist and promotes strict trade restrictions,. Each box in front of the stated item is checked (see results of searching for #blackpantherisaltright). Of course, such commentators, while not totally off base, ignore the gestures toward a world community at the end of the movie, not to mention that they substitute reel power dynamics for the real power dynamics we see every day. The King of Wakanda is not in league with those who favor a white ethnostate in a land that was already diverse before the nation's formal founding. *Black Panther* is not logically the filmic flag of white nationalism. That dubious distinction perhaps still belongs to *The Birth of a Nation*.[4]

To emphasize, never should white nationalism be confused with any progressive or left-nationalist responses to white supremacism. Critical inspection of discourses that seek to enroll us lies at the heart of rhetorical education. It would be instructive for students to review *Black Panther* but also research the Black Panther Party for Self-Defense, the Brown Berets, and the Young Lords to examine the platforms of those groups relative to the aims of those who favor a white ethnostate. Calls for Third-World solidarity, anti-capitalist and anti-imperialist organizing, embraces of Chicanismo, and celebrations of the fact that the blood of four continents flows through most Puerto Rican bodies—I've been handed personal versions of all these narratives—all stem from a liberating desire not to dominate, oppress, or be isolationist but to improve society for all. Progressive and radical Asian American nationalism was part of this activity as well, in such groups as the Asian American Political Alliance, the Red Guard, and the I Wor Kuen (Ogbar 2001). This last group advocated for the end of the geographic boundaries of the United States. I don't suggest that the position will prevail but do suggest that the idea and the reasoning behind it—given the history of imperialism as well as immigration and emigration harassment—should be on the table for discussion if we are to understand the full range of perspectives about national borders.

Almost naturally, as we guide students through discussion of various nationalisms, we will want to pressure the very idea of nationalism itself, sort of in the mode of philosopher Kwame Anthony Appiah (2018) in his recent book, *The Lies that Bind*. Appiah argues that nations, at least modern nation-states, are constructions that are not based on essential, self-evident factors. There is no always-already status to be assigned to nations or potential citizens. For example, he is a native Londoner who has traced his maternal ancestry back to thirteenth-century England. But Appiah, whose father was from Ghana, is almost never referred to as an Englishman. He is more likely assigned the identity *Ghanaian* in the American imagination, though he has never been a citizen of Ghana. Appiah understandably is perplexed by the question of what constitutes any *national we*. Ancestry is not the answer. As he points out, any family shares common ancestry, but so does the entire human species. Where does one draw the national line? We all, as the ever-popular DNA kits reveal, belong to several ancestry groups. If you want to build states around nations, Appiah concludes, it involves more than rounding up people and constructing constitutions: "You're going to have to *make* a nation: you will take a population most of whom wish, for some reason, to live under a shared government, and then, after wrestling them from whatever states they currently live in, you will need to build in them the shared sentiments that will make it possible for them to be productive together" (77). This seems to be a formula for creating the American people, which is an ongoing experiment, one which may or may not work in the long term. Documents and creeds by themselves do not ensure productive nations. Neither do overly constricting prescriptions concerning patriotism.

One could examine the white-nationalist project this way: of the various options that the descendants of an array of European ethnics could have chosen as a marker of peoplehood in the New World, whiteness was pushed by economic elites because it allowed them to distribute the policing of subjugated populations to whites in general. *White* meant boss or supervisor or defender of the constructed white peoplehood. Control and exploitation of *others* were essential to the project, and white identity was solidified in positive correlation with the status quo. Each generation has to be taught what this restrictive and restricting white heritage means. Some reject the narrative. White nationalists do not. They want white identity, Baldwin's projection notwithstanding, to be synonymous with citizenship and statehood.

Ojibwe/Dakota scholar Scott Lyons (2010) calls for realistic, nonessentialist nationalism. "Nations are produced by nationalists," he observes, "but they are *re*produced by citizens who articulate the meanings of their nation in locales like constitutions" (188). Lyons would hold on to the idea of nation, "while de-essentializing it," if the political initiative improves actual lives. The same applies, he contends, "for those legal fictions we call our 'identities' and the many practices and beliefs known as 'cultures': these too can be deployed in ways that might improve actual lives, problematic though they clearly are" (xii).

Narrow nationalisms set up a Rockwell-Muhammad, ethnic-nationalism-so-why-not-white-nationalism dialectic. Nonessentialist nationalisms, on the other hand, welcome historical nuance and complexities of identity. This understanding is like the notion developed by rhetoric scholar Marilyn Cooper (2004). She explained it this way: "the self is fluid and in process, but determinate at any particular moment; it is not necessarily hybrid but always complex, determined by its experiences to a certain extent but still also constructed or chosen with varying degrees of awareness; and it defines itself not in opposition to others or its community but in relation to others" (91). This line of inquiry holds great promise, and great challenge, for students. How do we best promote relational outcomes in a nation still becoming, while respecting the best tradition of nationalisms, which are, after all, how we even made it this far along a fraught path? This was, in fact, the danger of Martin Luther King Jr. and Malcolm X to the establishment—Black nationalist and organic enough to galvanize an African-American-led civil rights or religious movement and prophetic enough to issue a race-transcendent challenge in the name of fairness to restructure radically American political priorities. You can't get there from white nationalism. What you get from white nationalism is a synonym for white supremacism and a modern label for the same old white backlash against attempts at social progress by so-called minorities that has been around since the nation's inception. As Langston Hughes ([1967] 2001) expressed it:

> When I try to find a job
> To earn a little cash,
> Try to find myself a job
> To earn a little cash,
> All you got to offer
> Is a white backlash.

One would think that a multiethnic polis is eventually going to insist on better than this.

Not surprisingly, given the endurance of white supremacism both outside and inside the academy, scholars in rhetoric, composition, and literacy studies have employed critical race theory as an analytic tool and counterargument. They have been particularly attracted to the work of Derrick Bell (1993) and to the notion of "racist permanence" that he articulated in his fascinating and provocative book, *Faces at the Bottom of the Well*. As Bell wrote, "Black people will never gain full equality in this country. . . . This is a hard-to-accept fact that all history verifies" (12). These racial realists, as they term themselves after the *Faces* character Erika Wechsler, reject, along with Bell, a linear progress narrative and see no transcendence over racism possible in the American nation-state. It is beyond question that as a practical matter they are correct. American racism was, has been, or will be observable as alive and well by everybody they and Bell ever knew, know, or will know. On the other hand, it is worth exploring with students Bell's overall political vision. He was, after all, more a political liberal than a political radical, so it is fair to ask: was his conclusion the logical result of a constrained liberal vision that could not imagine American life beyond the clutches of a capitalist oligarchy? Moreover, it seems necessary to point out that in terms of social relations, history can predict but not verify the future. History is open-ended, that is, contingent and dependent on material conditions. A time existed, for many centuries in fact, way longer than this country has been around, when the absence of white supremacy could have been construed as a permanent feature of the territory we now call the United States. A point assumable from the analysis of racial realism is that if racism is defeated, that would mean that we would no longer be in the USA. Maybe someone will see that reality, though of course we won't be the ones. Or maybe Bell slipped an out-clause into his argument. He carefully said *this country* and sometimes *this society*, by which he could have been referring to the ongoing racist state and not making a prediction about the possibilities of a post-racist nation still called the United States (ix, 8).

But we rightfully can hit the pause button on theory and speculation. A theory can animate one's activism, but racial realists are right that to resist everyday racist oppression is sufficient rationale for political engagement. One doesn't need a theory for it. One need not theorize getting a knee off one's neck. However, it seems that if the encouraged political actions are connected to the premise of rejecting ideas of racial advancement, then racial realists at least owe students a definition of racial progress beyond the notion of resistance as self-fulfillment. Is only qualitative change to be seen as progress and quantitative change considered failure? I waver on this question; therefore, I imagine that it is a worthwhile one with which students can wrestle. My broader point, though I am possibly too circuitous in getting to it, is that I endorse the intellectual project of racial realists and of critical race theory overall, particularly its emphases on social justice and experiential knowledge. These precepts are needed in the struggle against white supremacy and its most high-profile verbal expression: white nationalism.

What America ultimately becomes will be largely a function of the story that gains the most traction. Will it be a romantic, essentialist state? Or a liberal one? Or radical? Appiah speaks to the first two possibilities:

> Liberal states depend upon a civic creed that's both potent and lean—potent enough to give significance to citizenship, lean enough to be shared by people with different religious and ethnic affiliations. The Romantic state could pride itself on being the emanation of one *Volk* and its primordial consciousness; the liberal state has to get by with much less mystical mumbo jumbo. The Romantic state could boldly identify itself with the General Will; liberal states must content themselves with a general willingness. The Romantic state rallies its citizens with a stirring cry: "One people!" The liberal state's true anthem is: "We can work it out." (103)

Students can participate in working it out—or not. We have no guarantee that romantic notions won't prevail. We can make a pretty good guess that liberalism insofar as it stresses individual rights will be persuasive to many. Radical restructuring at the institutional level at the expense of certain individual choices—what we have seen traces of in the left-liberal ideas of Barack Obama, Bernie Sanders, and Elizabeth Warren, and in a mix of other socialist or neo-Marxist formulations—may be an attractive proposal as well. This is some of the rhetorical action in play for students as they consider the semantic borders of white nationalism.

NOTES

1. A name for those who uncompromisingly rally around the words "Make America Great Again," Donald Trump's 2016 campaign slogan.
2. Marantz says of shitposting that it is "a style of discourse prevalent on some parts of social media (especially certain corners of 4chan, 8chan, Gab, some parts of Reddit). In the best case, the result is absurdist so-bad-it's-good humor; in the worst case, the result is bigotry or incitement to violence" (5).
3. In 1962, Rockwell, founder of the American Nazi Party, was invited to speak at a Nation of Islam rally in Chicago. The ANP and the NOI, white and Black organizations, respectively, the latter led by Muhammad, both espoused racial separation.
4. The 1915 film, directed by D. W. Griffith, denigrates African Americans and glorifies white supremacists, particularly the Ku Klux Klan.

REFERENCES

Appiah, Kwame Anthony. 2018. *Lies that Bind: Rethinking Identity*. New York: Liveright.
Baldwin, James. 1962. "As Much Truth as One Can Bear." *New York Times Book Review*, January 14, 1962. 1, 38.
Baldwin, James. 1998. "Notes on the House of Bondage." In *Collected Essays*, edited by Toni Morrison, 799–807. New York: Library of America.
Bell, Bernard W. 2005. *The Contemporary African American Novel: Its Folk Roots and Modern Literary Branches*. Amherst: University of Massachusetts Press.
Bell, Derrick. 1993. *Faces at the Bottom of the Well: The Permanence of Racism*. New York: Basic Books.
Burke, Kenneth. 1939. "The Rhetoric of Hitler's 'Battle.'" *The Southern Review*, No. 5, 1–21.
Cooper, Marilyn. 2004. "Nonessentialist Identity and the National Discourse." In *Rhetoric and Ethnicity*, edited by Keith Gilyard and Vorris Nunley, 87–102. Portsmouth, NH: Boynton/Cook-Heinemann.
Du Bois, W. E. B. (1897) 2004. "The Conservation of Races." In *African American Literature*, edited by Keith Gilyard and Anissa Wardi, 1087–97. New York: Penguin Academics.
Freire, Paulo. 1970. *Pedagogy of the Oppressed*. Translated by M. B. Ramos. New York: Continuum.
Hughes, Langston. (1967) 2001. "The Backlash Blues." In *The Collected Works of Langston Hughes*, edited by Arnold Rampersad, vol. 3, 142–43. Columbia: University of Missouri Press.
Lazere, Donald. 2009. *Reading and Writing for Civic Literacy: The Critical Citizen's Guide to Argumentative Rhetoric*. Boulder, CO: Paradigm Publishers.
Lee, Spike, director. 2018. *BlacKKKlansman*. 40 Acres and a Mule Filmworks.
Litman-Navarro, Kevin. 2018. "White Nationalists Are Co-opting 'Black Panther' to Push Their Own Agenda." *Inverse*, March 15, 2018. https://www.inverse.com/article/42350-white-nationalists-coopting-black-panther.
Lyons, Scott Richard. 2010. *X-marks: Native Signatures of Assent*. Minneapolis: University of Minnesota Press.

Marantz, Andrew. 2019. *Antisocial: Online Extremists, Techno-utopians, and the Hijacking of the American Conversation.* New York: Viking.

Ogbar, Jeffrey O. G. 2001. "Yellow Power: The Formation of Asian-American Nationalism in the Age of Black Power, 1966–1975." *Souls: A Critical Journal of Black Politics, Culture and Society* 3 (3): 29–38.

Orwell, George. 1946. "Politics and the English Language." *Horizon: A Review of Literature and Art*, April 1946, 252–65.

Paxton, Robert. 2005. *The Anatomy of Fascism.* New York: Vintage.

Serwer, Adam. 2019. "Only the Right Can Defeat White Nationalism." *The Atlantic,* August 21, 2019. https://www.theatlantic.com/ideas/archive/2019/08/the-right-bears-a-special-responsibility-in-the-fight-against-white-nationalism/596479/.

Vials, Christopher. 2014. *Haunted by Hitler: Liberals, the Left, and the Fight against Fascism in the United States.* Amherst: University of Massachusetts Press.

3
STRANGERS IN A STRANGE LAND
"The Foreign Student" at US Universities after World War II

Amy J. Wan

In January 2019, an email from Megan Neeley, the Director of Graduate Studies of the Master of Biostatistics Program at Duke, went viral. This email, which was sent to all of the Biostatistics master's students, explained that two faculty members came to her about a "small group of first-year students who they observed speaking Chinese (in their words, VERY LOUDLY) in the student lounge / study areas." In this reprimand of international students for speaking Chinese in the common areas of the program's building, the DGS warned students that their language practices might affect future research and internship opportunities (Blum 2019). She told the students that the faculty members had wanted to know the names of the students for future considerations of internships and master's projects and that "they were disappointed that these students were not taking the opportunity to improve their English and were being so impolite as to have a conversation that not everyone on the floor could understand" (Blum 2019). Such explicit hostility toward international students and their language practices in the US is not uncommon, and this viral moment exemplifies long-held tensions between institutional efforts toward globalizing and how these same institutional policies and practices govern language use.

The Duke example brings together some of the main issues surrounding increasingly visible international and multilingual student populations in the United States, especially given their context in the history of the growth of higher education. While institutions point themselves toward increasing student populations, US-centered educational and governmental policy cultivates spaces in which some students have more access than others to the full range of global citizenship offered within the structure of US higher education. The implications of these contradictions—that institutions want to internationalize their student populations but don't create multilingual spaces—are profound because they tell us who is being included in higher education and how these spaces are shaped by these nationalist language policies and practices.

This chapter examines the logic behind such messages communicated to international students, by connecting these types of contemporary examples of racialized judgments around language to a longer history of international students and anti-Asian sentiment in the United States. Even though strict national quotas and restrictions around immigration to the United States that were developed in the late nineteenth and early twentieth centuries were not lifted until the 1965 Hart-Cellar Act,[1] a small number of international students, who were an exception and could enter the country on nonimmigrant visas, still came to study in the United States after World War II with the understanding that they would return to their home countries after their studies were over (Bevis and Lucas 2007). These students, particularly those from Asian countries or who were seen as non-white, were constructed as "foreigners" entering mostly white university and community spaces. In order to construct an understanding of this earlier context for international students, this chapter examines higher education scholarship and policy responding to the expansion of higher education in the US after World War II and the presence of international students, as well as demographic data from New York City and the colleges within it, the top destination for international students in 1948 and in the years following (Institute of International Education 1948). I demonstrate how international student experiences were shaped both by a growing movement to use higher education to cultivate citizens who could participate in the postwar role of the US as a world power and by the persistent racialization and resulting anti-Asian sentiment that has been woven into the cultivation of American citizenship. And I argue that this mid-century expansion of higher education established the intertwining of many of the structures, assumptions, and beliefs about international students that continue to inform our policies today.

This argument depends on two main shifts in thinking about US citizenry, which this chapter examines more closely. First, the rise of mass education played a crucial role in the cultivation of US citizens; before this point, higher education had been slowly expanding (Levine 1987) but the logic that it should be an accessible broad-based public good for all citizens was not expressed until this moment. This expansion of mass higher education after World War II had explicitly "American" aims, with foreigners acting as both potential threats and allies to citizens who were the custodians of burgeoning US world power. Additionally, international students must be seen in the context of immigration laws and policies during this period. The laws that determined which few were in the country also constructed how individuals from outside the US were seen mainly as foreign and racialized bodies. By examining these two shifts, this chapter creates a more ecological sense about how US higher education constructed the "foreign student" and how writing, language, and literacy were being used, and are being used, to manage this population.

This chapter builds on scholarly work like Paul Matsuda's "The Myth of Linguistic Homogeneity in US College Composition" (2006), in which he provides historical background prior to the 1960s to understand the construction of writing classrooms as monolingual spaces, a myth that operates to contain linguistic difference. While much scholarship in second-language writing and translingualism counters this myth of linguistic homogeneity, in this chapter, I specifically talk about expanding this historical view to consider how institutions and their policies reinforce not just linguistic homogeneity, but homogeneity more broadly and the way racialization works hand-in-hand with language minoritization (Rosa and Flores 2017). To that end, I broaden the scope to consider how the influence of higher education policy and immigration policy and the role of racialization make altering the influence in language and writing policies more complicated than just changing a policy. By considering the deeply held historical foundations of how international students might be seen on US campuses, we can see how these Duke students and other students from Asian countries are racialized in mostly white university spaces, and that language policing contributes to this racialization. Although not the focus of this chapter (but part of my larger project on this topic), it must be noted that a consequence of this racialization is the continuing conflation of "international student" with Asian, providing a diversity alibi for US institutions that can increase the number of students of color while not addressing the long history of discrimination and exclusion of Black and Brown students. Linguistic homogeneity persists because the institution itself is in many ways homogenous, yet it also strives for pluralism in a way that brings students of color into hostile spaces that enforce monolingualism, monoculturalism, and whiteness. Because international student enrollment waned due to immigration policies enacted and enforced between 2016 and 2020,[2] as well as the decrease in transnational movement because of border restrictions stemming from the 2020 global pandemic (Fischer 2020) and because of new attention to persistent racial inequities shown by the uprising of spring

2020, institutions need to consider how their policies and the people can construct or transform these hostile spaces, especially if they want to continue their "global" missions. The late 1940s through the 1950s, both in higher education and immigration policy, set some of the policy terms for these current tensions.

EXPANDING HIGHER EDUCATION AFTER WORLD WAR II

The post–World War II era is often upheld as a moment of great potential in histories of higher education. Michael Fabricant and Stephen Brier (2016) describe how this expansion was based on a utilitarian need to prepare workers for "the technical and service jobs essential to the transformation and expansion of American capitalism in the postwar era," as well as a desire to provide educational opportunities to veterans who served and to enforce "enduring democratic ideals and values that had come to the fore in the war" (41). Veterans of World War II were given free access to higher education via the GI Bill, and the institution at large saw a rapid increase in funding, investment, and expansion. John Thelin (2004) describes how the shape of American higher education was altered after World War II because "its base was extended so as to move significantly closer to providing mass access to higher education" while simultaneously increasing the selectivity, prestige, and reach of certain kinds of programs and institutions, as illustrated by the increasing number of doctoral programs and junior colleges (260). During this period, Thelin notes, there was an 80 percent increase in enrollment, with just under 1.5 million enrolled in 1939–1940 and almost 2.7 million by 1949–1950 (261).

Often cited as a kind of "golden age," this mid-twentieth-century period of expansion for mass higher education is often characterized as the time in which the middle class was built (Fabricant and Brier 2016; Newfield 2008). With such expansion, the goals of higher education became much lauded: being a public good, producing citizens, and acting as a key part of the social engine and the cultivation of democracy. Colleges and universities were characterized as having a central role in the progress of the nation, and legislative motivators, such as the GI Bill, contributed to the large numbers of students who were enrolling. But according to Abigail Boggs, Eli Meyerhoff, Nick Mitchell, and Zach Schwartz-Weinstein (2019), such a characterization, common in critical university studies, "neglects the ways this expansion was underwritten by militarized funding priorities, nationalist agendas, and an incorporative project of counterinsurgency" (5). This period is when higher education developed into a public good that was inextricably linked to the success and power of the United States after the war.

The 1946 Commission on Higher Education and its resulting report, *Higher Education for American Democracy: A Report of the President's Commission on Higher Education* (1947), known as the Truman report, played a significant role in the "dramatic expansion" of higher education (Fabricant and Brier 2016, 40) and provide insight into this nationalist agenda. President Truman appointed this commission, comprised of various university presidents and educational leaders, to create a federal statement about how expanding higher educational opportunities for all citizens would support democracy. The report articulated a shift in national thinking toward support for mass higher education, establishing the rhetorical foundation for policy arguments that align accessible higher education with democratic values, one that still exists in our own current discourses on higher education. The report and the work of the commission laid the groundwork on a federal level for many continuing beliefs and policies and also language about the need for expanding access to college, and provided a rationale and government support to do so. It also helped establish the belief that access was crucial to help eradicate inequality in our society and strengthen our democracy. The Truman Commission created a kind of federal mandate to expand higher education beyond the elite by calling upon institutions of higher education to embrace their broadened charge of creating citizens.

In part, this broadening of higher education was explicitly framed as a necessary practice because of the United States' place as a new world power. Upon the report's release, the *New York Times* article (Fines 1947) summarized it: "American education today was not intended to fit young gentlemen for leisure in the old European tradition, the report stressed, but rather to develop citizens whose adult life would combine work with leisure and participation in the nation's affairs" (1). The connection to foreign European traditions in the post–World War II era provides a warning that elitist educational traditions in Europe did not prevent the rise of fascism. The Commission positioned higher education for democracy in contrast to education that served the authoritarian governments the US fought against, noting that the "social role"—the purpose of education in a democratic society—was quite distinct and that US institutions needed to take up that responsibility seriously. The Commission not only obliged higher education to broaden its constituency but also used the report to establish language and values presenting higher education as a public good, such that the work of colleges and universities would be to cultivate the engagement of citizens and a healthy democracy.

The Truman report imagined that American higher education could help students understand world politics and the responsibilities of the nation. As a result, the report is driven not just by a desire to improve the lot of US citizens but also by post-war concerns about the growing power and influence of the United States over "foreign" countries, as well as the desire to prevent something like World War II from happening again. The Commission characterized liberal education as "provincial" (1947, 16) and challenged higher education to prepare students for "world citizenship," making an argument for understanding world history and cultural diversity in order to "fit ourselves for the world leadership that has fallen to America in this crucial moment of history" (1947, 17). This is not to say that institutions were instantly more accessible, particularly to students of color and other marginalized communities. But the rhetoric existed as a way to animate certain policies built into the philosophy of public serving institutions such as the City University of New York (CUNY) and the rising number of regional and community colleges, whose development was partially driven by the mandates established in this report. The expansion of higher education was directly tied to its construction as a space where American ideals were being cultivated and propagated, particularly in contrast to those of foreign countries when the Cold War was shaping national alliances. And these connections, beween expanding access and strengthening democracy for US citizens and a need to consider the role of higher education in a global context and the heightened profile of the US as a world power, laid the groundwork for US institutions of higher education as an attractive space for foreign students.

WHO WERE FOREIGN STUDENTS?

In addition to the effort to broaden the student population of higher education and increase US effectiveness as a world power through higher education, colleges and universities in the US also saw a small but growing number of international students, a trend that ran separately from broader migration patterns to the US, which were established by the restrictive immigration quotas established in 1924. As part of a post–World War II effort to understand the rest of the world and to create citizens who would more effectively understand the US as a world power, both Fulbright and UNESCO were partially responsible for the growth when they began sponsoring international exchange in education. In 1939–1940, before World War II, there were 6,154 "foreign students" in the US, which rose to 25,464 in 1948–1949 (Institute of International Education 1948) and 30,462 in 1951 (Bevis and Lucas 2007, 5). Cora Du Bois (1956) provides a coeval rationale that students were coming to the US to study because their universities in their home countries in Europe were damaged after the war, but also more importantly that the US government "launched massive democratization and re-education programs in Austria, Germany, Korea, and Japan (5). Additionally, other nations saw the US as the only place where economic and social development" programs were available and where it was seen as superior in technology and science (Du Bois, 5–6). Du Bois also points to the growing ease of travel as well as the "importance of English as a world language" (6) as reasons for the increase in students. Countries were sponsoring students to come to the United States for training, with the understanding that they would return home and that their countries of origin would benefit from their education and training, which would include knowledge about the United States' benevolence and values.

Yet Bevis and Lucas (2007) write about how "postwar recovery problems loomed as a major determinant in many cases" (135) that precluded poorer countries from having the resources to support students to study abroad in the US. Increased political tensions between the United States and Soviet satellite countries also affected international student enrollment (Bevis and Lucas 2007, 135). The patterns of international student exchange were very much dependent on how geopolitical relationships shaped access. In 1948–1949, the top five countries of origin for foreign students were Canada, China, India, Mexico, and Cuba, with China, India, Mexico, and Cuba representing the visibly foreign or racialized groups of students; Germany did not break into the top five until the mid-1950s (Institute of International Education 1948). Altogether, there were a little over 7,500 students from these countries, about a third of the total number of international students studying in the country at the time. International students, especially those who were non-white, were still quite rare in university spaces. And their presence was explained by a foreign need to access US educational resources.

Both the presence and construction of "foreign students" after World War II are the result of a complex matrix of nationalist tendencies, racism, and exceptionalism around US higher education. I want to underscore that for many of the non-white students, they were among the few people from their race and ethnicity groups, not only on the campuses but also in the United States itself. While US higher education created policies and structures to increase international exchange, US immigration policy was doing the opposite. Because of the 1924 National Origins act, there was already a quota system, still in place after World

War II, that limited immigration according to countries of origin, with non-European countries given an annual immigration quota of one hundred people. As historian Mae M. Ngai (2004) reports, the 1924 immigration act marked a moment when immigration policy realigned and hardened racial categories in the law (7). She writes about how during the 1920s the ethnic and racial identities of European Americans became "uncoupled," while "Asians' and Mexicans' ethnic and racial identities remained conjoined. The legal racialization of these ethnic groups' national origin cast them as permanently foreign and unassimilable to the nation." She argues that "these racial formations produced 'alien citizens'—Asian Americans and Mexican Americans born in the United States with formal US citizenship but who remained alien in the eyes of the nation" (8). The culture of increased racialization of immigrants and the near elimination of non-European immigration meant that non-European international students were entering a space where people like them were marginalized and foreign. There was some tweaking in 1952 by the McCarran-Walter Act (a.k.a. the Immigration and Nationality Act), which revised the restrictions put in place by the 1924 National Origins Act, adding the screening of aliens to eliminate suspected security risks. And while this act in 1952 eliminated the racial bar to citizenship, which ended Japanese and Korean exclusions, what replaced it was a global race quota that restricted Asian immigration to the United States by race rather than country of origin.[3]

This picture of international students alongside immigration relies on an amalgamation of data from the Open Doors report and US Census, which often did not have analogous or parallel categories. But I place these data in concert with one another and present the result here in order to construct a sense of the atmosphere that international students were entering, one that was predominantly white, with a vast majority of the population born in the United States. For example, New York was one of the top states that international students were entering during this period. Out of 25,464 international students in the US, there were specifically 5,000, or 18.7 percent of them, in New York State (Institute of International Education 1948). The Institute of International Education reports that Columbia University and New York University were in the top five institutions for foreign student enrollment in 1948–1949, with 1,140 and 724 students respectively. Racial data on these students was not available, but even if we assume parallel proportions to the countries of origin as reported by the Institute of International Education, there were racialized "foreigners" attending these institutions from China, India, Mexico, and Cuba who were entering a vastly majority-white population and culture. According to the 1950 US Census, out of the over 12 million people living in the New York urban area, 8 percent were non-white. In New York County, the total population was 1,960,101, and 19,020 people were considered "Other Races,"[4] which was the category for people who were considered neither white nor Black. The total population in Queens County, now one of the most diverse counties in the country, was 1,550,849. Out of that number, 1,208,929 were white, 170,055 were "Negro," and 2,199 were "Other Races." That means that 11 percent of the population was non-white, and that out of the 1.2 million white people, 767,621 were "foreign-born white." And looking specifically at Asian populations in 1950, there were 1,742 Indian, Japanese, and Chinese people, equaling 0.1 percent of the population. This is all to say that American pluralism in the mid-20th century did not look like it does today, with a vast majority of the foreign-born population considered white and linguistic diversity very much based in European languages.

There was also relative homogeneity at institutions of higher education. In 1967, which is the earliest available date for demographic information I've found for the City University of New York (CUNY 1969), the city's public university system, 81.85 percent of students were white, 10.2 percent were Black, 2.9 percent Puerto Rican, and 4.1 percent other, and at senior colleges (which are the four-year colleges) 87 percent were white and 6.4 percent Black (a category which also included Puerto Rican students). The proportion of white students to non-white students was likely the same or larger in the years previous, and since CUNY is a public institution and therefore more open in its admissions compared to Columbia and NYU, a relatively safe assumption is that the private schools in New York were much whiter. Additionally, this means that racialized foreign students who were not studying in these more central locations close to immigrant communities did not have many other students around them who were from countries other than the US or spoke their languages.

As previously discussed, international students in the 1950s were assumed to be in the US for education and training that was not available in home countries. Institutions of higher education recognized that their role in providing this education for foreign nationals did not just mean providing skills but also that their experiences in the United States were important as well. M. Brewster Smith wrote in 1955 that "not so long ago, foreign students appeared to most college administrators as a marginal luxury. They brought to the campus a touch of exotic color; they enriched the educational milieu of American students" (1955, 231), noting that a shift had occurred:

we not only ask whether the foreign student is getting the education and training that he came for, but inquire whether his training will contribute to his country's social and economic development. Will his experience unfit him for a constructive role in his less-advantaged homeland? And perhaps most insistently, will his voice be heard as a friend of America in the forum of world ideological conflict? Sometimes, indeed, the question reduces to a plaintive, will he love us? (231–32)

While his exoticized casting of foreign students is problematic (and more on that later in the chapter), from this we can understand that, not unlike today, administrators at US institutions of higher education had very specific ideas about what they were gaining from or contributing to with this population of "less-advantaged" international students. While students were positioned as disadvantaged, needing education unavailable to them at home, they were also seen as valuable ambassadors of what the United States had to offer, exporting US nationalist values. Colleges and universities were seen as contributing to the soft power of the US's new status on the world stage, helping underresourced countries with knowledge and education, while also making a good name for the US. Yet their "exotic color" still persisted.

Since international students were only allowed in the United States for education and because there were so few other racialized non-Americans around, they were set apart from other people who surrounded them. Much like the contemporary "public charge rule" that is being pushed today, in which green cards are denied to immigrants who might be dependent on public benefits like Medicaid and food stamps (Liptak 2020, 27), the context of the international student in the late 1940s and into the 1950s, during the beginning of the anti-communist Cold War, established a view of good foreigners and bad, ones who were coming to the US for education and knowledge and those who sought to undermine the US.

MAKING THE "FOREIGN STUDENT" FOREIGN IN HIGHER EDUCATION

Because the rise of mass higher education and international student enrollment was born out of a nationalist higher education system and an isolationist immigration climate, it is unsurprising that writing and language instruction reflected a view in which the foreign student needed to learn the English language and American values as part of their study in the United States and was often racialized by those trying to understand their "exotic color." Like many other colleges in the US,

Queens College had an English Language Institute (ELI) that targeted international students (Matsuda 2006, 647).[5] The institute's mission described how it was designed to

> meet the language needs primarily of (1) visiting students from other countries who need to attain competence in English sufficient to enable them to pursue studies of collegiate and professional level in the United States colleges without linguistic handicap; (2) visitors from other countries who need to attain competence in English sufficient to enable them to meet their language needs while in this country; (3) members of the United Nations personnel and their families residing in the Metropolitan area; (4) new citizens and repatriates who have only recently arrived in this country. (Queens College 1949, 31)

These different categories of students included new citizens who repatriated (of which there were very few during this period) but for the most part focus on those with professional reasons to be in the US, usually temporarily.

Matsuda argues that because English language instruction was happening outside of the confines of general instruction and matriculation, it contributed to the linguistic containment of language learners. The funding for such programs provides additional insight into how Queens College positioned them and how English-language institutes across the country did as well. In the 1950s and 1960s, CUNY was free for all students, but not surprisingly those who enrolled in the ELI paid additional tuition and fees. In 1962 (which was the first time ELI fees were published in the course bulletin), these fees were $316 a semester, which is a little under $3,000 in 2019 money, a bargain compared to today's tuition but $3,000 more than nothing, which is what "citizens who are actual residents of the city" were paying (Queens College 1962, 53). How "citizens who are actual residents of the city" were determined is a question that goes unanswered in these materials, but it raises the concern about what part of the college foreign-born residents of the city attended.

Scholarship on English-language instruction during this period gives a sense of how those goals were translated in separated writing and language classrooms and of the experience that foreign students were receiving. Herbert Schueler (1949), the director of the Queens College ELI, wrote that this program is designed for "professional training of foreign students" and that a typical class enrolls students whose "native tongues are Turkish, Persian, Greek, Polish, French, German, Spanish, and Russian" (309), with a focus on mostly European languages. And the curriculum itself was completely in English: "No foreign dictionaries are ever used. No attempt is made to use translation exercises. All explanation, all teaching, all textual material, even at the most elementary level, utilizes English alone" (309). Not only is this a stark contrast to the translingual approaches of today, it clearly reflects the English-only cultural mandates of higher education in the US as well as any global spaces in which the US is an influence.

These questions about what to do with foreign students were represented at CCCC during this same time period. "The Foreign Student in the Freshman Course," a report on a workshop held during the 1956 meeting of CCCC, describes what might be a familiar scenario for modern readers, in which teachers and administrators of first-year writing classes asked: "what can be done where foreign students must be taught in the regular Freshman course?" (Cargill 1956, 123). The report indicates a dearth of institutional support and structures, citing the lack of "satisfactory materials for classroom use" (123), "teachers who have not had opportunity for special training in the teaching of English to foreigners" (123), and "an immense range in the kinds of programs (or lack of them) now existing" (122). The category of "foreign student" here, while not stated outright, is intended to show that this type of student was not like the others in the class. Even though, unlike in English-language institutes, students were not contained in a separate space or class, the notion of the "foreign student," a non-English-speaking body that is difficult to teach and is separate and different from the rest of the students and from the rest of the university yet given somewhat minimal institutional attention and resources, is one that persists.

As one might expect, there was a racialized (and racist) hierarchy to the kinds of international students who can succeed in US classrooms during this period. M. Brewster Smith (1955) talks about the importance of students adjusting, because otherwise "they are all too likely to feel beleaguered and diminished. Defensive reactions may then come to the fore that complicate rather than simplify their problems of coming to terms with life in America. Defensiveness easily becomes a self-perpetuating vicious circle" (235). While this warning is somewhat innocuous and speaks to the lack of support and isolation that international students might feel, he goes on to say that "students from certain countries, however, seem especially vulnerable. These are the representatives of underdeveloped countries imbued with the spirit of emergent nationalism" (234). He also talks specifically about students from India, "who cite American race relations as a counter to criticisms of caste, American materialism to balance home-country poverty, and so on through a long list of standard reactions to the probing of standard 'sensitive areas'" (236–37). He calls it "defensive nationalism," and points to

Scandinavian students, who "take a much more realistic, matter-of-fact view of their American experience" (237), and claims that "far from uncritical, their attitudes are too highly differentiated to be neatly characterized as pro or con. We came to refer to their Smorgasbord approach—an orientation that facilitates effective learning" (237). He continues, "Japanese seem especially prone to withdraw to themselves, cutting themselves off from potentially corrective processes of communication and swallowing their resentment. The Indian students. . . . were more likely to direct their hostilities outward, wearing a noticeable chip on the shoulder" (240).

It's hard not to read all these attitudes about the "defensive nationalism" against the backdrop of the internment of Japanese citizens during World War II or any other of the numerous examples of race discrimination, white supremacy, and nationalism. And in this article, Smith (1955) is not just expressing his own jingoistic and racist views but reporting on results from the Committee on Cross-Cultural Education of the Social Science Research Council, a committee that conducted three years of research on educational exchange, sponsored by the Carnegie Corporation, the Ford Foundation, and the Rockefeller Foundation and included researchers from UCLA, Harvard, Columbia, University of Michigan, and Michigan State (232). On their behalf, Smith writes, "The wider the cultural gap to be bridged—the more difficult the task of cross-cultural adjustment—the longer the student may have to flounder in the adjustive phase before he manages to come to terms with the requirements of life and study in America" (239). This language is obviously coded, with the cultural gap standing in for race. The level of suspicion toward Indian and Japanese students mirrored the suspicion around non-white foreigners that permeated these various institutions across the country and at large. International students were seen as potentially useful as part of the distribution of the soft power of the United States, but racialization made them ultimately suspicious, made them foreigners. The classroom space, particularly the writing classroom space, cultivates these attitudes by using language instruction as a way to reinforce the racialized and nationally oriented separation of students, reflecting what was happening within the United States.

On Chinese migrants to the US after World War II, M. Ngai (2004) writes about how "in a few short years the dominant image of Chinese lurched from despised oriental 'other' to wartime ally to dangerous Communist threat" (203). This sense of suspicion around certain groups of immigrants most certainly carried over to racialized, mostly Asian, international student populations, particularly as their status as either ally or other was unstable. The shifts in who was worthy and who was not, who was more easily assimilated and who wasn't, who was educable and who was not, stemmed from the intertwining of language and race, and also from the tension between US higher education as a pluralistic, accessible institution as opposed to one that upheld nationalist values.

Even though internationalization and understanding are the stated goals on behalf of the foreign student, these efforts come from a place of extreme nationalism rooted in the white supremacy of the United States. We've inherited these beliefs about language, race, and foreignness in the structures of higher education, and I believe that recognizing the influence of the geopolitical and racial context on our everyday activities as literacy instructors and administrators is the only way we can start to dismantle them.

ANTIRACISM AND THE GLOBAL UNIVERSITY

In this chapter, I have traced out the legacies of policies geared toward international students, with particular attention to the way racialization helps to construct these policies. As I've demonstrated here, there is a long history of expanding higher education in a way that racialized and othered "foreign students" as part of a larger project to realize nationalistic goals. In our current moment of US institutional dependence on international students for tuition money and for the cultivation of the "global university," particularly as that enrollment declines because of extreme nationalistic and isolationist policies at the federal level, writing and literacy educators in the US have an obligation to think about how we might actively work against and dismantle hostile spaces cultivated by these long-held and deliberate logics of foreignness.

Part of this dismantling involves recognizing the larger ecology in which our policies, practices, and beliefs emerge. Decisions we make about students, and the spaces that we help construct for them, are part of a longer history of nationalized and racialized discourse in the United States. For instance, when we dive into upholding the global university, we must be critical of what this means and what it looks like. Literacy and writing has a long history of being used both to uplift and free students, but also to project racialized standards onto them. Policies and practices that shape the international student experience are one small part of this legacy of white language supremacy (Inoue 2019); Black students and other students of color on campus are subject to language policing through these same modes of acceptability and appropriateness (Flores and Rosa 2015). And because campuses want (and at this point, need) international students, there is an opportunity to connect the project of supporting their language instruction to a larger ecology of linguistic justice, to explicitly advocate that the cultivation of supportive linguistic environments for international students must also be implemented more broadly on behalf of other language-minoritized students on campus. We need to fight for specific structures and supports and curricular changes, not just because they are ethical and support students, but because they are actively antiracist and work against the hostile environment cultivated by logics of standards and expectations.

But as this history illustrates, policies alone cannot do the job of dismantling this structure. It also means paying attention to our own expectations and the ways we support students' literacy practices. Perhaps our behaviors are not as overt as the rebuke made by the DGS at Duke, but how are educators and administrators actively thinking about ways to incorporate, support, and value people's various linguistic practices into school spaces? How does racialization come into play when we are judging people's language practices? In the Duke example, other administrators publicly stated that the DGS was wrong; there's no written policy that says everyone needs to use English at all times. But that doesn't mean there isn't a tacit one. How many other times and in how many other spaces is this kind of thing reinforced by people like the DGS, but not in writing and not in ways that can be virally distributed or tracked? How do the practices and beliefs about who belongs and who doesn't get filtered through in the ways that we respond, in who gets the internships, who succeeds? This happens not just through practices and policies but clearly also, as seen through the example at Duke, through attitudes and how they might be enforcing assimilation, the suppression of language as well as cultural and racial identities, or judgments about who "fits" into the larger systems. These attitudes have implications, not just to international students but to any students whose language might be deemed outside the norm (Inoue 2019). We need to be aware of these potential biases and also make space—curricular, physical, and ideological—where we can expand the institutional senses of what a global university can possibly mean.

And these practices extend far beyond the classroom into how we might see the work we do in relation to national immigration policies. The way restrictive immigration policies shaped demographics and the way international students were often an extreme minority shines a light on the experience of international students moving to the United States in 1955, sometimes to New York City where a third of the international students in the country were, and other times to places like Ann

Arbor for the University of Michigan, a top school for international students (Institute of International Education 1948), where the rest of the town was overwhelmingly white and English-speaking and US-born. We must also see how our work connects to the living contexts of students—whether they are allowed to speak the languages they are most comfortable with, or if they even have spaces where they can buy their groceries.[6] The lack of other racialized and language-minoritized students in those spaces to help normalize their language use—to normalize themselves—shapes their experiences. The policy and discourse around who is let into the United States and who earns suspicion shapes their experiences as well.

The extreme isolationist immigration policies of the White House, and the uprising and protests against police brutality in late spring 2020 sparked by the death of George Floyd as well as Breonna Taylor and countless others, put into question the way institutions reflect and embody racial biases. It also revealed the larger contexts around minoritization and how it is rooted in a history of race and language discrimination, as well as how policies of all scales uphold and perpetuate these beliefs and ideologies. We need to be actively antiracist and consider how the embedded values and the histories of these ideologies in our policies affect the ways we engage with students in order to think about new possibilities.

NOTES

1. Exclusionary immigration policy was developed in the US at the federal level beginning with the Supreme Court decisions *Chy Lung v. Freeman* (1876) and *Henderson v. Mayor of New York* (1875), which placed the responsibility of immigration laws on the federal government. The immigration policy beginning with the Angell Treaty of 1880 and the Chinese Exclusion Act of 1882 marked increased exclusionary and racialized policies, including the 1891 Immigration Act, the 1906 Naturalization Act, the Immigration Act of 1907, the 1917 Immigration Act, and the 1921 Emergency Quota Act. Johnson-Reed, or the National Origins Act of 1924, further codified restrictions based on race (Aleinikoff, Martin, and Motomura 2003; Briggs 1984; Kansas 1928; King 2000; Ngai 2004; Schneider 2001).
2. Wadhia (2019) outlines how the combination of proposed and implemented policies through executive-order action, like the Muslim ban, family separation policies, and the repeal of DACA, as well as increased enforcement of immigration policies on the books, creates a culture of increased fear around immigration, which translates to the transnational movement of nonimmigrant international students. Open Doors (Redden 2019) reports a decline in international students, from a peak of 903,127 in 2016–2017, partially due to concerns about visa and immigration policies in the US as well as anti-immigrant rhetoric and concerns about safety. In May 2020, the White House issued a proclamation that suspended entry of Chinese international students and researchers who were seen as benefiting the Chinese military (Watanabe 2020).

3. These immigration policies held relatively firm until the 1965 Immigration Act, which lifted the national-origins quota and created a path for family reunification through immigration (Aleinikoff, Martin, and Motomura 2003; Briggs 1984; King 2000; Ngai 2004; Schneider 2001).
4. The quotation marks here indicate 1950 US Census categories.
5. In late spring 2020, this institute was disbanded in the wake of the COVID-19 pandemic budget cuts and was projected to decline in revenue because of the falling enrollment of international students.
6. I'm thinking specifically of the interdependence of Asian grocery stories and Chinese international students in Champaign-Urbana, where I went to graduate school.

REFERENCES

Aleinikoff, T. A., D. A. Martin, and H. Motomura. 2003. *Immigration and Citizenship: Process and Policy.* 5th ed. St. Paul, MN: Thomson West.

Bevis, T. B., and C. J. Lucas. 2007. *International Students in American Colleges and Universities: A History.* New York: Palgrave.

Blum, S. D. 2019. "Speak Softly . . . or at Least Speak English." *Inside Higher Ed,* January 30, 2019. https://www.insidehighered.com/views/2019/01/30/academe-should-not-police-international-students-speech-opinion.

Boggs, A., E. Meyerhoff, N. Mitchell, and Z. Schwartz-Weinstein. 2019. "Abolitionist University Studies: An Invitation." *Abolition Journal,* August 28, 2019. https://abolitionjournal.org/abolitionist-university-studies-an-invitation/.

Briggs, V. M., Jr. 1984. *Immigration Policy and the American Labor Force.* Baltimore, MD: Johns Hopkins University Press.

Cargill, O. 1956. "The Foreign Student in the Freshman Course." *College Composition and Communication* 7 (3): 122–24.

Commission on Higher Education. 1947. *Higher Education for Democracy: A Report of the President's Commission on Higher Education, vol. 1, Establishing the Goals.* New York: Harper Collins.

CUNY. 1969. *CUNY Data Book, 1967–1968.* http://www.cuny.edu/irdatabook/rpts3_AY_archive/DBook1967_1998/CUNY%20Data%20Book%201967-1968.pdf.

Du Bois, C. A. 1956. *Foreign Students and Higher Education in the United States.* Washington, DC: American Council on Education.

Fabricant, M., and S. Brier. 2016. *Austerity Blues.* Baltimore, MD: Johns Hopkins University Press.

Fines, B. 1947. "Sweeping College Changes Would Double Enrollment." *New York Times,* December 16, 1947.

Fischer, K. 2020. "To Keep International Students during the Pandemic, Colleges Get Creative." *The Chronicle of Higher Education,* May 22, 2020. https://www.chronicle.com/article/To-Keep-International-Students/248838.

Flores, N., and J. Rosa. 2015. "Undoing Appropriateness: Raciolinguistic Ideologies and Language Diversity in Education." *Harvard Educational Review* 85 (2): 149–71.

Inoue, A. 2019. "How Do We Language so People Stop Killing Each Other, or What Do We Do about White Language Supremacy?" *College Composition and Communication* 71 (2): 352–69.

Institute of International Education. 1948. *Open Doors: Report on International Education Exchange.* CD-ROM, New York Public Library, New York.

Kansas, S. 1928. *U.S. Immigration: Exclusion and Deportation.* New York: Holland Publishing.

King, D. 2000. *Making Americans: Immigration, Race, and the Origins of the Diverse Democracy.* Cambridge, MA: Harvard University Press.

Levine, D. O. 1987. *The American College and the Culture of Aspiration, 1915–1940*. Ithaca, NY: Cornell University Press.

Liptak, A. 2020. "Supreme Court Allows Trump's Wealth Test for Green Cards." *New York Times*, January 27, 2020. https://www.nytimes.com/2020/01/27/us/supreme-court-trump-green-cards.html.

Matsuda, P. 2006. "The Myth of Linguistic Homogeneity in US College Composition." *College English* 68 (6): 637–51.

Newfield, C. 2008. *Unmaking the Public University: The Forty-Year Assault on the Middle Class*. Cambridge, MA: Harvard University Press.

Ngai, M. 2004. *Impossible Subjects: Illegal Aliens and the Making of Modern America*. Princeton, NJ: Princeton University Press.

Queens College. 1949. *Queens College Bulletin*. Queens College Library, Special Collections and Archives, Queens, New York.

Queens College. 1962. *Queens College Bulletin*. Queens College Library, Special Collections and Archives, Queens, New York.

Redden, E. 2019. "Number of International Students Drop." *Inside Higher Ed*, November 18, 2019. https://www.insidehighered.com/admissions/article/2019/11/18/international-enrollments-declined-undergraduate-graduate-and.

Rosa, J., and N. Flores. 2017. "Unsettling Race and Language: Toward a Raciolinguistic Perspective." *Language in Society*, no. 46, 621–47.

Schneider, D. 2001. "Naturalization and United States Citizenship in Two Periods of Mass Migration: 1894–1930, 1965–2000." *Journal of American Ethnic History* 21 (1): 50–81.

Schueler, H. 1949. "English for Foreign Students." *Journal of Higher Education* 20 (6): 309–16.

Smith, M. B. 1955. "Some Features of Foreign-Student Adjustment." *Journal of Higher Education* 25 (5): 231–41.

Thelin, J. R. 2004. *A History of American Higher Education*. Baltimore, MD: Johns Hopkins University Press.

United States. 1950. US Census. https://1950census.archives.gov/.

Wadhia, S. S. 2019. *Banned: Immigration Enforcement in the Time of Trump*. New York: New York University Press.

Watanabe, T. 2020. "'It's the New "Chinese Exclusion Act'": How a Trump Order Could Hurt California Universities." *Los Angeles Times*, June 7, 2020.

4
"TO SUPPLANT IGNORANCE REQUIRES INSTRUCTION"
Literacy as Transnational Racial Project in the Colonial Philippines

Florianne Jimenez Perzan

> "I had a friend, a young Filipino girl, who has been one of the most diligent among the pupils of the American schools. She was staying with me two or three years ago when my publisher sent me a copy of a primer intended for use in the Philippines. . . . This Filipino girl had heard me use the expression 'poor white trash,' and I had explained to her how the Southern Negroes use the words as a term of derision of those who fail to live up to the traditions of race and family. When I took my book to her in the joy of an author in her first complete production, she looked at it a minute and burst into tears. 'Poor Filipino trash!' was all she could say for a long time, and I finally pieced it out that she was enraged because the Filipino boys and girls in my book were sometimes barefooted, sometimes clad in chinelas, and wore native camisas instead of American suits and dresses.[1] I pointed out to her that not one Filipino child in a hundred dresses otherwise, but my argument was of no avail. The children in the American readers wore natty jackets and hats and high-heeled shoes, and winter wraps, even at play, and she wanted the Filipino children to look the same." (94)
>
> —Mary H. Fee, *A Woman's Impressions of the Philippines*

The American schools to which Mary Fee refers in her memoirs were a crucial arm of US colonial power in the Philippines at the turn of the twentieth century. Having seized the Philippines (along with Puerto Rico, Cuba, and Guam) from Spain in the Spanish-American War, the US embarked on an ambitious project of mass public education, with English as the primary language of instruction. Under American colonial education, students had to navigate the multiple contradictions and inconsistencies of imperialism. On the one hand, the schools intended to fundamentally alter Filipino bodies, language, and discourse in the name of civilization: to remain too Filipino, and to resist change, rendered one unacceptable to the colonial regime. But on the other hand, to become "American," and to express that one had the rights and capabilities of an American, was inappropriate. The exchange between Mary Fee and her young friend is an example of the paradox of belonging that many Filipinos faced at this time. Fee intended the primer that she wrote to be a realistic, relatable representation of Filipino life for young Filipino readers, not a denigration of native customs or dress.[2] However, the young girl saw the illustrations and felt a deep sense of disappointment. The girl was hurt by the idea that her teacher could not see her like the American children she had read and heard so much about: on the contrary, she was more similar to a derided form of whiteness. Furthermore, the insult of "Filipino trash," coming from Black discourse ("the Southern Negroes"), placed Filipino bodies below Black ones in the American context of inequality. The epigraph thus calls us to ask, as readers, how US racial discourse maps onto the colonial context in the Philippines, and how colonized Filipinos responded to this discourse. Being centered around a written text, it also calls up questions about how literacy shapes, and is shaped by, this racial discourse.

This chapter thus reframes literacy during colonial education in the Philippines as a *transnational racial project*. Following the definition of the "transnational" offered by scholars such as You (2018), this chapter aims to "highlight and work to build connections, crossings, and spaces between the existing national, ethnic, racial, and linguistic boundaries" (2). As asserted by histories of transnational writing education in Indonesia (Engelson 2011), Syria (Arnold 2014, 2018), You (2010), and Jamaica (Milson-Whyte 2015), US imperialism and English literacy education outside of the United States are deeply connected, and writing education has been used as a colonial tool. Thus, I call attention to the movement across the geopolitical borders of the ideology of literacy as white property, how this ideology operated differently in the racial politics of the colonial Philippines, and how this transnational racial project became visible in student writing from the colonial period. This essay thus offers two central contributions: first, through a review of historical sources, I map out the tensions and contradictions in the history of writing education in the Philippines. Through this mapping, I demonstrate that the notion of racialized subjects' "fitness" thoroughly informed colonial policy and the teaching of writing in English in the Philippines. Second, I analyze an essay written by a Filipino student during US colonization and, using rhetorical analysis, show how literacy as a transnational racial project becomes visible in her arguments on the benefits of literacy for social change. With these two major contributions, I examine on multiple scales the discourses on race and class that were circulating around US imperialism, and the responses to these discourses from colonized subjects. Through this analysis, I argue that students drew upon a consciousness of their racial subject-position to critique the inequality of US imperial rule.

The essay analyzed in this chapter, Macaria Allarey's "The importance of education," is one among 153 student compositions in the personal papers of Frederick G. Behner, a teacher from Michigan who traveled on the USS Transport *Thomas* in 1901. Behner was part of a group of over five hundred American teachers, who were selected by an examination, to establish the Philippines' first public schools. The entire archive of student essays totals about nine hundred pages of loose-leaf, handwritten text in English on various topics such as science, folklore, travel, reading, and education. Many students, including Macaria, signed their names and added dates to their essays. Over half of the essays were marked with corrections, word substitutions, deletions, and marginal comments, and in some cases, a numerical grade and a verbal assessment ("Very good"; "Please correct and hand back"). Based on the content and tone of these annotations, I assume that these annotations were made by a teacher. In this chapter, I represent teacher annotations as faithfully as possible through strike-through, insertion, and spacing, and I indicate their written commentary on the student texts in italics. As for the students, I estimate that Macaria and the other students were between fourteen and seventeen years old when these essays were written.[3]

My method of rhetorical analysis is informed by the persistent presence and co-occurrence of significant themes across the archive. "Literacy" and "race" did not readily emerge as major themes in my initial thematic coding. During the first pass, I noted that several students repeatedly echoed three sentiments in different words: *Education can make people equal; Education makes people better;* and *Better people make better leaders.* After I noted the significance of these sentiments in student essays, I used rhetorical analysis to reflect on how students were positioning themselves, what kind of reader they implied or assumed, how they made certain claims such as the three sentiments above, and why these would occur. I supported my interpretations with archival research on the Filipino experience during American colonization. By examining primary and secondary sources, I have established a historical context for student writing and writing education in English that recognizes Filipino agency and resistance.

THE IDEOLOGY OF LITERACY AS WHITE PROPERTY

The cultural power of literacy—its benefit to individuals, as well as to communities on larger scales—has been witnessed over and over again throughout history. This ideology of literacy, or "literacy myth" (Graff 1979), promises that it will improve *everyone*'s moral, social, intellectual, or economic lot, regardless of actual individual or societal circumstances. In the field of literacy studies, scholars have found that literacy holds promise, but for individuals at the mercy of social and political forces it can by no means guarantee progress (Brandt 2001; Graff 1979; Graff 1995; Street 1984).

Among these larger social and political forces, race and its connections to literacy have also been studied intently. The scholarship has shown repeatedly that for people of color in the US, literacy has been present at moments of marginalization and domination (Hoang 2015; Young 2004; Royster 2000). Literacy (or lack thereof) has been used to keep fundamental rights such as suffrage, citizenship, and education from people of color. As Catherine Prendergast has argued in *Literacy and Racial Justice* (2003), embedded within the ideology of literacy is the notion that literacy belongs to whites. Specifically, Prendergast argues that "the ideology of literacy has been sustained primarily as a response to perceived threats to White property interests, White privilege, the maintenance of 'White' identity, or the conception of America as a White nation" (7). Through historical study, Prendergast demonstrates how literacy has been a stand-in for white property in pivotal moments in US history. Her argument shows that literacy's imbrication in bigotry and white supremacy is not accidental—it is a purposeful *racial project*, which Omi and Winant (2015) define as "an interpretation, representation, or explanation of racial identities and meanings, and an effort to organize and distribute resources (economic, political, cultural) along particular racial lines" (125). In other words, literacy remains a constantly moving target for people of color in the United States, and even when it is acquired, it does not always deliver on its promises.

While Prendergast's argument has focused on events within US borders, my research shows that this notion of literacy as white property also holds transnational implications. Through the movement of US ideology to and upon the Philippines, and through the deliberate construction of the US colonial project, the ideology of literacy as white property was replicated in the Philippines. In the next section, I articulate a short history of race during the Spanish and American colonial period in the Philippines, and show how this history informed writing education during US colonization. I thus argue that the teaching of writing in the Philippines during American colonization was a *transnational racial project*—an effort to redistribute the benefits of literacy along racial lines that crossed national boundaries and fortified the lines of race that justified US colonization. This claim demonstrates, on a macro scale, the pressures upon literacy and writing education, and how literacy was used to create race and class stratification in the Philippines.

The role of race in US imperial rule cannot be understood in a historical vacuum: the racial politics of the Philippines at the turn of the twentieth century was shaped by encounters with its Southeast Asian neighbors, Spanish Catholicism, European whiteness, and Chinese immigration. The subjugation of the Philippines by Spain, specifically the lack of political representation in the Spanish Cortes, was justified by the assumed savagery and superstition of the Filipino people. As "recalcitrant savages and potential subversives" (Rafael 2009, 347), Filipinos were treated as the exception among Spain's colonial territories.

This geopolitical inequality thus created racial hierarchies within the Philippines. At the pinnacle of nineteenth-century Filipino society were the *peninsulares* or those who claimed bilinear Spanish ancestry and who had been born in Spain. Below them were the *creoles*, who also claimed bilinear Spanish ancestry but were "corrupted" by their birth in the Philippines. One could also be marked by blood mixture, or *mestizaje*: these were the Spanish mestizos, who were typically the children of Spanish men and native Filipino women, as well as the Chinese mestizos. As a burgeoning middle and upper middle class, both Spanish and Chinese mestizos would become economically prosperous but remain socially excluded. A third marker of difference was inclusion or exclusion from the Spanish Catholic church: those who were evangelized or baptized into Catholicism but did not have Spanish or Chinese ancestry were called *indios*. Those outside of the Church—the Chinese, the *infieles* or unconquered highland animists, and the members of Muslim communities in the south—remained on the fringes of Spanish colonial society (Kramer 2006). In this highly stratified and unequal social context, we see a complex overlapping of nation, race, ethnicity, and class as determinants of power.

By the late nineteenth century, towards the end of Spanish colonial rule, some Filipinos would begin to resist these Spanish colonial hierarchies by "satirizing Spanish imperial racism and [holding] Philippine peoples up favorably to some of its standards" (Kramer 2006, 41). Sociocultural achievement through writing, education, and scientific training thus became the favored mode of resistance, because it begged the question: if Filipinos could be as cultured as Spaniards, why couldn't they be given the same rights? The irony of this resistance is not only in how it reified racist colonial standards but also in how sociocultural achievement as a mode of resistance was only accessible to elite Filipinos. Filipino elites' exposure to European liberalism was largely due to their education and travel in Europe, which families or individuals financed themselves. Thus, challenging racism under Spanish colonial rule was predicated upon class, and the individual merits of the elite made to speak for an entire nation.

Class and race inequality would remain salient during American colonial rule. Strategically, however, whatever racial formation the United States led in the Philippines needed to be markedly different from the inequality of the Spanish colonial era while still justifying the lack of self-governance for Filipinos. According to Kramer (2006), this was exercised as "a regime of collaboration between Americans and Filipinos, one in which US officials recognized provincial and metropolitan elites as unequal political partners" (142). Because of their education, Filipino elites were seen by American civil administration as the most rational members of Filipino society and were thus given a measure of agency over governance through membership on committees or civil service appointments. Education became a cornerstone of US colonial rule in two ways. The few who already possessed it were considered the most fit for inclusion in colonial management, while the majority, who were uneducated, justified US control. Thus, education served as a means for the US to position itself as a benevolent and tutelary empire, with the first American teachers as its emissaries.

In line with many other colonial educational movements, pushing the English language was justified by reason of its connections to white culture and norms. In 1902, William Howard Taft, the first civil governor of the Philippines, declared that "through the English language certainly, by reading its literature, by becoming aware of the history of the English race, they will breathe in the spirit of Anglo-Saxon individualism . . ." (as quoted in Tupas 2008, 52). Educational planners took this idea seriously: English classes often revolved around literary texts from the canon of British and American literature. In the US's project of benevolent assimilation, reading and writing remained tethered to a white American ethos: as argued by Wesling (2011), the American literary text as deployed in the pedagogy of the colonial classroom served as "evidence of the cultural and moral superiority of America's Anglo-Saxon civilization, thus providing the ideological justification through which the United States' imperial interventions were recast as 'civilizing' missions" (6). While Wesling's work is focused on the texts that circulated in the colonial school, their work implicates literate activity—the reading of literary texts, the modeling of American literary style for student writing (Ick 2000; Martin 2004)—more broadly. For a Filipino to participate in the English classroom was to be in dialogue with white American culture, but, as the anecdote from Mary Fee illustrates, it also meant learning that you were not white, and furthermore, you were *beneath* whiteness.

When writing in English was explicitly mentioned by educational administration, it was often deemed less important than oral composition and conversational English. But it is clear that students did write: *The Filipino Teacher's Manual,* an instructional volume on pedagogy for American teachers in the Philippine Islands, had an entire section dedicated to teaching composition: "the art of putting words together properly in sentences to express our thoughts" (Theobald 116). The author, F. C. Theobald, recommended that students write one to two new compositions a week, that teachers should mark students' composition notebooks "in order of excellence," and that the best student writing be shown to local leaders ("the *concejales* or *tenientes*"). Teachers were also instructed to provide conscientious feedback, and it was recommended for students to correct one composition and return it to the teacher before starting another. Composition thus had a social function: to instill obedience, discipline, and perseverance through written exchanges between student and teacher, and to showcase the success of the American school to local stakeholders. Thus, both the process of acquiring literacy in English for Filipino students and the performance of this acquisition were part of the colonizing process.

Writing education in English at the colonial schoolhouse thus occurred in the collisions between the racist assumptions that shaped the decision for the US to "liberate" the Philippines from Spain, the racial politics of *mestizaje* and racial/ethnic stratification in the Philippines, and the fraught politics of race and literacy circulating in the US at the time. In the next section, I focus on competing ideas on the "fitness" of Filipinos and examine literacy's imbrication in these ideologies.

FILIPINO FITNESS AND UNFITNESS FOR LITERACY

The US colonization of the Philippines was tied to a white ethos: politicians framed the US's involvement in the Philippines not as colonization but as an ethical and moral imperative to civilize downtrodden savages. In a speech to Congress on January 9, 1900, Senator Albert Beveridge argued stridently that US dominion over the Philippine Islands was "the mission of our race, trustee under God, of the civilization of the world" (as cited in Wesling 2011, 1). In other words, the inherent superiority of whiteness, and the unspoken inferiority of non-whiteness, rationalized the US colonization of the Philippines. This racialized discourse of American empire would continue to persist throughout the American colonial era in different forms, especially in education.

The whiteness of the American ethos is also tied to the history of literacy in the United States. In *Writing against Racial Injury*, Haivan Hoang (2015) explores the entrenchment of language and literacy in the American ethos, and the implications of this ethos for Asian American writers. Ultimately, she argues, "To become lettered *in English* . . . was to become an American self whose virtue was defined by morality, intellectual talent, civic engagement, and socioeconomic worth" (6). However, literacy education was often distributed and manipulated along racial lines: some communities of color were declared fit only for certain kinds of literacy, and others were not offered literacy at all. Hoang continues, "If literacy symbolized the path toward becoming the 'good' American, then legacies of racism undoubtedly seated racial minorities in opposition to this ethos" (7). Literacy education became not about redistributing the goods of literacy but about converting (or coercing) people of color into white ideologies of Christian faith, industriousness, and heterosexuality without giving them the rights and privileges afforded to white people.

Over in the Philippines, notions of Filipino "fitness" served US imperial ambition by placing Filipinos outside of the American literate ethos. This was no accident: US engagement with Filipinos was shaped by administrators' knowledge of people of color in the United States, specifically Native Americans and Black Americans. Even as educational policy toward Filipino literacy would shift, the unfitness of the Filipino race for literacy remained the bedrock of colonial education. The first superintendent of schools in the Philippines (1900–1902) was Fred Atkinson, formerly a principal of Springfield High School in Massachusetts. Atkinson's tenure as superintendent was distinguished by his strong push for industrial education, which was heavily influenced by the manual training in Massachusetts public schools and the Hampton and Tuskegee industrial schools for Black students. In his unpublished manuscript, *The Present Educational Movement in the Philippines*, Atkinson wrote: "In this system we beware the possibility of overdoing the matter of higher education and unfitting the Filipino for practical work. We should heed the lesson taught us in our reconstruction period when we started to educate the negro. The education of the masses here must be an agricultural and industrial one, after the pattern of our Tuskegee Institute at home" (as cited in May 1980, 93). In this way, white American discourse on Blackness and its racist assumptions informed the paternalistic relationship between American educators and Filipinos.

Atkinson's successor, David Barrows, held a very different vision. For Barrows, the aim of colonial education, and of US civil government in general, was the destruction of *caciquismo*—the political and cultural overdominance of a small number of landed elite, usually of Spanish or Chinese mestizo lineage, over large swaths of peasantry. Thus, Barrows's administration (1903–1909) advocated for the creation of "peasant proprietors" who could cultivate and profit from their own small farms, rather than "a great body of unskilled labor, dependent for living upon its daily wage, willing to work in great gangs, submissive to the rough handling of the 'boss'" (as cited in May 1980, 99). To achieve this, Barrows wanted a greater emphasis on academic and literary subjects—reading, writing, civics training, geography, arithmetic—and to shift away from manual training.

While Atkinson's industrial education and Barrows's liberal education were at odds, both administrations engaged with the myth of literacy and the so-called question of whether Filipinos were, as a race, "fit" for it. Atkinson believed that an overabundance of literacy would dissuade Filipinos from engaging in physical labor—thus, under his rule, the myth transforms into physical labor being transcended by literacy that Filipinos did not deserve. Barrows, on the other hand, believed that Filipinos were worthy of literacy, but only insofar as it could supplant old ways of thinking and improve Filipinos as a race.

As for the response of Filipino students and their communities to this discourse, we can infer from a public debate in the *Manila Times* that Filipinos chafed at the overwhelming power that foreign bureaucrats had to dictate their destinies. The *Manila Times* is the Philippines' oldest English-language newspaper, with origins in American colonial rule. Its first publisher, Thomas Gowan, started publishing the paper in 1898 to meet the demand for an American paper in Manila, specifically for US Army soldiers. The paper's masthead announced itself as the "Pioneer American daily in the Far East" ("About Us" n.d.). The following exchange, a debate between "Filipino Student" and "W. H. F." in the Public Forum section of the paper, is indicative of the investments that advocates and detractors of industrial education held, and shows one among many possible perspectives that Filipino students may have taken. More crucially, we see at work the ideology of literacy as white property and its underside, the unfitness of Filipinos for literacy.

On May 26, 1908, the letter of an anonymous writer, Filipino Student, appeared in the *Manila Times*'s Public Forum section:

> A student without money, upon leaving school, would immediately cast about for the occupation that would yield him the largest salary. What would it be, that of a farmhand receiving a maximum of ten pesos per month, that of a mechanic receiving seventy-five centavos to one peso and fifty centavos per day, or that of a clerk with a minimum of twenty-five and a maximum of say two hundred pesos per month? . . . What we Filipino students wish to know is, where we can get the best salaries and where there is the best opportunity for advancement and promotion . . . if *The Times* will devote more space to telling us where we can make a good living and less to talking about the learning of trades which, if acquired, will scarcely support a man in comfort, we'll all subscribe for the paper. (Filipino Student 1908)

This anonymous student made an argument that was conscious of his or her class and racial position. Filipino Student approached the issue pragmatically: jobs involving heavy manual labor did not pay as much as white-collar jobs, therefore he or she was interested in training for the latter type of jobs. The student then leveraged his or her literate position as a potential *Manila Times* reader and subscriber to demand an improvement of the discourse on Filipino industry, and thus that readers like him or her be informed about better opportunities.

On May 27, 1908, the *Manila Times* published the scathing reply of W. H. F.:

> It seems to be the ambition of our 'Filipino Student' just to wriggle thro' life as a menial, or subordinate cog in the great wheel of industry. He dreams of the ecstasy of roll-top desks and delusive click-click of the typewriter, while he swoons in horrible nightmares of the honest trader and tiller of the soil.
>
> . . . Ask yourself these questions: What have I done to boast of? What have I done, or what am I now doing, to raise my country from the slough of chaotic decline? Take a cursory glance through the immediate history of your own people, and then ask, Who are the great men of my country? You will find, that outside of a few politicians and literary blubbers you would be able to count them all on your nimble digits.
>
> . . . So, we would advise our erudite "Filipino Student" to dismantle his garb of egotism, and throw aside, for the present at least, his prejudice to that honest toil worthy its hide. (W. H. F. 1908)

The response from W. H. F. is dripping with condescension. In the span of a few sentences, the writer attacked both Filipino Student's individual aspirations, and then Filipino identity more broadly. Filipino Student's desire for a higher salary was dismissed as a fetish, and the aversion to manual labor dismissed as a melodramatic reaction. Then, the writer made an appeal based on national character: because the

Philippines had produced so few "great men," there was no point in students aspiring to be like "politicians and literary blubbers." W. H. F. then signs off by dismissing white-collar ambition as "egotism," implying that the Filipino student was overreaching his station. While we do not know what race W. H. F. was, or whether he or she was an American, we can infer, based on the writer's use of **"your** own people," that they didn't identify as Filipino. Clearly, W. H. F. saw literacy as *not* Filipino property, and deemed it inappropriate to believe anything else. This echoes what Hoang and Prendergast have argued: even as Filipino Student professed that he or she bought into the literacy myth, the rewards of literacy—a professional career with a higher income—were still kept firmly out of reach.[4]

Ultimately, the Atkinson-Barrows debate and this brief interlude in the *Manila Times* demonstrate that under US colonization, literacy became a stand-in for the ability to transcend one's circumstances, to improve one's lot, and to engage (or not engage) in specific kinds of labor. *The debates over Filipinos' fitness for literacy were never about whether literacy was good or bad, or whether the educational system was capable of making change.* It was a debate about whether or not Filipinos deserved agency over their intellectual and physical labor. As a transnational racial project, literacy worked because it aligned itself with two vectors of power: class and race. Literacy was, and had always been, more accessible to Filipino elites that could collaborate with and inform US rule, and thus represented a form of socioeconomic mobility that was threatening to the colonial project. Literacy also represented the possibility that Filipinos could transcend their individual circumstances and follow ambitions that did not align with US visions of Filipino capacity. Thus, under US rule, literacy was simultaneously the criterion for receiving its rewards, and the reward itself.

In the next section, I analyze a student essay on literacy to examine how these discourses of fitness are made visible in a piece of Filipino student writing. The writer positions herself as both a potential beneficiary of literacy, and a critic of the inequality that literacy has created. My analysis will show that an examination of Macaria's subject-position as deployed through the use of "we" is a critique of how colonial ideology limited access to literacy and its potential for social mobility.

INDIVIDUALISM AND SOCIAL CONSCIOUSNESS

Championing the individual over the collective was an important part of the discussion on Filipino fitness, particularly in the liberal model that

Barrows endorsed. Barrows, the ardent believer in literacy that he was, advocated for the individual by claiming that by cultivating the peasant-proprietor, education would sever the social link between landowner and peasant. Writing instruction also echoed this discourse: the previously mentioned *Filipino Teacher's Manual*, a handbook for teachers of all subjects in the Philippines, championed the individual voice in composition, and reminded teachers that "the aim of composition work is the natural expression in simple, clear English of the child's own thought, not that of the teacher" (Theobald 1907, 123). The unquestioned dominance of the individual over the collective is rooted in the ideological dominance of Western individualism over the past two centuries (Mao 2006). Under US colonial rule, individualism clearly held sway at multiple scales.

How can we read student writing against the discourses on individualism that existed at larger scales? Macaria's essay, as well as many of the essays in the Behner archive, expresses arguments in the royal "we." One might say this could be a consequence of instruction, but this particular essay, "The importance of education," *never* uses "I," while other compositions from Macaria and other students go back and forth in the usage of "we" and "I." We can assume, then, that for this essay's specific topic, Macaria's consistent deployment of "we" and complete absence of "I" is purposeful and intentional.

Macaria opens her essay by explaining the connections between education and success:

> [In order that existence of] To supplant ignorance [be passed away, the first thing] require[s] d is instruction.
>
> If we intend to be ourselves important in this world and desire to [accomplish] live a happy life, we might be successful by means of getting an education.

The "we" that Macaria invokes in her essay has an indefinite referent, and this indefiniteness opens up a range of interpretive possibilities. Is this a general "we" that speaks to all mankind? Or is it her classmates and fellow Filipinos? Or is "we" inclusive of her American teacher/reader? The "we" that Macaria invokes here is a body that is partaking, or is about to partake, of education. Based on this premise, her "we" includes herself and her fellow students and Filipinos, and excludes her American reader. In this case, she pointedly draws a line between herself and her American teacher-audience, forcing them to listen to her desires for national and racial progress. As Macaria continues her discussion of why education is valuable, we see her ardently advocating for literacy as a collective good: her use of "we" to describe the subjects of colonial education articulates a perspective that considers literacy as good, but only insofar as it benefits everyone.

In the next part of her opening paragraph, Macaria articulates that getting an education has two benefits: it has the ability to improve intellectual capacity and can create social change:

> It not only makes people intelligent and widens their horizon and inspires them with a desire to become something more than they are, but gives equal opportunities and *is* the cause of equality.

Macaria's use of "not only" to connect the two promises of literacy sets up an unequal relation between "mak[ing] people intelligent," which focuses on gaining intelligence as individual attribute, and "giving equal opportunities and is the cause of equality," which are social benefits. This use of "equal opportunities" and "equality" alludes to some prior consciousness on Macaria's part: for her, the world is already deeply unequal, and education can correct this. This statement is an echoing of the literacy myth that Barrows's administration endorsed.

However, there is a subversive edge to Macaria's identification with literacy, due to her consciousness of her subject-position as a colonized subject and as Filipino: as we saw in the debate between W.H.F. and Filipino Student, Filipinos were not viewed as entitled to literacy. We see this consciousness coming through in her allusions to justice:

> We find it beneficial, *for* as we gain [a] knowledge [which is necessary for a] *just as for we* understand[ing] the best ways to do anything; we get modern ideas about all the world; [different] our thoughts [in each time] change as we get more education and we come to know in all the current events in *from* all over this globe by reading different kinds of books, magazines and newspapers which are all parts of education. More than these, we learn to get our own respective rights [*sp.*] and justice[,] which are *of* [the most important in our lives] greatest importance, and to defend and protect ourselves.

When Macaria says, "we learn to get our own respective rights and justice . . . and to defend and protect ourselves," she does not explicitly name the conditions or circumstances that demand rights and justice, nor does she say why rights and justice trump the intellectual benefits of literacy. If we step back and imagine the scene of the colonial school, we see how oppression and inequality might loom large in her mind. In the wake of the Philippine-American War, Filipino society was very much in flux, and Filipinos were caught between competing geopolitical and cultural alliances, between languages, and between desires to resist or cooperate with US imperialism. In fact, although the Philippine revolutionary government had declared loyalty to the

American government as early as April 1901, armed resistance and insurrection movements would continue all over the country until 1913 (Steinbock-Pratt 2019). Given this context of unrest, as well as the long histories of Filipino oppression, it is easy to see how a consciousness of resistance and injustice might permeate the writing of a Filipino student.

While Macaria's writing does show a keen awareness of marginalization, and a strong desire for social change on behalf of her country, it also shows the writer caught in the contradictions of the literacy myth. By the end of her essay, Macaria's writing seems to shore up the myth of literacy as a pure meritocracy, and to endorse literacy as a means for the redistribution of power:

> People who did not receive instructions,[5] usually are those who have the simplest forms of life, those who have the simplest forms of life, those who have queer customs and ideas, whose thoughts [*sp.*] having ~~not~~ received *no* intellectual trainings are so poor that they ~~could~~ can not be ~~needed~~ in any important affairs about government or *even* ordinary matters; they have a steady course of life, *as long as a stronger mind governs them but* self-government is unfit for them; while learned [~~ones~~] men are those who climb~~ed~~ the ladder of fame and greatness, who hold and entertain [~~at present~~] high professions, who occupy influencial employment *yet* who have a quiet and happy lives, and who become one of the enlightened peoples of the world.

Macaria characterizes education as a means to distinguish between leaders and followers, and the "self-government" as the right of the educated. This echoes the US colonial perspective that placed the elite, who already had access to education, in seats of power. Thus, while she expresses an earnest desire to make the world more equal, she is also buying into the literacy myth that made things *more* unequal.

However, as she closes her essay, Macaria adds a level of nuance to her running theme of inequality by discussing class. She claims that, through education, poor and rich people can become equal:

> Poor and rich may have the same hope and equal chances [~~by the process~~] of getting an education which in a large sense is the necessity of the times among every people who desire either material or spiritual prosperity.

While this statement may constitute another instance of buying into the literacy myth, she, like Filipino Student in the *Manila Times*, spells out one very clear, pragmatic benefit of literacy: "material prosperity." As we saw in the exchange between W. H. F. and Filipino Student, the ability of Filipinos to control their economic destinies and to have agency over the rewards of literacy was directly inimical to US imperial rule.

Thus, coming from a writer such as Macaria who identifies strongly as Filipino and writes with the collective nation in mind, the claim that education can solve material inequity and political disenfranchisement reads almost like a threat. To a certain kind of reader, literacy becomes dangerous because it allows the marginalized to alter their social position. Macaria's hope for education as a great equalizer between social classes directly engages with the overlapping discourses of class and race in the Philippines. While race is not explicitly mentioned in Macaria's essay, her seizure and redistribution of literacy as a common good, and her characterization of inequality as a matter of class, interrogates the history of colonial rule that has allowed literacy to concentrate among the elite.

CONCLUSION

The essays in this section of *Writing on the Wall* have cast a critical eye on nationalism and ethnonationalism in the United States. This is for good reason: as the past few years of the Trump administration have taught us, a desire to close off a nation's borders on the basis of "making it great again" can only cause further injustice for those who have been historically excluded. It serves both scholars and the public well to be critical of the deployment of nationalism and to interrogate who gets to deploy it and why.

However, I hazard that it's possible to recuperate nationalism in a form that strengthens connections and civic relations, rather than centering on who does and doesn't belong. In the Philippines, where I grew up, and where this research is focused, nationalism—the love of one's country and its people, the desire to appreciate the local rather than default to the foreign—is seen as deeply necessary, because until relatively recently nationhood had never been ours in the first place. When your country has been colonized for hundreds of years, and continues to suffer its effects, nationalism is not necessarily a bad thing. Seen from the colonial wound (Anzaldúa 2012), nationalism can also be about strengthening a collective formation by making conditions more equal. Macaria, the student writer whose composition is the focus of this chapter, does exactly that. In the face of colonial suppression, Macaria writes about the radical and empathetic potential of education—the hope that education enables its possessors to advocate for themselves and for others. Moreover, though she never says it directly, Macaria is conscious that she writes not just as an individual but as a representative of her people, who all deserve the rewards of literacy. In Macaria's writing, then, we find a form of nationalism that considers other people, and wants conditions to change in order to benefit everyone, not just the individual. What this example from a colonized nation suggests is that there are other, better, ways to advocate for one's status as a nation, beyond strengthening borders.

Furthermore, this chapter also examines the commonplaces and germinal theories in writing studies that often "travel" in transnational scholarship: literacy, race, and class. What this chapter contributes is a "slowed down" analysis of how discourses of race, class, and literacy move through history and have traveled from the United States to one of its colonies. The chapter shows that national legacies of literacy, race, and class can disembed themselves from their national contexts: thus, we need approaches that are attentive to movement, hybridity, and replication across locations and scales. The role of history in our scholarship, in the necessity of both (re)writing history and drawing from it in our analyses, cannot be overstated. The mapping of history in this chapter demonstrates that literacy adheres to vectors of inequality, but always in historically and culturally specific ways.

Second, this chapter contributes to conversations that acknowledge the entanglements between various racist discourses that marginalize people of color. To acknowledge these entanglements as rooted in long histories of oppression, and to observe how these problematic discourses inform each other across national boundaries, adds another dimension to our understanding of race and white supremacy. Simply put: the oppression of one marginalized community begets the oppression of multiple communities. But within this entanglement also lies the hope of solidarity across national, racial, and ethnic lines. As scholars engage with issues of identity on a transnational scale, our analyses must consider how whiteness and race move and operate along this scale, and pursue the dismantling of these structures on these scales as well.

Acknowledgment. The author wishes to thank her research assistants, Kyle Arena and Danielle Jin, for their meticulous transcription, the staff of the University of Michigan Bentley Historical Library for providing scans of the student papers, and the staff of the American Historical Collection at the Ateneo de Manila University for their invaluable assistance. The archival research in this chapter was supported by a Dissertation Fieldwork Grant from the University of Massachusetts Amherst Graduate School.

NOTES

1. *Chinelas* are slippers or sandals; *camisas* are Filipino native blouses or shirts.
2. *The First Year Book*, by Mary H. Fee, Margaret A. Purcell, Parker H. Fillmore, John W. Ritchie (1907).
3. This estimate is based on the content and vocabulary of the essays, as well as inference based on other archival sources. In a 1905 report on schools in the Philippine Islands, the Superintendent reported that Victor Oblenas, another student whose work appears in the archive, received a scholarship for further study in the United States. His age was reported as seventeen years old.
4. The heated discussion on Filipino education in the paper did not end here. Exchanges by letter between Filipino Student, various anonymous writers, American politicians in the US and the Philippines, educators, and administrators would continue in the pages of the *Manila Times* for several months more.
5. In the margins, a teacher has commented, "Here did you mean uneducated or uncivilized?"

REFERENCES

"About Us." n.d. *Manila Times Online.* https://www.manilatimes.net/about-us/.
Allarey, Macaria. "The Importance of Education." Box 1, Frederick G. Behner Papers, Bentley Historical Library, University of Michigan.
Anzaldúa, Gloria. 2012. *Borderlands/La frontera: The New Mestiza.* San Francisco: Aunt Lute Books.
Arnold, Lisa R. 2014. "'The Worst Part of the Dead Past': Language Attitudes, Policies, and Pedagogies at Syrian Protestant College, 1866–1902." *College Composition and Communication* 66 (2): 276–300.
Arnold, Lisa R. 2018. "'Today the Need Arises' اَلحاجة تستدق موِيلا: Arabic Student Writing at the Turn of the Twentieth Century." In *Transnational Writing Education: Theory, History, and Practice*, edited by Xiaoye You, 95–112. New York: Routledge.
Brandt, Deborah. 2001. *Literacy in American Lives.* Cambridge, UK: Cambridge University Press.
Engelson, Amber. 2011. *Writing the Local-Global: An Ethnography of Friction and Negotiation in an English-Using Indonesian Ph.D. Program.* PhD diss., University of Massachusetts Amherst.
Fee, Mary H. 1910. *A Woman's Impressions of the Philippines.* Chicago, IL: A. C. McClurg.
Filipino Student. 1908. "Look for the Largest Salary." *Manila Times*, May 26, 1908.
Graff, Harvey. 1979. *The Literacy Myth: Literacy and Social Structure in the Nineteenth-Century City.* New Brunswick, NJ: Transaction Publishers.
Graff, Harvey J. 1995. *The Labyrinths of Literacy: Reflections on Literacy Past and Present.* Pittsburgh, PA: University of Pittsburgh Press.
Hoang, Haivan. 2015. *Writing against Racial Injury: The Politics of Asian American Student Rhetoric.* Pittsburgh, PA: University of Pittsburgh Press.
Ick, Judy Celine. 2000. "Ilonggos, Igorrottes, Merchants, and Jews: Shakespeare and American Colonial Education in the Philippines." *Humanities Diliman*, no. 1, 110–34.
Kramer, Paul. 2006. *The Blood of Government: Race, Empire, the United States, and the Philippines.* Chapel Hill: University of North Carolina Press.
Mao, LuMing. 2006. *Reading Chinese Fortune Cookie: The Making of Chinese American Rhetoric.* Logan: Utah State University Press.
Martin, Isabel. 2004. "Longfellow's Legacy: Education and the Shaping of Philippine Writing." *World Englishes* 23 (1): 129–39.
May, Glenn Anthony. 1980. *Social Engineering in the Philippines: The Aims, Execution, and Impact of American Colonial Policy, 1900–1913.* Westport, CT: Greenwood Press.

Milson-Whyte, Vivette. 2015. *Academic Writing Instruction for Creole-Influenced Students*. Mona, Jamaica: University of the West Indies Press.
Omi, Michael, and Howard Winant. 2015. *Racial Formation in the United States*. 3rd ed. New York: Routledge / Taylor & Francis Group.
Prendergast, Catherine. 2003. *Literacy and Racial Justice: The Politics of Learning after Brown v. Board of Education*. Carbondale: Southern Illinois University Press.
Steinbock-Pratt, Sarah. 2019. *Educating the Empire: American Teachers and Contested Colonization in the Philippines*. Cambridge, UK: Cambridge University Press.
Rafael, Vicente. 2009. "Introduction: War, Race, and Nation in Philippine Colonial Transitions." *Japanese Journal of Southeast Asian Studies* 49 (3): 347–55. https://doi.org/10.20495/tak.49.3_347.
Royster, Jacqueline Jones. 2000. *Traces of a Stream: Literacy and Social Change among African American Women*. Pittsburgh: University of Pittsburgh Press.
Street, Brian. 1984. *Literacy in Theory and Practice*. Cambridge, UK: Cambridge University Press.
Theobald, Harry. 1907. *The Filipino Teacher's Manual*. New York: World Book Company.
Tupas, Ruanni. 2008. "Bourdieu, Historical Forgetting, and the Problem of English in the Philippines." *Philippine Studies*, no. 56, 47–67.
Wesling, Meg. 2011. *Empire's Proxy: American Literature and U.S. Imperialism in the Philippines*. New York: New York University Press.
W. H. F. 1908. "Look for the Largest Salary." *Manila Times*, May 27, 1908.
You, Xiaoye. 2010. *Writing in The Devil's Tongue: A History of English Composition in China*. Carbondale: Southern Illinois University Press.
You, Xiaoye. 2018. "Introduction: Making a Transnational Turn in Writing Education." In *Transnational Writing Education: Theory, History, and Practice*, edited by Xiaoye You, 1–17. New York: Routledge.
Young, Morris. 2004. *Minor Re/Visions: Asian American Literacy Narratives as a Rhetoric of Citizenship*. Carbondale: Southern Illinois University Press.

5

SCALING COSMOPOLITANISM IN THE AGE OF PRECARITY

Tony Scott

This chapter was primarily drafted in 2020, a time during which the lives of most people on Earth changed substantially. As COVID-19 quickly made its way through populations across the globe, governments and scientific institutions struggled to respond; hospitals and healthcare systems were overwhelmed; the global economy was shocked into recession; and borders were closed, bringing an unprecedented era of global mobility to an at least temporary halt. Amid this crisis, the question "when will we be back to normal?" emerged as a common refrain. In "The Pandemic Is a Portal," a widely circulated article published in April 2020, writer and activist Arundhati Roy countered that the pandemic did not bring about a deviation from normalcy; rather, it exposed and amplified already-existent global crises. The dramatically unequal effects of the pandemic on the already vulnerable and marginalized; the confused, politically polarized, and often simply unaccountable responses of governments; the lack of established national safety nets and civic infrastructures that would have served to more efficiently alleviate hardships and marshal and distribute information and resources; and the months-long inability of civic institutions to quickly coordinate research and authoritatively shape policy across organizational, national, and international boundaries—all brought into relief in 2020 the deep political economic problems that were evident in 2019. Roy argued that a return to the normative crisis of pre-2020 global neoliberalism was neither desirable nor tenable. In this frightening time of rupture and possibility, rather than asking when we will be back to normal, we should be asking, what comes next and how can we make it better?

Prior to the pandemic, higher education had also become conditioned to normative crisis due to the neoliberal and austerity-driven economic policies that have become globally dominant over the past four decades. In the US, governmental support for higher education peaked over forty years ago in 1975, when state funding accounted for 60.3 percent of total funding. By 2010, after decades of tax cuts and rising enrollments, the share of state funding for higher education had dropped to 34.1 percent (Mortensen 2012, 27).[1] As states have steadily diminished per-student funding the cost burden was shifted directly to students and their families. Among public institutions, tuition accounted for only 20.9 percent of total revenue in 1980, but by 2019 tuition had risen to account for almost half (49%) of total revenue (SHEEO 2019). A College Board study found that the average cost of tuition at public four-year colleges and universities increased 50 percent between 2003 and 2013 alone (2013, 15). As tuition has risen, so too has individual debt accumulation, especially for postsecondary degrees (See NCES 2017). This sharp increase in debt has happened during a period in which over two-thirds of faculty members in the US are now on contingent appointments and over 50 percent of faculty members are employed part-time overall (AAUP 2020). Whether they work in North America, Africa, Europe, Australia, or Asia, most postsecondary writing and language educators work in a profession in which transience and precarity are normal conditions of work (see, for instance, Barrett 2019; Block 2002; Cardozo 2017; Cohen 2017; Hazelkorn 2017; Nixon 2017; Pérez and Montoya 2018; Ryan, Burgess, and Connell 2013; Welch and Scott 2016).

It is within this precarious professional environment that the call for papers for this collection solicited work that challenges racism, xenophobia, and nationalism through "endeavor[ing] to cultivate cosmopolitan and translingual dispositions in students and faculty." Importantly, cultivating cosmopolitan and translingual *dispositions* in students and faculty is a more expansive goal than for instance refining, or laying particular claim to, emergent terms in the scholarly forums of rhetoric, composition, and writing studies (RCWS). Approached as *dispositions*, cosmopolitanism and translingualism are tethered to *material* time-space experiences and enactments—the everyday activities and living relations in which composing and writing education happen. Dispositions develop and manifest in practice. It is through this valence that You's *Cosmopolitan English and Transliteracy* puts moral obligation at the center of his inquiry into language use and literacy education, binding cosmopolitanism and translingualism to active questioning and critique and placing focus on how "people are conversing across borders to form new alliances on specific issues and [developing] regional or global affiliations." These affiliations, he argues, "will conceivably break down the borders between nations and between cultures, enabling one to embrace his or her moral obligations to neighbors and strangers. This is the pathway towards a true cosmopolitanism" (2016, 10). Canagarajah similarly describes a "new ethics of cosmopolitanism and diversity whereby people are engaging with more tolerance, understanding, and reflexivity with other communities and cultural norms, even within structures of power difference" (2020, 73). Canagarajah's "negotiated literacies" similarly emphasizes attunement to difference. and the ethical dimensions of meaning-making among others (74–79). Likewise, his description of the translingual subject locates a moral stance in invested attunement to positionalities and inequities as they relate to everyday relations (61–63).

Extending from this materialist, situated understanding of cosmopolitanism, this chapter is intended to bring attention to the varied political-economic conditions in which cosmopolitan dispositions will need to be fostered if they are to have widespread, ideologically consequential influence on teaching and learning in postsecondary writing education in the US. It will draw on some of the research from a qualitative study that focuses on how ideas about writing and writers have moved across diverse time/space scales in postsecondary writing education. The study gives particular attention to the transience and precarious terms of work of writing teachers, exploring how work and work conditions shape curricular uptake and writing pedagogies. The chapter will first use published descriptions of curricular change in two writing programs as the basis for a discussion of how the programmatic scaling of curricula that are informed by cosmopolitan ideas are complicated by resource constraints and entrenched programmatic rhetorics and architectures. The descriptions will highlight tensions between scholarship-driven curricular constructs and the goals and the conditions that writing programs respond to and create. A short case study that follows will focus on an experienced part-time teacher who is struggling to do conscientious teaching work with linguistically, culturally, and economically diverse students in an institution that is in economic crisis. The study will highlight some of the complex factors that are often at play in the formation of pedagogies that respond to superdiversity outside of direct influence from RCWS scholarship and under conditions of precarity.

STUDY DESCRIPTION

Two of the questions that shaped the study focus on the scaling of ideas about writing within, and across, writing programs were:

- How do the ideas about writing that circulate in established scholarly forums of RCWS relate to, and travel among, everyday artifacts and practices of writing education? How, for instance, are ideas about writing education scaled—translated, authorized, and recontextualized across actually-existing institutional contexts?
- How do teachers relate to prevailing constructs about writing education in the various institutions in which they work? This question subsumes research on terms of work, institutional architectures and procedures, and how transient teachers move among, and adapt to, diverse work environments, vocabularies, and curricula.

These questions have to do not only with the scaling of scholarly ideas and program administration but also with the precarity of postsecondary writing work. Though not often directly acknowledged, theories and research on writing curricula that circulate in RCWS scholarship have relied primarily on the existence of writing programs to give abstract disciplinary ideas reach and material life in actually-existing teaching and learning environments. Most of the people who teach postsecondary writing are not writing scholars; most don't have advanced degrees in RCWS, and the majority are also not long-term faculty at single institutions. Postsecondary writing courses are primarily taught by teaching assistants who will graduate and move on to other jobs; part-time teachers who teach across institutions; and full-time non-tenure-line faculty who, while often on longer-term contracts, also move across jobs and institutions more often than tenure-line faculty (an ever-shrinking category). Writing programs have evolved, in part, to create stabilities and economies of scale in these conditions of labor precarity. This scaling function enables programs to serve as conduits between the realms in which scholarly discourses circulate—for instance, journals, monographs, conference presentations, and statements issued by the National Council of Teachers of English, the Conference on College Composition and Communication, and the Council of Writing Program Adminstrators—and the diverse places where everyday teaching practices are happening. The entanglements of genres and procedures that we immediately recognize as constitutive of writing programs—defined curricula, course outcomes and sequences, placement processes, program assessments—scale curricular aims through channeling the labor of trans-institutional and -disciplinary teachers toward institutionally specified goals. Those who work as writing administrators know, or quickly learn, that their work will involve attention to some or all of these scaling elements, and those who do introductory teaching work in writing programs must become adept at recognizing typified structures and practices and adapting to them across the institutions at which they find work.

The study includes twenty-one non-tenure-line participants who teach writing in a variety of postsecondary settings: public and private research institutions, regional public institutions, two-year colleges, and liberal arts colleges. The participants' backgrounds vary, but only three had advanced degrees in RCWS at the time of the study. Others had degrees in English literature, creative writing, comparative literature, English education, and linguistics. Primary data is from interviews, site visits at institutions where some participants worked, and a considerable body of artifacts collected from teachers and institutions, including syllabi, assignments, grading matrices, programmatic curricular statements and outcomes statements, and assessment benchmark drafts.

As part of the interviews, participating teachers shared their work histories, which included a striking amount of occupational precarity and movement: across the institutions at which they are educated and work (sometimes simultaneously) over periods of years; and across cities, counties, states, and in some cases nations where they teach. The majority of the teachers had spent most of their careers working at clusters of schools located within a particular region or city. One teacher, for instance, had taught in part- and full-time positions for over two decades, but at only three schools located less than ten miles apart. Other histories covered more distance and had more variance in types of teaching jobs. One participant had started as a secondary English teacher before moving on to becoming an introductory writing teacher at the postsecondary level. She had taught at eight different schools in three states and at the time of the study was working part-time at three institutions. Another had taught in three countries and four US states and had worked part- and full-time in both introductory writing programs and in English language learning programs.

To understand more of how transience and precarity shape the development and transfer of ideas and practices in writing pedagogy, I adopted a hybrid approach that draws on methods in institutional ethnography as well as in scalar and mobility studies. Institutional ethnography provided a useful frame for studying what happens when disciplinary concepts from RCWS scholarship enter complex fields of circulation and uptake shaped by an array of work ecology factors in writing education: for instance, diverse professional discourses, bureaucratic prerogatives, personal and professional economic constraints, racialized and classed perspectives on language and learning competencies, technologies, and varied or competing disciplinary epistemologies (LaFrance 2019). By design, however, the study isn't located at a single institutional site, so the approach also adapts elements of methods from mobility and scalar research conducted across several disciplines (see, for instance, Collins, Slembrouk and Baynham 2009; Compton-Lilly and Halverson 2014; Lorimer Leonard 2017; Nordquist 2017; Stornaiuolo and LeBlanc 2016; Tsing 2017; Vieira 2016). This work has opened new ways of understanding how the times-spaces of "communities of practice" extend beyond particular moments and singular, immediately apparent locations. Finally, the study draws on scholarship in writing program administration that describes how the relative cross-institutional stability of writing program architectures enables the scaling of curricular ideas across programs and classes.

In what follows I will share two published accounts of efforts to remake writing programs, at Arizona State University and Northeastern University respectively, to better serve more diverse students. Both of these sites are relatively well resourced in comparison to the broader national scene in US postsecondary education, and both are led by groups of faculty scholars who are invested in using research to inform programmatic processes and curricula. I then describe a short case study centering on Ethan, who at the time of the study was working part-time in two writing programs at urban institutions that are under economic stress and serve extraordinarily diverse student populations. Ethan's case study opens an opportunity to consider how pedagogical ideas about language and learning are shaped within learning environments that are characterized by a relative scarcity of professional development resources and high levels of transience and precarity—a "normal" condition in writing education that is not proportionally represented in RCWS scholarship (see Hassel 2013).

PROGRAMMATIC SCALING AND COSMOPOLITANISM

To what extent do the imperatives of programmatic scaling hinder our field's ability to be responsive to diverse language practices, writers, and cultures in everyday pedagogy in the locally adaptive ways that a cosmopolitan disposition demands? Ideas in scholarship can function to critique pervasive writing program practices, but scholarly ideas in RCWS also gain authority through their incorporation and regularization across sites. For example, "basic writing" and "basic writers" emerged as progressive constructs during an era of rapidly expanding college enrollments in the 1960s and 1970s. The reproduction of the category was further substantiated by the replication of basic writing courses across postsecondary writing programs in the US (see Horner and Lu 1999). Writing program placement assessments, course sequences and goals, and even pedagogical expertise continue to be anchored to, and productive of, categories like "basic writers," "advanced writers," "underprepared writers," "native English speakers," "L2 [English as a second language] students," and "international students." The institutional embeddedness of these categories has been important for the establishment of coherence between research, curricula, and administrative practices. Their embeddedness can also lead, however, to calcified discourses, structures, and assumptions that prevent responsiveness to both local situations and evolutions in research and language ideologies over time.

Some of the challenges with making progressive structural changes to writing programs are evident in work like Katherine Daily O'Meara and Paul Kei Matsuda's (2017) description of the creation of a new infrastructure of support for L2 writers at Arizona State University (ASU). Daily O'Meara and Matsuda explain that ASU has a student enrollment that is among the largest in the country, and the writing program offers over one hundred L2-designated writing courses. Importantly, the goal for changes at ASU wasn't just focused on improving how well the program serves its international students, it was also to "capitalize on the size of the program and people [at ASU] to achieve national prominence" (205). So, while the descriptions of programmatic efforts to internationalize the ASU program are mostly centered on distinctly local processes, structures, and administrators, another important goal was to gain authority and potentially broader professional influence through offering a model that could be scaled across other writing program sites (204–5). Local program change, scalability, curricular authority, and national professional standing are deeply entangled in this effort as it is described. With the goal of creating a local model with national influence, Daily O'Meara and Matsuda anchor their explanation of program changes in established disciplinary sources, referencing the *CCCC Statement on Second Language Writing and Writers*; the *WPA Outcomes Statement*, an external review conducted by the WPA Consultant-Evaluator Service; and scholarship in "curricular design, teacher professional development, and placement options and procedures" in L2 writing (203–4). The infrastructural mechanisms that the group initiated to foster the curricular change likewise followed established blueprints for other types of change in writing program administration discourse at research-extensive institutions. For instance, the group sought new teaching and administrative positions specializing in L2 writing, developed L2 professional development opportunities for teachers already working in the program, established a graduate course on the teaching of L2 writing, and sought to foster greater community among teachers, with the goal of creating a "culture of L2 writing" (210–13). A rub is that the established, recognizable categories that make models of change like the one described by Daily O'Meara and Matsuda more scalable across sites can also continue to reproduce overly-generalized notions of students' experiences, language practices, and cultures—not through philosophical intent but due to their embeddedness in scholarly discourse and programmatic practices. New ideas gain wider influence and authority more readily when they don't require fundamental changes in course types and nomenclatures, conceptions of professional goals and expertise, or understandings of students' histories, competencies, and needs.

In a contrasting depiction of programmatic change at Northeastern University, Jonathan Benda, Michael Dedeck, Chris Gallagher, Kristi Girdharry, Neal Lerner, and Matt Noonan sought to analyze how well their program served international students and "quickly recognized that the designation *international* is insufficiently robust as an analytical category" (2017, 79). The questions that Benda and colleagues began asking quickly complicated established categorical distinctions among students, based on cultural, national, and linguistic backgrounds and competencies:

> Are students international by virtue of their visa status? By country of origin? By citizenship status? By history of schooling? By racial, cultural, linguistic, religious, or tribal-group membership? Moreover, among our students, nationality and language often do not neatly align: many of our international students are fluent (and sometimes L1) English speakers, just as many of our US students are multilingual—and sometimes L2 (or L3) speakers. Even within national and language or cultural groups, we see huge ranges in academic preparation, language and literacy experiences, and cultural perspectives. (79)

Based on these questions, the group conducted research into students' experiences and competencies and found that the students had experiences with language and writing that belied the categorical distinctions on which programmatic placement processes and corresponding courses and curricula had been based. Placements and curricula based on characteristics like current residency, national citizenship, and primary language simply did not adequately respond to the students' diverse cultural identifications, experiences, and language competencies. The program questioned the fundamental constructs of language and learning on which its categorical distinctions, programmatic structures, and curricula were based, reflecting for instance on how "administrators (both inside and outside the writing program), instructors, students, writing center consultants, and so forth—[were] constructing and using the concepts of *nation* and *international* as contexts for understanding and working with each other" (94). Benda and coauthors' account provides a model through which programs might not just *respond to* superdiversity through installing a scholarship-driven cosmopolitan curriculum within broadly replicated program architectures, but also *enact* cosmopolitanism through a more fundamental change in stance toward how writing education is conceived and structured.

The fine-tuned, locally responsive placement and pedagogical work undertaken by the Northeastern group requires a substantial amount of stability and resources. The ranks of faculty in the writing program at Northeastern are constituted by PhD students, full-time lecturers, and tenure-stream faculty (Benda et al., 84). Likewise, the process of review and change at ASU described by O'Meara and Matsuda was undertaken at a research-extensive, flagship university. Nevertheless, in a short section near the end of their chapter about internationalization, Daily O'Meara and Matsuda indicate that the working conditions of teachers at ASU were having a negative impact on their efforts to make progressive programmatic changes. As they tried to enact their transitions, the workload for sixty non-tenure-line, full-time teachers in the program was changed from a 4/4 teaching load (four classes per term in fall and spring) with service and professional development requirements to a 5/5 load with no service or professional development requirements. This change predictably "led to a decline in teacher participation and involvement in professional activities [and] despite best efforts in planning workshops and potlucks to suit busy teachers' schedules, we have at times experienced low attendance and participation" (213). Daily O'Meara and Matsuda report additional strains on the program's resources, including requests for the L2 expertise developed within the department from other units across campus. Even at a highly regarded university like ASU that is comparatively well funded and where research faculty with nationally recognized expertise in postsecondary writing education and administration are working toward change, material resources considerably constrain curricular options.

The writing programs at ASU and Northeastern certainly face many challenges, including recognizing and addressing the assumptions baked into institutional architectures, which can structurally inhibit and even contradict curricular and pedagogical evolution. Nevertheless, they are stable and resourced well enough to bring the programs into conversation with current, ongoing research in RCWS and language studies.

What of programs that are less well resourced or are much more reliant on part-time instructors—for instance, two-year colleges, where, according to the latest National Center of Education Statistics (NCES) data, 67 percent of teachers are part-time? A persistent complaint within the broader field of postsecondary writing education has been that scholarship has little connection to the concerns and material conditions of introductory writing teachers, and that when conditions are portrayed, they are usually at more selective and better-resourced research-intensive institutions (see, for instance, Hassel 2013; Lamos 2011; Penrose 2012). Meanwhile, research on demographics in higher education shows that a disproportionate number of students of color, low-income students, and nontraditional students are in open-enrollment and otherwise less selective institutions. A College Board study, for instance, found that 44 percent of Black and 56 percent of Hispanic college students were enrolled in two-year institutions (Ma and Baum 2016). Published research in RCWS does not reflect the full spectrum of postsecondary institutions, nor does it proportionally represent the perspectives, work environments, and practices of the non-tenure-line writing teachers who deliver most writing instruction.

Like the instructors Daily O'Meara and Matsuda describe at ASU, most of the participants in the study I conducted didn't have much, or any, formal education in RCWS. Given this lack of disciplinary moorings in RCWS, these teachers formed their primary ideas about writing education "on the job" as they taught across various institutions over time. For many, professional transience created a sensibility in regard to writing education knowledge that is experiential and not clearly tethered to the theories or questions about writing education that circulate in any particular discipline or body of research. What follows is a brief case study of Ethan, who at the time of his participation in the study was a part-time teacher at two very diverse urban universities: City University and Victoria College.[2] Ethan is in some ways typical of those participants in the study whose teaching practices have been formed in work environments that, primarily due to a lack of resources, are not brought into direct conversation with disciplinary scholarship in RCWS. He makes pedagogical decisions with minimal direct institutional oversight, and his curricular understandings and pedagogical practices are substantially shaped by his individual work experiences, work environments, and professional affiliations over time. The presentation of Ethan's case study will put emphasis on the material terms of teaching work, in part to provide an opportunity to consider the relationship between the terms of everyday work in writing, and dispositions toward students' language and learning.

ETHAN

Ethan has an MFA and a Masters in English Literature from a well-regarded university, and for over twenty years he has been a part-time teacher, primarily of introductory writing and creative writing, in a large city in the US. He reported that he typically teaches eight to ten courses per year at a combination of three to four institutions. At the time of the study, he was working at two institutions at which he had regularly taught courses for over a decade. The commute between the two schools is about eleven miles, and traveling between them during off-peak hours takes about an hour and ten minutes.

One of the schools at which Ethan works is a branch of City University that is housed in a cluster of buildings in a highly diverse area of the city. Ethan's small, shared office is in a large building that also houses classrooms as well as street-level commercial spaces for businesses. City University was founded in the early decades of the twentieth century with the mission of offering an affordable college education to people from a variety of national, ethnic, and socioeconomic backgrounds—particularly recent immigrants. This progressive mission has made the university a magnet for many teachers who, like Ethan, see higher education as a pathway toward greater social justice and equity. Like many private universities and liberal arts colleges throughout the US, however, City has fallen into dire financial difficulties over the past two decades, and in recent years it has been enacting increasingly draconian budget cuts. At the time of the study, enrollment was in decline, and the school was in a protracted and contentious contract dispute with the union to which Ethan belonged. Even as the dispute wore on, the school was in the process of consolidating programs, cutting courses and teaching positions, and selling or renting out some of its properties. Wear and tear in the form of broken desks, missing lights, and damaged ceiling tiles was evident in offices and classrooms. Ethan was being offered fewer classes than in the past at City, and even some long-term faculty were not getting contract renewals. This was especially troubling for Ethan because other institutions in the city had also been steadily reducing course offerings over recent years.

City University enrolls roughly equal percentages of students who identify as African American, white, Asian, and Latino. Within those broad categories, students exhibit the very rich variety of language, national, ethnic and religious backgrounds, citizenship statuses, and identities that characterize the superdiversity of the broader neighborhood that encompasses the school. City targets its advertising toward first-generation college students and students who speak a variety of languages, and its acceptance rate approaches that of open-enrollment institutions. Almost two-thirds of the student body are considered low-income, as indicated by Federal Pell Grant Aid statistics. Nevertheless, tuition and fees have risen to over $30,000 per year, and its six-year graduation rate is below the national average for schools in its category. Ethan's everyday teaching work was shaped in significant ways by the pervasive signs of precarity at City: the austerity measures, labor conditions, and problems with infrastructure, as well as the fact that the majority of City students are first-generation, from economically disadvantaged families, and accumulating debt without completing degrees. A substantial contrast with Northeastern and Arizona State Universities, City is what highly cosmopolitan institutions often look like.

The resources for large-scale reflection and change in curriculum and programmatic processes described at ASU and Northeastern were simply not available at City. At the time of the study, the writing program conducted an annual orientation and offered periodic workshops, but they were not required for experienced teachers and were poorly attended. Like most of the participants in the study, Ethan did not describe his teaching using a particular disciplinary idiom. Likewise, teachers who participated in the study typically answered questions about departmental or program philosophies and outcomes for writing courses by enumerating what is explicitly required of students and teachers, such as minimum pages of polished prose, numbers of assignments that go through multiple drafts, a specific textbook or designated readings, required modes, and so forth. When Ethan described the curriculum at City, he compared the requirements there unfavorably to the requirements at Victoria College, where he was also teaching: "At Victoria College it is fifteen pages of edited writing, like high-stakes essays, and then you have these other ancillary writing requirements. At City University they stipulate four essays . . . I give them three essays, but then two in-class essays that are done in two parts. In Victoria College it is also three essays, but that is the extent of it. So the anthologies—whatever you do—it is on your own." Ethan did not see significant differences in the curricula at the institutions at which he regularly taught. Like many introductory writing curricula across the US, the introductory writing course sequences at City and Victoria assume a generally linear progression in writing proficiencies, with definable, generalizable skills (topic development, grammar, academic conventions) that are expected to transfer across academic writing contexts. The description of the introductory course sequence at City emphasized critical reading, writing process, and proficiency with "academic" or "scholarly" writing. Victoria also emphasized writing process and "proficiency with academic writing." Because the courses are not very distinct in terms of their underlying philosophies or requirements, teachers who teach at both institutions can do their own versions of efficiency-scaling. Ethan was able to use some of the same pedagogical materials—assignments, readings, exercises, and so on—for classes at both institutions. Understandably, this is also a common practice among study participants across institutional types. Teachers' use of materials and practices among the institutions at which they teach is enabled by the structural similarities—in course sequences, outcomes, assignment genres, et cetera—across writing programs throughout the US.

In terms of language ideology, City is more explicit in its curricular description than Victoria, but the explicitness highlights a somewhat contradictory stance that is embedded in the program's placement process, course descriptions, and outcomes. The general curricular description indicates that "second-language" and "non-standard dialects" should be respected and students need not abandon them at City, yet the curriculum also aims for proficiency in a "standard English" construct, and "standard English" is used interchangeably in course descriptions with "academic writing." A placement process is used to determine which of the school's three sequenced courses is appropriate for each incoming student. Those students who can't meet the program's standard for English-language proficiency, based on "weak or insufficient" writing on submitted samples, must take a course or courses in the school's English education program before entering the writing sequence. Further complicating the institution's stated position of respect for "second-language" and "non-standard dialects" found in the general curricular description, City lists "social inequities, lack of familiarity with English, segregated discourse communities, and/or poor schooling" as reasons that students might be placed into the university's developmental writing class. So, use of the term "academic writing" as a curricular goal (still very common in institutional lexicons and placement assessments) creates the context for required remediation and obfuscates an underlying institutional nativism. Language practices exhibiting "second language" or "non-standard dialect[al]" characteristics are valued as a general philosophical position yet also categorically equated with the outcomes of historical and social inequities and subpar education.

While Ethan teaches his classes at City and Victoria using many of the same materials, he nevertheless adjusts his approaches based on his perceptions of the differences in students' backgrounds and preparedness at the two schools. Victoria College is a public school that is part of a system that is also under financial duress, but it is nevertheless better resourced and more selective than City, and the writing program is a part of a well-regarded English department with a thriving major. Likewise, Ethan's perception of Victoria College in terms of how teachers are treated, the overall quality of the school, and the preparedness of the students is substantially higher than his perception of City:

> The student populations are so drastically different. At Victoria College you are getting very good, well-prepared, academically grounded students that have been groomed for college. Then you go to City University, and you get students who are writing at the level of a junior college. They are the first in their family to be in college, which is very nice, but they don't have the academic infrastructure at home to prepare them for this. So I use different kinds of anthologies. I use different kinds of approaches. The students from Jamaica [at Victoria], the non-American students who have been schooled in places where there is more of a European model. They get it. But the Americans . . . might have come out of these flimsy inner-city high schools. So there is a lot of that going on, and . . . in the classroom in real time it definitely affects how I present the material.

Though he uses many of the same teaching materials in writing courses at both schools, Ethan describes choosing different readings, giving more feedback on grammar, and spending more time on reading comprehension at City. He therefore calls much of his work at City "remedial," and he does vocabulary-building and reading aloud exercises in his writing classes at City because he feels that many students have insufficient vocabularies and reading skills for college-level work. When he spoke of his pedagogical approaches across schools, he emphasized students' relative levels of preparedness for advanced reading and writing in "academic English," rather than for instance referencing the students' linguistic resourcefulness and competencies.

Ethan's perceptions of his status and work at City—the increasingly precarious terms of his employment, his judgment of the overall character and quality of the institution, and the backgrounds of the students—shaped what and how he teaches. At the time of the study, Ethan had begun to regret that his circumstances required that he continue to work at City. He indicated that he felt "attacked" and "devalued" there, because the institution was cutting teaching positions without warning, defunding its infrastructure, and communicating disrespectfully with faculty. He also believed that the material condition of the classrooms at City University had become so poor that they significantly affected his ability to do his job well: "You call up buildings and grounds to fix some light, and then three months later they fix it. We are huddled in one part of the classroom because there aren't any lights elsewhere. It's sad." Stating it bluntly, Ethan said that he felt "shat upon as a worker" at City, and while he said that he would never consciously "cut back on his work" with students because of his feelings about the university, he nevertheless worried that he might be spending less time responding to writing at City due to his resentment of the school. He was also troubled about the ethics of how City was treating its students, with its high tuition, low graduation rates, and targeting of low-income, first-generation, recently immigrated families in its marketing. Overall, his pedagogical goals and practices at City were deeply entangled with his feelings about the demographics and ethics of the school:

> I have to give the students the best education I can, because it is like on some level they are, you know, it's, I mean, they come to this school and take a six-credit remedial course. It's not called "remedial," but that is what it is—and they are not prepared for it, and they fail. They drop out and they are left with this big bill, and it is really a shame. I feel like I can't pass them if they are not worthy of it, but on the other hand I feel like I have to make up for . . . really the moral deficits of this place.

Ethan expresses empathy for City students, and he is deeply troubled by his positionality in an institution that he feels is ethically compromised by its financial difficulties and austerity practices.

PRECARITY, MATERIALITY, AND THE PORTAL

Ethan's pedagogy is shaped by a complex array of factors, including institutionally driven stratifications of language differences, his own experiences as a veteran writing teacher who has taught writing at various institutions for several decades, and the daily necessities of teaching courses across multiple institutions under difficult conditions with few guarantees of additional work beyond a given semester. He also expressed considerable empathy for the economic circumstances of his students, and it was clear that he understood and adjusted his teaching to the fact that many of the students at City were balancing school with demanding work and family responsibilities. He makes a point of inviting students to speak in languages other than English in classes and, if they choose, to do some informal writing in languages other than English. This work is performed against the grain of his institutional work ecology though, which does not provide support or incentivize sustained exploration of translingualism and cosmopolitanism as they relate to writing education. In the absence of resources and conditions that might foster a climate in which teachers and students are able to pursue their work together as ongoing, collective, critical inquiry into language and learning in their own lives, the program at City adopts the common programmatic practice of constructing its curriculum out of static, abstract constructs: for example, "academic writing," "standard English," and "non-standard dialects."

How might the term "cosmopolitan disposition" more explicitly address the conditions and possibilities at City and elsewhere? You proposes a "border-crossing model" for teacher development that incorporates content knowledge of scholarship, interactions with teachers with experience and expertise with multilingual writers, and direct interactions with multilingual students. You's model is not based on a language standard and positions teachers as "decision-makers" who "make their tacit knowledge and decisions explicit," rather than as "knowledge sources channeling wisdom to their students" (2016, 204). The pedagogical stance that You advocates extends from a conception of cosmopolitanism as materially situated, intellectually creative, and critically evolving in response to everyday encounters and environments. In this way, You's cosmopolitanism is aligned with the way that Bruce Horner describes teaching and intellectual work in *Rewriting Composition: Terms of Exchange.* Horner critiques the tendency to define students and writing teachers in RCWS theory and writing program discourses as categorical types, which, he argues, extends from the need to commodify composition work for exchange—making it "easily recognizable by readers" (2016, 33). Horner encourages RCWS theorists to "recognize that knowledge resides not only in discursive consciousness but also in practical consciousness . . . in what actors 'know how to do,' not just in 'what actors are able to talk about' " (169). In a more recent epistolary article written with Jan Blommaert, Horner further argues for making standards in writing education themselves the subject of situated pedagogical inquiry, approached as historical and contestable "sites of contest and change" (2017, 16). Ethan's example, however, shows how difficult it is in postsecondary learning environments without material stability and resources to foster and scale the cosmopolitan and translingual dispositions and practices advocated by You and Horner. Ethan has little support for exploring the emergent scholarly constructs that might help him to pursue more progressive innovations, and the effects of the economic practices of his institution on students make him feel morally compromised. The question of moral obligation as it relates to cosmopolitanism and translingualism should be extended to encompass the moral contradictions that the economics of our institutions create.

Now is a particularly important time to investigate these questions. In this historical moment, COVID-19 has made the precarity of bodies and institutions a daily concern. The pandemic has pushed many of us to become more deeply aware of our own immediate material environments and actions, and it has brought greater awareness of our mutuality with others. As we move through this volatile and potentially transformative time, heightened awareness of bodies, institutions, and precarity presents opportunities for more focus on the diverse terms of work that constitute everyday material relations in higher education. Because work in translingualism and cosmopolitanism is concerned with movement and time/space scales that connect practices to broader ideological, national, and cultural relations, it also opens pathways toward better understanding of, for instance, the scaling architectures of writing programs as well as the terms of work and ontologies of knowing of writing teachers and students. Toward the end of transforming not just curricular vocabularies and stated goals but also the spaces and conditions of work and learning in which those goals might be possible, RCWS scholars might pursue more granular research that collapses artificial, abstract distinctions between disciplinary ways of understanding writing and learning as opposed to the complex material environments in which knowledge is taken up by teachers (see, for instance, Hassel and Phillips 2022; LaFrance 2019; Martins 2015; You 2016; and Zawacki and Cox 2014). The problems with which Ethan struggles at City University are primarily due, not to individual shortcomings or inadequately argued positions in scholarly research, but rather to the failure of economically strained institutions to create the conditions for collective reflection and research-informed curricular and pedagogical innovation. Ethan's case is an example of how conditions of precarity can prevent the development of sustainable, mutually informing connections between RCWS scholarship and the teachers and students doing language work in economically stressed institutions. As we move through what Arundhati Roy calls a "portal" of change, and as neoliberal political economy rapidly loses credibility and unravels, professionals in postsecondary writing education have the opportunity to anticipate what comes next and imagine how we can make it better.

NOTES

1. This is a decline of 43.3 percent. For an excellent, nuanced analysis of funding decline and changes in US higher education over the past four decades, see Isaacs 2018, 37–43.
2. The names of participants and other identifying information, such as the names of schools, have been changed in an effort to protect identities.

REFERENCES

American Association of University Professors (AAUP). 2020. "The Annual Report on the Economic Status of the Profession." Accessed November 1, 2020. https://academeblog.org/2020/05/28/annual-report-on-the-economic-status-of-the-profession-2019-20/.

Barrett, Beverly. 2019. "Higher Education in Austerity Europe." *European Journal of Higher Education* 9 (2): 238–41.

Benda, J., M. Dedek, C. W. Gallagher, K. Girdharry, N. Lerner, and M. Noonan. 2017. "Confronting Superdiversity in US Writing Programs." In *The Internationalization of US Writing Programs*, edited by S. K. Rose and I. Weiser. 79–96. Logan: Utah State University Press.

Block, David, and Deborah Cameron, eds. 2002. *Globalization and Language Teaching*. New York: Routledge.

Canagarajah, Suresh. 2020. *Transnational Literacy Autobiographies as Translingual Writing*. New York: Routledge.

Cardozo, Karen. 2017. "Academic Labor: Who Cares?" *Critical Sociology* 43 (3): 405–28.

Cohen, Rosetta Marantz. 2017. *The Work and Lives of Teachers: A Global Perspective*. Cambridge, UK: Cambridge University Press.

College Board. 2013. "Trends in College Pricing 2013." Accessed November 1, 2020. https://research.collegeboard.org/trends/college-pricing.

Collins, James, Stefaan Slembrouck, and Mike Baynham, eds. 2009. *Globalization and Language in Contact: Scale, Migration and Human Contact*. London: Continuum.

Compton-Lilly, Catherine, and Erica Halverson, eds. 2014. *Time and Space in Literacy Research*. New York: Routledge.

Daily O'Meara, K., and P. K. Matsuda. 2017. "Building the Infrastructure of L2 Writing Support: The Case of Arizona State University." In *The Internationalization of US Writing Programs*, edited by S. K. Rose and I. Weiser, 203–15. Logan: Utah State University Press.

Hassel, Holly. 2013. "Research Gaps in Teaching English in the Two-Year College." *Teaching English in the Two-Year College* 40 (4): 343–63.

Hassel, Holly, and Cassandra Phillips. 2022. *Materiality and Writing Studies: Aligning Labor, Scholarship, and Teaching*. Studies in Writing and Rhetoric. Champaign, IL: National Council of Teachers of English.

Hazelkorn, Ellen. 2017. *Global Rankings and the Geopolitics of Higher Education: Understanding the Influence and Impact of Rankings on Higher Education, Policy and Society*. London: Routledge.

Horner, Bruce. 2016. *Rewriting Composition: Terms of Exchange*. Carbondale: Southern Illinois University Press.

Horner, Bruce, and Jan Blommaert. 2017. "Mobility and Academic Literacies: An Epistolary Conversation." *London Review of Education* 15, no. 1 (March): 2–20.

Horner, Bruce, and Min Zhan Lu. 1999. *Representing the "Other": Basic Writers and the Teaching of Basic Writing*. Urbana, IL: National Council of Teachers of English.

Isaacs, Emily. 2018. *Writing at the State U: Instruction and Administration at 106 Comprehensive Universities*. Logan: Utah State University Press.

LaFrance, Michelle. 2019. *Institutional Ethnography: A Study of Practice for Writing Studies Researchers*. Logan: Utah State University Press.

Lamos, Steve. 2011. "Credentialing College Writing Teachers: WPAs and Labor Reform." *WPA: Writing Program Administration* 35 (1): 45–72.

Lorimer-Leonard, Rebecca. 2017. *Writing on the Move: Migrant Women and the Value of Literacy*. Pittsburgh: University of Pittsburgh Press.

Ma, Jennifer, and Sandy Baum. 2016. "Trends in Community Colleges: Enrollment, Prices, Student Debt, and Completion." *College Board Research Brief*. Accessed June 15, 2020. https://research.collegeboard.org/pdf/trends-community-colleges-research-brief.pdf.

Martins, David. 2015. *Transnational Writing Program Administration*. Logan: Utah State University Press.

National Council of Education Statistics (NCES). 2017. "The Debt Burden of Bachelor's Degree Recipients." https://nces.ed.gov/pubs2017/2017436.pdf.

Nixon, John. 2017. *Higher Education in Austerity Europe*. London: Bloomsbury Academic.

Nordquist, Brice. 2017. *Literacy and Mobility: Complexity, Uncertainty, and Agency at the Nexus of High School and College*. New York: Routledge.

Penrose, Anne. 2012. "Professional Identity in a Contingent-Labor Profession: Expertise, Autonomy, Community in Composition Teaching." *WPA: Writing Program Administration* 35 (2): 108–26.

Pérez, Marta, and Ainhoya Montoya. 2018. "The Unsustainability of the Neoliberal Public University: Towards an Ethnography of Precarity in Academia." *Revista De Dialectología y Tradiciones Populares* 73 (10): 9–24.

Roy, Arundhati. 2020. "The Pandemic Is a Portal." *Financial Times*, April 3, 2020.

Ryan, Suzanne, John Burgess, and Julia Connell. 2013. "Casual Academic Staff in an Australian University: Marginalized and Excluded." *Tertiary Education and Management* 19 (2): 161–75.

State Higher Education Executive Officers (SHEEO). 2019. *State Higher Education Finance FY2019*. Boulder, CO: State Higher Education Policy Center.

Stornaiuolo, Amy, and Robert Jean LeBlanc. 2016. "Scaling as a Literacy Activity: Mobility and Educational Inequality in an Age of Global Connectivity." *Research in the Teaching of English* 50 (3): 263–87.

Tsing, Anna Lowenhaupt. 2017. *The Mushroom at the End of the World: On the Possibility of Life in Capitalist Ruins*. Princeton, NJ: Princeton University Press.

Vieira, Kate. 2016. *American by Paper*. Minneapolis: University of Minnesota Press.

Welch, Nancy, and Tony Scott. 2016. *Composition in the Age of Austerity*. Logan: Utah State University Press.

You, Xiaoye. 2016. *Cosmopolitan English and Transliteracy*. Carbondale: Southern Illinois University Press.

Zawacki, Terry Myers, and Michelle Cox. 2014. *WAC and Second Language Writers: Research towards Linguistically and Culturally Inclusive Programs and Practices*. Ft. Collins, CO: WAC Clearinghouse; Anderson, SC: Parlor Press.

PART II

Resisting Ethnolinguistic Stereotypes

Community-Engaged Literacies and Pedagogies

6
WRITING TO MEND LITERATE FRAGMENTATION

Rebecca Lorimer Leonard

This chapter explores how community writing shapes the critical language awareness of multilingual writers. If literacy educators and researchers must cultivate cosmopolitan and translingual dispositions in isolationist eras, as this collection's introduction suggests, what are the literate mechanisms that dismantle isolation? How might writing, in community settings in particular, impact multilingual writers' understandings of their own critical dispositions regarding cross-border language and literacy practices in nationalist times?

In pursuit of these questions, I describe below a partnership between an undergraduate literacy studies course and a community language school and then show how the writing undertaken during that collaboration changes writers' awareness of their literacies' critical dimensions. Drawing on qualitative analysis of data collected over two years with project students, teachers, and staff, the chapter details the lived experience of the collaboration from the point of view of one multilingual writer, who uses his writing to, in his words, "recover," "reestablish," and put back together parts of his literate identity that had become "fractured." The nationalist politics that intensified during the project inflected participants' writing with the cries and images of family separations, at borders, among languages. Analysis of project data shows that opportunities to put things back together through writing, to recover the whole across fragments, allowed participants to recognize and begin to mend their own, more metaphorical, experiences of separation. The chapter shows how community-engaged writing activities in particular shape writers' language awareness in ways that help them reconnect literate selves that political or educational contexts actively seek to separate.

CRITICAL AWARENESS OF LANGUAGE AND LITERACY

My approach to critical awareness draws on several scholarly conversations that aim to acknowledge or heighten writers' critical awareness of language and literacy. An array of scholarly terms and theories offers insight into what "critical" and "aware" might mean when it comes to literacy and language. I synthesize this array below both to offer a frame for the chapter's analysis and to show why this research sought to understand what "critical" and "aware" look like, experientially, in writers' lives.

For example, "metalinguistic awareness" indicates a type of metacognition wherein language becomes the object of discussion when language users are engaged in a conscious reflection on language itself (Jesson 2016), whereas "multilingual awareness" is treated as a beneficially critical trait of the multilingual individual (Jessner 2014; Kramsch 2006; Pavlenko 2006). Critical language awareness (Alim 2005; Fairclough 1992) and critical language pedagogies (Baker-Bell 2013; Metz 2018) seek to heighten students' awareness of the power-laden consequences of language use. Critical literacy (Freire [1970] 2000; Janks 2010), sociocritical literacy (Gutiérrez 2004), and critical global literacies (Yoon 2016) focus this heightening on reading and writing as powerful practices of social change. Theories of mestiza consciousness (Anzaldúa 1987), cosmopolitan English (You 2016), rhetorical attunement (Lorimer Leonard 2014), translingual awareness (Seltzer 2020), and rhetorical sensibility as critical awareness (Guerra 2016), all seek to name the already-heightened knowing of writers who traverse language and geopolitical borders as a matter of daily life. Framing these writers as cosmopolitan intellectuals (Campano and Ghiso 2011) or citizen sociolinguists (Rymes 2014) highlights and values the existing critical awareness of everyday writers.

This broad reading draws together like-minded approaches to highlight the ways they seek to give name to the forms of critical awareness that already exist or might be taught. These approaches share an understanding of criticality—recognizing the inequity, volatility, and contradictions built into social order—but they differ in their placement of awareness. Enactments of language or literacy "awareness" depend on a goal or focus—on a pedagogy that results in awareness, on the awareness that language users already possess, or on the goal of heightened awareness that everyone should head toward.

Therefore, in the larger project from which this chapter draws, I take critical awareness to mean both multilingual writers' inward-facing awareness—of individual and family language identity—and their outward-facing awareness—of literacy and language in the world. My goal in this two-part lens is to trace how participants' critical awareness evolves iteratively through painful and productive senses of self. While Chiang and Schmida (1999) have found that multilingual student writers experience "serious disjunctures between the way they conceptualize their linguistic identities" (86), Pavlenko (2006) has observed that multilingual writers who "position themselves discursively as whole" may not necessarily "perceive such sharp differences between their linguistic selves" (26–27). Therefore, a navigation of fractured and "whole" language identification is not incidental but potentially central to writers' critical awareness. My theoretical frame thus attempts to illuminate the language ruptures that participants feel *and* see in the world.

THE COURSE AND COMMUNITY PROJECT

This chapter's data is drawn from a larger study of a community-engaged literacy partnership between the University of Massachusetts Amherst and the International Language Institute of Massachusetts (ILI) in Northampton, Massachusetts. ILI is a nonprofit community language school whose official mission is to promote intercultural understanding and strong, diverse communities through language instruction and teacher training. ILI runs a wide variety of programs, using a two-part funding model wherein they offer TESOL certification and world language courses to fund free English programs for immigrants and refugees. During a faculty fellowship with UMass Amherst's Center for Civic Engagement and Service Learning, ILI's executive director and I identified which immediate needs of the school might be met by undergraduates taking a course with me.

Thus, in spring 2018, I first offered "English 391: Multilingualism and Literacy," an upper-division elective that introduces undergraduates to literacy studies through the lens of language diversity. English 391 asks students to make meaning not only *through* literacy but also *of* literacy, exploring the social significance of literacy in all of its routines, values, and belief systems (Brandt 1994). By thinking across classroom and community contexts, students especially encounter the tension between academic theories (for example, English as hegemonic global language) and urgently expressed community needs (English as workplace necessity). Like similar community-engaged courses in TESOL (Blum 2015; McLaughlin, Rodriguez, and Madden 2008; Rabin 2011), literacy studies (Katz 2012), or linguistics (Fitzgerald 2009), English 391 aims to be functional, by providing writing support for a local school and community experience for UMass students, as well as important, through complicating commonplace assumptions about literacy's problems and promises.[1]

The course introduces undergraduates to theories of transnational and multilingual writing (Lam and Rosario-Ramos 2009; Lippi-Green 2012), as well as approaches to literacy as a fraught mechanism of power (Brandt 1994; Gee 2012; Freire [1970] 2000; Scribner 1984). This groundwork prepares students to discuss three focal ethnographies that examine transnational and translingual literacy (Kalmar 2015; Prendergast 2008; Vieira 2016), each of which is intended to scaffold connections across the course's academic and community writing activities. Assigned writing in the course offers students the opportunity to challenge and extend this scholarship. Students write eight informal reflections posted in the online course management system and three formal literacy theory analyses, and they complete a community project of their choice. Midway through the semester, UMass students begin working at ILI alongside ILI's students, teachers, and staff on four ILI-requested projects: (1) a weekly pop-up writing center to support the academic writing of ILI's international students studying in their Intensive English Program, (2) an editorial revision of ILI's host family guidebook, (3) one-on-one tutoring for immigrants and refugees taking courses in ILI's free evening English program (FEEP), and (4) a driving curriculum for ILI students who need to get their driver's licenses in the US. As they write, project participants are guided by models of community literacy that decenter universities as the locus of language and literacy expertise (Auerbach et al. 2013; Marko et al. 2015), always aiming to reflect on their social locations, build coalitional energy at the community site, center community members' experiences, and work toward a shared vision of social change (Campano, Ghiso, and Welch 2016; Carney 2014; Mitchell 2008).[2] In particular, the class explored questions about the kinds of social change "service learning" can and can't offer: access to power generated by literacy or disrupting the privilege that gathers around certain forms of multilingualism but not others. We aimed to arrive, by the end of the class, at a conversation about the literate injustices that have created the need for service to community literacy organizations in the first place.

Peck, Flower, and Higgins (1994) explain that community-engaged writing especially supports "critical awareness, strategic thinking, and reflective learning—a style of learning that unlike the slow shaping of acculturation can rapidly reflect on itself, experiment, and adapt" (12). As Sara P. Alvarez's and Layli Maria Miron's chapters in this collection so compellingly show, community-engaged writing can illuminate, if not always complicate, the stakes of writing across the boundaries of nation, language, and self. I initiated this study to understand exactly how community-engaged writing might impact the "critical awareness" of public and academic writing collaborators across school and community settings.

DATA COLLECTION AND ANALYSIS

While I have been building a relationship with ILI and its staff since 2015, I started formally collecting data with IRB approval in spring 2018 while teaching the first iteration of the UMass course. Since then, data collection has proceeded through the phases detailed in table 6.1. Participants in this project, and in the resulting study I describe below, include UMass students, ILI students, and ILI teachers and administrative staff. Therefore, "student participants" in this study include UMass students as well as multilingual community students who attend ILI.[3] Collected data fell into three main groups: (1) student texts, including written reflections, course assignments, and community writing projects; (2) observation notes of my own teaching and of student and teacher collaborations at ILI; and (3) interview transcripts across participants (see table 6.1).

My analysis of these data used several qualitative data analysis coding methods, moving through open and comparative rounds of coding common to grounded theory (Charmaz 2014). Following Saldaña's (2015) "codes to theory model for qualitative inquiry," figure 1 shows how my analytic process moved from initial open coding to the "literate mending" theory I use in this chapter to explore critical language awareness. In a first open coding cycle, process coding, values coding, and in vivo coding allowed me to track the constituent elements of critical awareness, often in terms participants themselves used. In a second coding cycle, I used axial coding to distill codes into groups until two strong categories came to the fore—connection and separation. At this point in the process, I wrote an analytic memo about synonymous codes that exemplified the connection-separation tension: mending and tearing, pushing and pulling, assembling and separating, and the in vivo codes "whole-some" (from participant Riya) and "fragment" (from participant Eli). Turning back to coding, comparisons of "connection" codes and "separation" codes allowed me to see that participants were not simply progressing from less to more aware during the course of the project, but were in fact sorting out the tension between connection and separation. Participants were in one week recognizing their own

Table 6.1. Data collection

Phase	Participants	Participant Activity	Collection Artifacts and Activities
Spring 2018	UMass students (n=16)	Online reflective journal	Written reflections (n=128)
		Final course paper	Formal literacy philosophies (n=16)
			Focal post-course interviews (n=8)
		Community projects	ILI project materials (driving curriculum, guidebook)
			Semi-structured interviews (n=8)
Fall 2018	UMass students (n=8)	Online reflective journal	Written reflections (n=64)
		Final course paper	Formal literacy philosophies (n=8)
			Focal post-course interviews (n=2)
		Community projects	ILI project materials (driving curriculum, guidebook)
			Semi-structured interviews (n=4)
Spring 2019	ILI teachers and staff (n=10)	Professional development reading group (which ILI requested and the author led)	Semi-structured interviews with ILI teachers and staff (n=8)
Summer 2020	ILI students and teachers (n=6)	Driving curriculum course	Semi-structured interviews with ILI students and teachers (n=6)

fragmented linguistic identities and the next week realizing ways to put them back together.

Importantly, the data analysis shows that critical language awareness is an emergent phenomenon that evolves alongside the shifting values, beliefs, and ideological pressures writers experience. That is to say, the analytic coding described above captured *change* in awareness over time but not *progress* of awareness. In this way, separation and connection are not the ends of a linear progression from less to more critically aware. Instead, these categories of codes are intimately bound, opposing forces that characterize the energy of participants' ongoing critical language awareness.

Based on this analysis, I present below one ethnographically informed case from the larger study. Focusing on an explanatory case in this way allows me to highlight the meaningful but "mundane particulars"

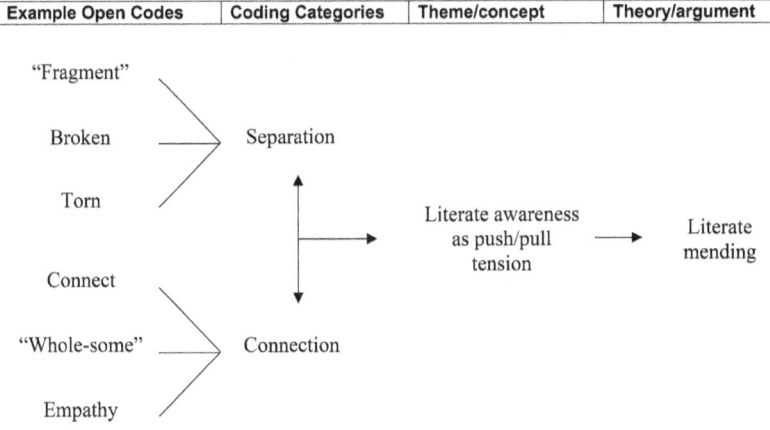

Figure 6.1. Coding Process that Led to Chapter's Theoretical Insight.

(Dyson and Genishi 2005, 3) that gather "detailed insights into mechanisms, motives of actors, and constraints" to understand a larger social phenomenon (Hancké 2009, 62). A case is particular but also heuristic: the focus on one project participant below shows how commonly experienced sociopolitical pressures shape critical language awareness in one individual life (Khan 2017, 61). In order to elaborate the tension that animates participants' critical awareness, I describe here the case of UMass participant Eli, a self-identified Asian American English major. Eli's case demonstrates how one writer's navigation of separation and connection resulted in the kind of critical awareness I am calling literate mending.

ELI'S LITERATE MENDING: FRACTURE AND RECOVERY

UMass students, ILI students, and ILI staff all engaged in literate mending across the project, in their written texts, conversations with me, and conversations with each other. But because Eli's responses generated the in vivo code "fragment," which pointed to tension in his critical language awareness, his writing and thinking especially demonstrate, in fine-grained contours, the kind of critical awareness participants experienced throughout the project.

Eli engaged in the course and community projects especially through writing, explaining at one point in an online reflective post, "I don't talk much but I type much." Eli grew up speaking English and Cantonese, hanging out in the library while his mother took evening ESL classes, deciding that "books were basically my parents." Eli was an English major who had always wanted to teach; he knew he wanted to be an ESL teacher even prior to college. Thus, Eli opted to work in the pop-up writing center project at ILI, supporting the academic English-language writing of students in the intensive English program. The writing center "popped up" at ILI once a week when a small group of UMass students visited ILI and created a writing center in one of ILI's classrooms. ILI students brought essay drafts into the room to work with UMass students one-on-one or in small groups. Eli adopted a pragmatic approach to working with these multilingual writers, explaining that his feedback on English-language rules and norms in students' writing ranged from "flexible" to "sorta wishy washy," with a common response of "you could say this, but honestly no one really cares if you say it like this." He explains that his disposition came from his own language-learning experience, understanding that "there's no line because that's just not the way language works."

Eli's own writing shows that he grappled with critical approaches to language and literacy throughout the course, especially in terms of assimilation, family lineage, and racism. Each of these themes in his course writing and interview conversations with me is characterized by the tension of fracture and recovery. Reflection on assimilation, family, and race caused felt fracture that he was attempting to, as he says, "reestablish" through his course writing. In an early reflective notebook entry Eli explains:

> There are a few theories as to why English literacy is taught even though it doesn't aid particularly in successful or complete assimilation or social mobility. The simple answer is communication, conformity, and show of power. The complicated one stems from a history of colonialism and insidious ethnic cleansing of sorts. How long does it take for a person to forget and try to reestablish where they came from fragments?

This early reflection shows that Eli continued building upon his previously existing critical awareness by asking hard questions about language and literacy throughout the project. His reflection asks these questions about a "person" in general, but his interview data show that he is also asking these questions about himself: in his interview he describes himself as a multilingual immigrant writer whose "identity fractures over time" and wonders aloud how can he move beyond "insidious" forms of literacy domination to "reestablish" who he is. How much recovery does it take to mend those literate "fractures"? Below I describe in two takes Eli's critical language awareness as a knowing navigation of this tension.

Chosen and Forced Assimilation

Because of his life experiences, Eli placed issues of assimilation at the center of his course inquiries, often pairing the potential benefits and pitfalls of assimilating to dominant language norms like standard American English. He identifies the access and belonging that comes with use of standard language in writing, even as he highlights the required shedding of ethnic, racial, or language identities deemed less desirable to a dominant culture. The relationship Eli creates between these two forms of assimilation is a defining feature of his critical awareness.

In online reflective posts throughout the semester, Eli grants that writing in standard English garnered him success in school. Narrating his early memories of reading and writing in both Cantonese and English, he explains that "reading and writing in English were equally as important because it was seen as an assimilation tool while learning Chinese was more crucial in preserving my heritage." In another post, he explicitly acknowledges the social and economic value of assimilating to language norms in particular, saying that journaling in his childhood was "more than personal pleasure, writing and reading used to only be sources of currency to me as an immigrant." Elaborating on this notion in yet another post, this time taking up scholarly framing from Prendergast's (2008) *Buying into English*, Eli explains at length: "English is a type of currency: you have it or you don't. And if you don't, you're in trouble. And like money, English has no inherent value besides the one unnamed value in that we prioritize it over other languages." In this way, Eli's ambivalence about writing appears as an almost resigned suspicion of performing access to standard forms of English in writing.

But in a course assignment that asked students to use their ILI community writing experiences to challenge an academic literacy theory read in class, assimilation takes on a decidedly less empowering tone. In his paper, Eli explored the impact of the monolingual ideologies he saw circulating in the community space and through instructors' writing assignments. Describing a writing center interaction with one student, Eli explains:

> A student wrote about immigration and how she endorses it because it helps diversify America. But she used words like "other people" and "they," which I found to be curious because she herself was an immigrant, and when she wrote about "them assimilating," she was doing that right in front of me in the classroom. I pointed this out to her and she seemed to light up and said "oh, that's my experience too!" which gave me pause: Some ESL students aren't even aware that they are part of the assimilation

system. How could ESL students negotiate and make decisions on how much assimilation leaks into their daily lives when they aren't even made aware that they are already integrated in the progress of assimilation? ... ESL schools contribute to the narrative where students strive to pack away their culture and submit into assimilation.

As he worked with the student on her writing, Eli noted the dissociation the assignment initiated between the writer and the generalized figure of the immigrant. In making that connection for the student, pointing out how her life may challenge her own argument, Eli articulated for himself the kind of assimilation quietly required in what he saw to be an "ESL school." In this case, Eli's framing of assimilation is less positive or even utilitarian: He names assimilation as a "system" that "leaks" into immigrant lives and sweeps them into its forward "progress." In his terms, ESL students "submit" to assimilation and are made to "strive to pack away their culture" to gain its promises.

Eli's reframing of cultural and linguistic assimilation was likely influenced by assigned course reading, which at that point was critical of literacy's social promise. But this stance was also informed by his lived experiences, primarily those which made him question the notion of choice—choosing to assimilate—as well as proof of authenticity—being made to validate one's assimilative credentials over and over again. In his interview, he wonders aloud whether or not it was really his "free will to learn English, to obtain literacy," because his "*need* to do that is not part of my free will," particularly because he was supposedly making this choice "as a baby." He similarly says his mother likely would not have chosen to live in the US or learn English, let alone assimilate to both, if "it was her free will and we weren't living in such a patriarchal man-dominated society." In written reflections, Eli further complicates the purported choice to assimilate in terms of the ongoing work involved in doing so. He says his life has helped him "understand it is extremely physically and mentally exhausting to always have to prove that your voice is valid." He writes, "I'm a God-fearing English-speaking nerd who doesn't know what a kilometer is and wears Timberlands so if that's not enough to prove that I'm an American I really don't know what else would." He responds to this point in a later interview by identifying literacy itself as the ultimate validator, continually affiliating English language literacy with social and cultural value. He says, "Literacy is just like, it means so much to us cause that's almost proof, like un-negatable proof that we spent time trying to be the American part of Asian." The literacy to obtain papers, to succeed in school, to navigate dominant language systems is the proof Eli holds up, both for himself and his parents, of their assimilative success. Thus, Eli's critical language awareness holds in tension the choice and compulsion to assimilate through literacy alongside his deep knowledge of that fragmented belonging.

Literacy Spans Lineage; Literacy Ends Lineage
Throughout his course writing and in follow-up interview conversations, Eli also stresses the power literacy has to simultaneously connect and fragment families. In a follow-up email to me he writes, "I would like for the general American population, and perhaps even the international population, to understand that literacy spans over generations." His belief that "literacy's impact spans much more than we initially believe" motivated him to write me a further email about a question that lingered with him after our initial interview. Because much of his writing and thinking over the course took place in terms of his family, Eli especially emphasized literacy's power to span, or connect across, generations of families. He explains the ways that literacy can connect these generations to create lineage:

> The decisions that we make about the standards about who and who is not literate, or how much literacy is "enough" are crucial not simply because they affect a certain general population or individual, but they run through peoples' entire lineages. Literacy also does not stay in its technical framework of "documents" or "literature" or "books," but its impact can leak into people's actions and emotions, which may last forever.

Literacy's connective power here is not benign—this is not the simple passing down of literacy's practices or values from parents to children. Instead, Eli notes that dominant literacy norms—the standards wielded to characterize language learners such as immigrants—"run through" generations, creating dispositions toward languages that echo across "entire lineages." In this way, literacy connects families, but not in the warmhearted ways often characterized by long-promoted images of parents reading to children. Because, as Eli writes, literacy "can leak" beyond the objects of books and papers and live instead in "actions and emotions," and the less beneficial dispositions toward language and literacy "may last forever" in children's, and thus entire families', desire or motivation to learn certain literacies in particular languages.

But Eli also knows deeply the ways literacy can separate families, creating the impossibility of lineage. Reflecting in his interview on his parents' struggles to respond to racist assumptions of their literacy deficits, Eli described how his mother's frustration with English-language learning after immigration to the US shaped his entire family. He explained that "her lack of literacy isolated her" to their home and "threw her into a deep depression," which he says was exacerbated by the quicker pace of his own English-language learning. This isolation not only physically separated her from the daily routines of her husband and child but also affected her ability to find a job, causing her to direct larger frustrations toward her family:

> There should have been something out there for a woman willing to work. If the doors didn't close on her, she wouldn't have closed the doors on me, forcing a toddler into the position of being a scapegoat for their family's suffering. I fully believe that America's obsession with people's lack of literacy and displacement of those people, all rooted in racism, came very close to ruining my family. And perhaps, the system is built that way on purpose, to segregate and eradicate certain groups of people, as it has been well-practiced in the past.

No matter how many English courses Eli's mother took at night at their local library, and no matter the effort she put into finding work appropriate to her pre-immigration qualifications, professional "doors" were closed on her, creating barriers to self-worth which she then turned toward Eli. These closed doors, which Eli places first in the hands of literacy-obsessed employers and then more broadly in America's "well-practiced" racist enactments of literacy in general, are the symbols of family separation. Literacy lineage is not possible with no avenues for passing, and Eli is savvy in knowing that the power of literacy to separate "is built that way on purpose."

Further, as an adoptee to Chinese immigrants to the US, Eli understands the ways that literacy intervenes to push families apart. In another course paper, Eli was asked to use course concepts to analyze the role of literacy in a contemporary news story on migration. He enacted Vieira's (2016) theory of sociomaterial literacy to analyze the case of Phillip Clay, an adopted undocumented Korean adult living in the US who was deported to Korea, where he had never lived. Eli explains that such adoptees with secure social and professional lives are deported and "separated from all that" and are "expected to make something out of nothing" in countries they have rarely or never visited. Eli argues that Phillip Clay's case shows that "all that literacy means nothing if there isn't the literacy that the American government is obsessed with," namely, documentation of citizenship. In his essay, Eli locates literacy in family lineage quite literally, noting that after deportation and much struggle with mental health and social isolation, Phillip Clay in fact committed suicide. Eli understands this tragic event in terms of literacy: a "lack of documentation as well as his lack of Korean literacy" exacerbated his social isolation to the extent that "literacy ultimately ended his lineage; he never had a wife nor children." Eli imbues literacy with a connecting as well as dividing power, in this way critically aware of the simultaneously beneficial and detrimental forces literacy enacts on families.

LITERATE MENDING: "THE WAY YOU LOOK IS A LITERACY"

In these two takes, Eli's critical language awareness is marked by the fragmentation of an isolationist era. But he also uses writing activities and relationships to, as he says, "recover" aspects of his linguistic self and feel "relief." Such recovery writing shows him mending the frayed edges of his language identity. Thus, the criticality of language awareness is shaped not only through disappointment, disillusion, and disgust but also through inspiration and hope. The latter characterizes what I call literate mending, the use of writing and writing relationships to stitch fractured selves back together.

In discussing interactions at a workplace in which customer dissatisfaction was expressed at him in race-based insults, Eli states that even with his "perfect American boy manners . . . in English and with a decent GPA" and with the "literacy that got [him] this job—[he] passed the interview, did the paperwork," he was still subjected to racist slurs about his English language capabilities, initiated not by his accentless spoken fluency but by his racial appearance. Reflecting on these interactions during his interview, Eli concludes that "literacy doesn't have to be words on a page . . . it's in the way you look too; the way you look is literacy." Here Eli is in conversation with scholars who argue that "the way you look" always mediates how you are heard (Flores and Rosa 2015). Like these scholars, Eli observes that racialized and language-minoritized writers are required to constantly validate their literate belonging, no matter their fluency. But Eli's articulation adds a helpful duality: that "the way you look"—the way you set your eyes on someone—also is a literacy, an evolving critical awareness of, in this case, the relationship between race and language.

Eli says experiences like these "split you apart," but Eli's case also suggests that scaffolded encounters with literate difference, such as those enabled by community-engaged writing activities, can help mend what has frayed. In response to my question about what the purpose of community-engaged writing might be, Eli depicts the tension of fracture and mending in vivid and lasting terms:

> Being part of a community, or being in a place where people want your help or seek out your help, helps you sort of recover things that you feel

like you've lost over the years. That you didn't even know that you had lost. Like there was a strong period of time that I rejected being Asian, rejected being Chinese. . . . But then if you're working with a community, it's kinda like, oh but I have a place in this community. I'm like a bridge for this community and I have a lot of power in this community. I need to respect that power; I need to respect my own community. I can't turn my back on them. Because, well, they need me. And it's a great relief. I know I see a lot of great relief for Chinese people and even LGBTQ Chinese people to see me and be like, oh, you're not dead. [laughing] Like pure cynical survival tactics, like oh you're not dead. You're still here thriving and going to school, getting a job in America. That's possible for me.

Eli's ability to recover pieces of his literate identity through his relationships with community members—here he is describing tutoring English in libraries—is remarkable. He responds in terms of what can be lost and recovered through language: respect, power, thriving, possibility. He is critically aware that his presence in a community writing space is an opportunity for others to recognize him and for him to recognize himself. In the present volume, as Miron shows in her exploration of public pedagogy and as Alvarez argues in her analysis of self-sponsored writing, the learning that occurs beyond the often monolingual walls of formal education can open up the literate experiences that are deemed worthy of recognition.

This community-engaged writing—both the tutoring and the later written analysis of it—allowed Eli to navigate the fragmentation and reintegration of his own language identity. Eli's own navigation created the contours of his critical language awareness, unique to his life but common to many of the multilingual writers in this study. However, critical language awareness is not an arrival. It is instead an evolving knowing that writers foster across their literate encounters, both damaging and restorative. As an ongoing practice then, community-engaged writing holds promise as the kind of literate mechanism that dismantles isolation, both in the self and in the world.

NOTES

1. For a full description of this course, see Lorimer Leonard, Pappo, and Piscioniere (2020).
2. Writing projects between ILI and UMass are sustained through new offerings of English 391 as well as through UMass students staying on as volunteers at ILI and enrolling in studies with me.
3. Of twenty-four UMass student participants, eight self-identified in class surveys as a child of immigrant parents, nine as multilingual, and ten as having proficient knowledge of languages other than English. Of ten ILI teacher and staff participants, two identified as coming from immigrant families, three as multilingual, and seven as having proficient knowledge of languages other than English.

REFERENCES

Alim, H. Samy. 2005. "Critical Language Awareness in the United States: Revisiting Issues and Revising Pedagogies in a Resegregated Society." *Educational Researcher* 34 (7): 24–31.

Anzaldúa, Gloria. 1987. *Borderlands/La Frontera: The New Mestiza*. San Francisco, CA: Aunt Lute Books.

Auerbach, Elsa, Byron Barahona, Julio Midy, Felipe Vaquerano, and Ana Zambrano. 2013. *Adult ESL/Literacy from the Community to the Community: A Guidebook for Participatory Literacy Training*. New York: Routledge.

Baker-Bell, April. 2013. "'I Never Really Knew the History behind African American Language': Critical Language Pedagogy in an Advanced Placement English Language Arts Class." *Equity and Excellence in Education* 46 (3): 355–70.

Blum, Denise. 2015. "'Because I Want to Serve the Gringos': Critical Race Pedagogy and Teaching English in Mexico." In *Learning the Language of Global Citizenship: Strengthening Service-Learning in TESOL*, edited by James M. Perren and Adrian J. Wurr, 541–68. Champaign, IL: Common Ground.

Brandt, Deborah. 1994. "Remembering Writing, Remembering Reading." *College Composition and Communication* 45 (4): 459–79.

Campano, Gerald, and María P. Ghiso. 2011. "Immigrant Students as Cosmopolitan Intellectuals." In *Handbook of Research on Children's and Young Adult Literature*, edited by Shelby Wolf, Karen Coats, Patricia Enciso, and Christine Jenkins, 164–76. New York: Routledge.

Campano, Gerald, María P. Ghiso, and Bethany J. Welch. 2016. *Partnering with Immigrant Communities: Action through Literacy*. New York: Teachers College Press.

Carney, William. 2014. "Keyword Essay: Critical Service Learning." *Community Literacy Journal* 9 (1): article 6. https://digitalcommons.fiu.edu/communityliteracy/vol9/iss1/6.

Charmaz, Kathy. 2014. *Constructing Grounded Theory*. London: SAGE Publications.

Chiang, Yuet-Sim D., and Mary Schmida. 1999. "Language Identity and Language Ownership: Linguistic Conflicts of First-Year University Writing Students." In *Generation 1.5 Meets College Composition: Issues in the Teaching of Writing to U.S.-Educated Learners of ESL*, edited by Linda Harklau, Kay M. Losey, and Mary Siegal, 81–98. Mahwah, NJ: L. Erlbaum Associates.

Dyson, Anne Haas, and Celia Genishi. 2005. *On the Case: Approaches to Language and Literacy Research*. New York: Teachers College Press.

Fairclough, Norman. 1992. *Critical Language Awareness*. London: Routledge.

Fitzgerald, Colleen M. 2009. "Language and Community: Using Service Learning to Reconfigure the Multicultural Classroom." *Language and Education*, no. 23, 217–31.

Flores, Nelson, and Jonathan Rosa. 2015. "Undoing Appropriateness: Raciolinguistic Ideologies and Language Diversity in Education." *Harvard Educational Review* 85 (2): 149–71.

Freire, Paulo. (1970) 2000. *Pedagogy of the Oppressed*. New York: Seabury.

Gee, James P. 2012. *Social Linguistics and Literacies: Ideology in Discourses*. 4th ed. Abingdon, UK: Routledge.

Guerra, Juan. 2016. "Cultivating a Rhetorical Sensibility in the Translingual Writing Classroom." *College English* 78 (3): 228–33.

Gutiérrez, Kris. 2004. "Developing a Sociocritical Literacy in the Third Space." *Reading Research Quarterly* 43 (2): 148–64.

Hancké, Bob. 2009. *Intelligent Research Design*. Oxford, UK: Oxford University Press.

Janks, Hilary. 2010. *Literacy and Power*. New York: Routledge.

Jessner, Ulrike. 2014. "On Multilingual Awareness, or Why the Multilingual Learner Is a Specific Language Learner." In *Essential Topics in Applied Linguistics and Multilingualism, Second Language Learning and Teaching*, edited by Miroslaw Pawlak and Larissa Aronin, 175–84. New York: Springer.

Jesson, Rebecca. 2016. "How Teachers Might Open Up Dialogic Spaces in Writing Instruction." *International Journal of Educational Research*, no. 80, 164–76.

Kalmar, Tomas Mario. 2015. *Illegal Alphabets and Adult Biliteracy: Latino Migrants Crossing the Linguistic Border.* 2nd ed. New York: Routledge.

Katz, Mira Lisa. 2012. "Critical Pedagogy Meets 'Survival English': One Community Based Workplace Literacy Program's Approach to Educating Immigrant Women in California." *International Journal of Innovation in English Language Teaching* 1 (2): 139–58.

Khan, Kamran. 2017. "The Risks and Gains of a Single Case Study." In *Researching Multilingualism: Critical and Ethnographic Perspectives*, edited by Marilyn Martin-Jones and Deirdre Martin, 60–72. New York: Routledge.

Kramsch, Claire. 2006. "The Multilingual Subject." *International Journal of Applied Linguistics* 16 (1): 97–110.

Lam, Wan Shun Eva, and Enid Rosario-Ramos. 2009. "Multilingual Literacies in Transnational Digitally Mediated Contexts: An Exploratory Study of Immigrant Teens in the United States." *Language and Education* 23 (2): 171–90.

Leonard, Rebecca Lorimer. 2014. "Multilingual Writing as Rhetorical Attunement." *College English* 76 (3): 227–47.

Lippi-Green, Rosina. 2012. *English with an Accent: Language, Ideology, and Discrimination in the United States.* 2nd ed. London: Routledge.

Lorimer Leonard, Rebecca, Danielle Pappo, and Kyle Piscioniere. 2020. "Course Design: English 391 Multilingualism and Literacy in Western Mass." *Composition Studies* 48 (1): 103–14.

Marko, Tamera, Mario Ernesto Osorie, Eric Sepenoski, and Ryan Catalani. 2015. "Proyecto Carrito—When the Student Receives an 'A' and the Worker Gets Fired: Disrupting the Unequal Political Economy of Translingual Rhetorical Mobility." *Literacy in Composition Studies* 3 (1): 21–43.

McLaughlin, John, Maria Rodriguez, and Carolyn Madden. 2008. "University and Community Collaborations in Migrant ESL." *New Directions for Adult and Continuing Education*, no. 117, 37–46.

Metz, Mike. 2018. "Pedagogical Content Knowledge for Teaching Critical Language Awareness: The Importance of Valuing Student Knowledge." *Urban Education* 56, no. 9 (October): 1456–84. https://doi.org/10.1177/0042085918756714.

Mitchell, Tania D. 2008. "Traditional vs. Critical Service-Learning: Engaging the Literature to Differentiate Two Models." *Journal of Community Service Learning*, no. 14, 50–65.

Pavlenko, Aneta. 2006. "Bilingual Selves." In *Bilingual Minds: Emotional Experience, Expression and Representation*, edited by Anita Pavlenko, 1–33. Clevedon, UK: Multilingual Matters.

Peck, Wayne, Linda Flower, and Lorraine Higgins. 1994. "Community Literacy: Can Writing Make a Difference?" *The Quarterly of the National Writing Project and the Center for the Study of Writing and Literacy* 16 (2): 10–14, 34–35.

Prendergast, Catherine. 2008. *Buying into English: Language and Investment in the New Capitalist World.* Pittsburgh, PA: University of Pittsburgh Press.

Rabin, Lisa M. 2011. "The Culmore Bilingual ESL and Popular Education Project: Coming to Consciousness on Labor, Literacy, and Community." *Radical Teacher*, no. 91, 58–67.

Rymes, Betsy. 2014. *Communicating Beyond Language: Everyday Encounters with Diversity.* New York: Routledge.

Saldaña, Johnny. 2015. *The Coding Manual for Qualitative Researchers.* 3rd ed. Los Angeles: SAGE Publications.

Scribner, Sylvia. 1984. "Literacy in Three Metaphors." *American Journal of Education* 93 (1): 6–21.

Seltzer, Kate. 2020. "'My English Is Its Own Rule': Voicing a Translingual Sensibility through Poetry." *Journal of Language Identity & Education* 19 (5): 297–311. DOI: 10.1080/15348458.2019.1656535.

Vieira, Kate. 2016. *American by Paper: How Documents Matter in Immigrant Literacy*. Minneapolis: University of Minnesota Press.
Yoon, Bogum. 2016. *Critical Literacies: Global and Multicultural Perspectives*. Singapore: Springer.
You, Xiaoye. 2016. *Cosmopolitan English and Transliteracy*. Carbondale: Southern Illinois University Press.

7

MULTILINGUALISM BEYOND WALLS
Undocumented Young Adults Subverting Writing Education

Sara P. Alvarez

> *"My finest and only haiku."*
> —Jung

It is the spring of 2017 in Queens, New York. Jung and I sit across from each other at a small table in the rear corner of a South Korean bakery, a franchise called *Tous les Jours*. Between the register to the right and the business's large windows to the far left, we can overhear laboring in multiple variations of Korean, English, and Spanish. Drawing on Korean and English, one of the two cash attendants jokes with her coworker about the pronunciation of a new orange-flavored drink. In her next breath, she turns her attention to one of her coworkers, a bussing employee, and directs him in Spanish. The two elderly women sitting at the table directly to our left speak to one another in Korean and smile at Jung and me. Jung and I have met here a number of times over the course of a year and a half, and when Jung first selected this location for our meetings I vividly recall him making light of the name of the place—saying, "It's like me, Korean and speaks French."

The image in figure 7.1 shows Jung's poem "dream haiku," which he had included as part of his portfolio for an immigrant community organizing fellowship application four years before in 2013. Through this fellowship, Jung, a South Korean national and an undocumented US recipient of Deferred Action for Childhood Arrivals (DACA), hoped to build on his activist leadership practices while continuing his college education as a history major. Since then, however, one wall after another have systematically confronted his momentum.

Composed on a background stamped with Chinese characters and three white cranes, something that Jung identified as a seemingly

https://doi.org/10.7330/9781646423248.c007

Figure 7.1. Dream Haiku, 2013.

"stereotypical Asian background," and written in what he downloaded as "resembling calligraphy" font, Jung's poem powerfully comments on the failure of the Development, Relief and Education for Alien Minors Act (DREAM Act) to pass in 2010. "dream haiku" is a critical and complex political commentary, purposefully subverting what Jung understood as a "Japanese form of art, often characterized as soft and gentle in Americans' minds." Jung's poetic writing piece labors in the transformation of assumed linguistic, cultural, racial, national, and artistic boundaries, as it also produces an "academic" argument about immigration policy impacting immigrant students and our transnational communities. More so, Jung's writing carefully weaves in lived experience with language practices as critical factors building and shaping academic language literacies.

As the "global turn" has gained full force in the field of literacy studies, and collided with what Brandt (2015) has come to identify as the "rise of writing" beyond college contexts and around the world, a number of educational writing premises have focused on what writing *can do for* and *with* writers deemed as multilingual (Alvarez 2018; Gonzales 2018; Ray and Theado 2016; You 2016). This seemingly global turn—along with its rising writing premises—however, "has not accounted for how racialization and nation-state boundaries function for our growing transnational and multilingual student body" (Alvarez and Wan 2019, 213), specifically how boundaries function in ways that can systemically reinforce white-gazed educational practices that limit these students' opportunities and possibilities of lifetime enrichment. These white-gazed educational practices operate from a colorblind ideology in a systemically racist and racialized society, making multilingualism a valuable practice without accounting for the how and histories of the bodies that sustain it. Therefore, the global turn has not contended with how these "newly" adapted writing premises reinforce deeply embedded monolingual and monocultural ideologies in US writing classrooms, such as the three I outline below:

- A compulsive attention to multilingual practices in ways that undermine the lived realities of racialized and immigrant students, who make up the majority in our transnational student populations (Alvarez and Wan 2019; Brooks 2017, 2020; Dovchin and Lee 2019; Lee and Alvarez 2020).
- A writing discourse, which consistently views and controls the language and literacy practices of historically underrepresented students as *in need of* or *approximation to* monolingual and white-gazed forms of writing—because such approaches are seen as "foundational" for these students' "future real-world" professional experiences (Baker-Bell 2017, 2020; Flores and Rosa 2015; Green 2016; Kynard 2013).
- An understanding of multilingual writing as a set of strategic "moves" or "crafty" and "creative" liberties, rather than as an embodied meaning-making practice and language and literacy labor that contributes to critical literacies and local and transnational community networks (Flores 2020; Horner and Alvarez 2019; Wang 2019).

In this manner, these premises have extended the white-gazed illusion that these rich practices are not dynamically participatory in the cultivation of widely valued schooling and academic literacies—which simultaneously constructs a wall between lifelong community literacies and so-called legitimate, academic literacies.

Drawing on one part of a three-year qualitative study working with twelve self-outed undocumented young adults in the US South and Northeast,[1] this chapter closely examines Jung's understanding and treatment of his own multilingual literacy practices at the margins of *nation*. As a South Korean national, whose named language practices include Tunisian French, Korean, Spanish, and English, and whose lived experience includes two migrations in a period of less than ten years, Jung's rich literacies demonstrate how multilingual writers explicitly contest monolithic views of language, nation, belonging, and the white-gazed ideology of academic writing. I argue that the practices of racialized immigrant writers, like those of Jung, cultivate a conscientious multilingual language architecture[2] that is attuned to how citizenship and immigration impacts people's literacies—in ways that expand writing educators' understanding of academic writing.

More so, these practices show writing educators how Brandt's (2015) posing of "the rise of writing" is also the result of the extraordinary language and literacy labor that immigrant and multilingual students contribute (and have contributed) to this shift. For writing educators in particular, because of their institutional context which walls conceptualizations of academic literacies according to a white gaze, a first step toward cultivating these rich practices is to acknowledge this labor and co-construction of literacy, toward a better understanding about how immigrant-generation and multilingual students' lived experiences intersect and shape academic literacies.

To contextualize how Jung's rich language and literacy practices pertain to larger scholarly and global discussions about writing education and students broadly categorized as multilingual, I first discuss how undocumented immigrant and traditional college-age adults offer an important lens for understanding multilingual practice beyond walls. In developing this discussion, I outline the walls of US writing as "academically" conceived, embedded in the set of premises I highlight in the introduction. I explain how these uncritical writing premises have been adapted amidst the global turn to uphold monolingual and monocultural writing approaches. I then turn to how the structured inequalities of "walled-in" contexts for writing education demand approaches that account for racialization and how the white gaze surveils citizenship. Adopting Flores's (2020) "language architecture" approach to examining the language and literacy practices of racialized students like Jung, I forward a writing research framework that more carefully accounts for—and answers to—the lived experiences of racialization and immigration status as vectors for analysis. Next, I outline the data collection and highlight how the methods involved in the larger research contributed great insight on how to consider writing education as a cyclical trajectory. For the next two sections, I turn my attention to Jung's upbringing and use of multilingual language theories, and how these shape and impact his writing. I return to Jung's writing and the ways in which he consistently navigates language and nation, as he layers vectors of identity in advocacy and professional writing. Finally, I offer some takeaways for writing scholars and educators in thinking about the broader implications of this work.

MULTILINGUAL AND UNDOCUMENTED YOUNG ADULTS IN US WRITING EDUCATION

Scholars focusing on studies of migration and social movements have paid attention to undocumented youth, but their studies have not considered the languages and literacy practices these youths enact and produce as transnational and multilingual students (Gonzales 2008; Muñoz 2015; Nicholls 2013). These migration scholars have mainly focused on the obstacles that first-generation immigrant children and second-generation children of immigrants face in completing higher education in the US. In doing so, these scholars have importantly offered educators and policy-makers important insight into the lives of "1.5-generation" documented and undocumented individuals. It is also important to note the limited scope of these studies in examining the educational paths and lived experiences of Asian-identifying undocumented and immigrant youths and communities (Pila and Escudero 2018).

The 1.5-generation of undocumented immigrants arrived in the US as children and have lived most of their lives in the US. Because of the 1982 Supreme Court ruling in *Plyler v. Doe*, which guaranteed all children in US territory the right to K–12 education regardless of immigration status, undocumented 1.5 youths have attended US schools and become a part of the so-called mainstream population. That is, they move in and out of English-speaking contexts on an everyday basis, and they have envisioned their lives as US people (Gonzales 2016; Iyer 2015; Patel 2013). But despite this vision, undocumented students face state and national policies that deter them from attaining higher education or seeking social mobility. For instance, in states like Georgia undocumented students are ineligible for in-state tuition and unable to obtain driver's licenses—even if they have been granted DACA status. Thus, these immigrant youths' educational paths to higher education and curricula that accounts for their lived experiences is further complicated by the ways in which federal and state policies and their divergent ways of enforcement in each state both wall them in to segregate them (Trivette and English 2017).

Undocumented young adults participating in immigrant rights' advocacy who also defy assumed racial categories tied to immigration, like Jung, embody the fierce language and literacy practices of racialized immigrant students in US post-secondary institutions and writing courses. In fact, as I have co-argued elsewhere, these immigrant-generation students, at the intersections of multiple vectors of identity that have been historically excluded and underserved in schooling settings, "are the [core body of the public] university" (Wan, Lee, and Alvarez, forthcoming). On the one hand, students like Jung often confront being treated as the "face of diversity" for large urban settings and public institutions of higher education such as the City University of New York (CUNY); and, on the other hand, school curricula often subtract racialized students' ontologies, languages, and lived experiences as well as histories of survivance and transformation—to the extent that they have had to labor upon their educational and employment paths via inadequate conditions and materialities (Hall 2014; Kynard 2013; Lee, Alvarez, and Wan 2021). Immigrant-generation students like Jung, whose embodied transnational and cultural ways of knowing also intersect lived experiences of contesting the walls of *nation*, offer writing educators an important window into the global realities of transnationalism and the damage caused by student learning goals tainted with vague and uncritical uses of the idea of citizenship as literacy (Alvarez and Wan 2019; Turner and Mangual Figueroa 2019).

It is precisely in this consideration of how transnational and immigrant-generation students make up and inform US universities (and institutions of higher education across the world) that the global turn in literacy studies has adapted monolingual-oriented and racialized writing premises that continue to reinscribe deficit models of education that harm multilingual students. That is, the dominant narrative of writing education—amidst the global turn—assumes that multilingual students "need" writing, and that "academic" writing will be the solution and "end all, be all," specifically in the context of societal, structural, and historical racism.

As literacy scholars working toward justice have importantly highlighted, it is the discussions on multilingualism and multiculturalism that often frame the paradigm that looks to serve white-imagined walls or white-gazed and monolingually conceived "norms" (Alim and Paris 2017; Kinloch, Burkhard, and Penn 2020; Rosa and Flores 2017). For this reason, the dominant white-gaze view studies the practices of racialized multilingual populations in ways that erase students' communities, making it so that language-minoritized students rarely see, hear, or have opportunities to weave in, expand, and "amplify" their own voices in the curriculum (Flores 2018; San Pedro 2017). This dominant narrative reinforces deeply embedded monolingual and monocultural ideologies in US writing classrooms, and further occludes how multilingual students have long contributed to (and transformed) highly valued literacies in school-like settings, performing labor often viewed as "academic writing." More so, this dominant narrative fails to capture how immigration and immigrant status impact students' educational and life paths (Camela 2019; Reyes 2020; Kleyn 2018).

RACIALIZED REALITIES AND CITIZENSHIP IN WRITING EDUCATION

Current and ongoing language and literacy theories have called for several terms, stances, and dispositions in response to the global turn in education and in the teaching of writing (Horner et al. 2011; Lee and Canagarajah 2019; Lorimer Leonard 2014). Among these orientations, translingualism (in college settings) and translanguaging (in mainly K–12 and bilingual education) have gained particular momentum in the Americas (García and Li 2014; Horner and Alvarez 2019), but critical applied linguists Flores and Rosa (2015) have further advanced these formulations, by arguing for "raciolinguistics" as a way to critique language ideologies linking so-called academic language with whiteness.

Rosa and Flores (2017) have cultivated important discussions and research about language and power that openly address how racialization functions in communicative interactions that pertain to educational assessment of language in writing. In forwarding this raciolinguistics framework, the work of these scholars has focused on the project of unsettling ideologies of linguistic and written "appropriateness" by explicitly addressing how the white gaze extends in communicative discourses.

Flores and Rosa (2015) highlight how the white gaze—as an ideological positionality—functions as a mode of racialized perception towards the design and assessment of writing identified as academic (151). The white gaze operates as a systematized ideological positionality, a vantage that establishes "the" walls and seeks to control, devalue, and limit opposition. Those nearest the walls are the most policed, and for the white gaze of academic writing, they are racialized as non-white or multilingual because they are viewed as being in opposition to the monolingual vantage point. By understanding how this white gaze operationalizes in writing education, raciolinguistics scholars have crucially shifted the ways in which the language practices of racialized students are (and should be) considered in the context of an unequally global and increasingly racist and anti-immigrant US society (Alim and Paris 2017; Menjívar, Abrego, and Schmalzbauer 2016). This attention to how the white gaze is operationalized has direct implications for the global turn in writing education, because its discursive walls are embedded in our educational approaches. As Rosa and Flores (2017) contextualize via research focusing on students who are termed "long-term English learners and heritage Spanish speakers," a shift to raciolinguistics demands that researchers and educators "engage with, confront, and ultimately dismantle the racialized hierarchy of U.S. society . . . This is a powerful shift from teaching students to follow rules of appropriateness to working with them as they struggle to imagine and enact alternative, and more radically inclusive realities" (186–87).

It is in considering more "radically inclusive realities" that Flores (2020) "proposes language architecture as an alternative conceptualization of language to counteract the concept of academic language that typically reifies deficit perspectives of racialized students" (28). This language architecture approach calls on educators and researchers to offset the systemic walls of the white gaze in the context of globalization, which can present multilingualism as a valuable asset and at the same time work to further racialize and disregard the means and bodies of knowledge in these rich practices (Baker-Bell 2020; Lorimer Leonard 2017; San Pedro 2017). As Flores (2020) explains, a language architecture framework views and treats so-called academic language as "a raciolinguistic ideology that frames the home language practices of racialized communities as inherently deficient," and rejects the idea that academic language is "a list of empirical linguistic practices" (24).

In this manner a language architecture framework asks that educators and researchers work to "make connections between [students' and writers'] existing knowledge and the seemingly unfamiliar tasks demanded by the [writing demands and practices in the curriculum]" (26). This is different from assuming that the practices of multilingual students (or those racialized as such) are being practiced or operationalized in service of furthering academic language as conceptualized through the white gaze.

In adopting Flores's (2020) language architecture framework, my examination of Jung's literacies forwards the following practices: (1) the view that Jung's already existent language and community practices are in consistent dynamicity with the production of so-called academic language and the practices often associated to it, and not in opposition or approximation to them; (2) a lens that directly addresses the walls that systematically treat Jung's literacies as deficient, as dissociated from "academic" literacies, and as disconnected from his lived experiences as an immigrant at the margins of the state; (3) an approach to writing research that centralizes the expertise, knowledge, and lived experience that Jung brings to his own understanding of multilingual practice; (4) an analysis that proposes a reconsideration for thinking about citizenship—in its political, cultural, and state definitions and practices, and as confronted with the white gaze. Here, I want to emphasize that my examination contests with how the white gaze racializes citizenship in its architecture of building borders, and ultimately how it racializes multilingualism.

Additionally, in advancing this adoption of the concept of language architecture—with a careful eye toward the ways in which the white gaze racializes citizenship, and the ways in which it racializes multilingual immigrants at large—I purposefully focus on how Jung labors language as an Asian, a Korean- and French-speaking undocumented activist. Jung's intersecting vectors of identity challenge the US racialization and misguided historicization of undocumented and immigrant activists—often attributed to Latinx/e and Spanish-speaking communities, in particular those of Mexican descent (Lee 2015; Santa Ana 2002). Jung's lived experience, as he notes in figure 7.2: "11 years a prisoner," contests the white-gazed walls of nation and US schooling by turning the "myth of the model minority" on its head. As seen in "dream haiku," Jung directs his audience's attention to vectors of his Asian identity, but he does so in ways that do not place Asian communities as "superior," "more deserving," or of greater merit, because his goal is to urge the passage of the DREAM Act. Instead, Jung captures these elements of identity in ways that progressively push against the walls of the US immigration system.

DATA COLLECTION

This chapter reports on two articulations of patterned codes emerging out of the larger data research (Saldaña 2015): (1) how language and lived experience labor and transform one another; (2) how multilingual immigrant young adults view their language practices. By focusing on these codes and placing them in conversation with one another, under Flores's (2020) call for thinking about the language practices of racialized youths as architecture, the analysis in this chapter centralizes the critical and transformative language-work that multilingual students do in subverting the monolingual and monocultural walls of writing education.

In order to understand how undocumented college-age immigrant activists have practiced and enacted their multilingualism and academic and professional writing, I carried out semi-structured qualitative interviews with participants over the course of three years. The first set of interviews focused on getting to know the participants' backgrounds and their language and writing interests. Follow-up interviews focused on writing samples participants provided and the discussions about language and writing that participants brought up during initial interviews.

Fieldwork for this research included observations and action research during immigration-related meetings and rallies, both national and local, as well as visits to participants' homes and their educational and working spaces. This was at their discretion. Over the course of this research, I collected over 450 pages of field notes and interview transcripts from nearly thirty hours of audio recordings and five hours of video footage; two hundred photographs of the spaces in which these college-age adults participated, noting how they positioned themselves to write; and sixty different multimodal and alphabetic-based writing texts that the youths in this study produced in relation to immigrant rights advocacy.

Given that the main method of analysis in this ethnography was an adaptation of text-ethnography (Lillis and Curry 2010), youths' writing also added to the data, including cyclical conversations via text messages and emails. Additionally, participants' own notes for their own writing (as time progressed) also informed our recurrent conversations. This can be seen in figure 7.2: "11 years a prisoner."

Because this chapter focuses exclusively on Jung, I offer a brief example on how these cyclical conversations took place with him, focusing on figure 7.1. Jung shared the poem in figure 7.1 early in the first few months of this ethnographic research, but this piece only came up in our conversations a year later when Jung and I began to discuss what and who motivated him to write. I then selected a number of similar pieces to discuss with him in our follow-up meetings, and in some cases asked him to annotate how he felt about seeing and reading these pieces in that moment, which in some cases was near the end of data collection (see figure 7.2). Conversations about the writing pieces, and their implications, however, did not end at the culmination of our in-person interviews. Conversations would continue over messaging apps, such as Facebook Messenger, and with added elements of writing like emojis, memes, GIFs, and audio files. Many of these conversations have continued beyond the point of data collection, as part of the trust relationship

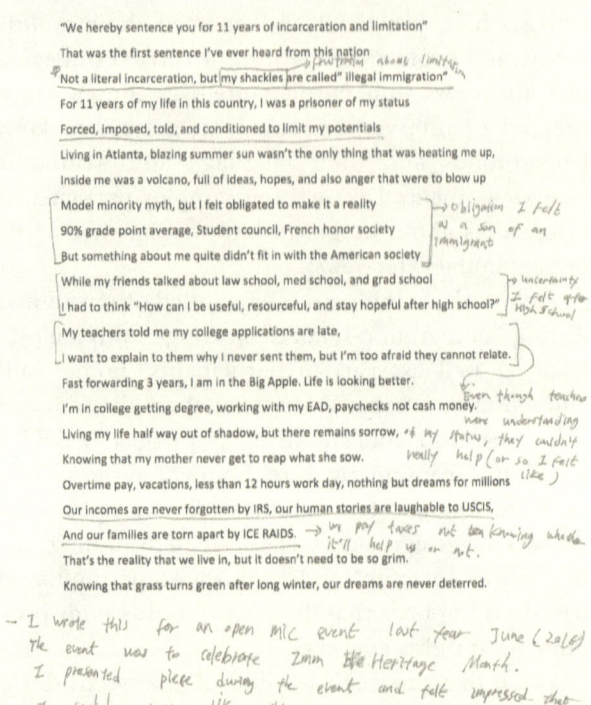

Figure 7.2. "11 years a prisoner," 2016.

we have built across the years—*en confianza* (Alvarez 2017)—and perhaps as part of our shared interest in understanding our own multilingual, immigrant, activist, and scholarly practices.

JUNG

"These Language Schools"

Born in Anyang city, 안양시, South Korea, Jung immigrated to Tunisia with his mother at the young age of thirteen. Together, Jung and his mother adapted to a new cultural and linguistic landscape, and then after two years of immersion in Tunisian French, they migrated once more—to the US South. Working seasonal jobs within ethnic communities, they endured many forced physical migrations, and Jung learned to identify and adopt some of the English accent variations between North Carolina and metropolitan Atlanta.

Moreover, while growing up in the US South, Jung adapted his rich language practices as a way to gain entry into Spanish. Socializing with

Spanish-speaking immigrant peers at school and work, Jung both developed a method for language support when English or Korean presented a challenge and cultivated friendships and community. Jung's migration story is therefore also about the ordinariness with which at least four named languages became a part of his daily life and how he strategically and consciously adapted them to serve his communicative and educational purposes. However, in observing how English came into his life, Jung positions himself differently than how he does with Korean, for instance. As our exchange that follows shows, Jung critically weaves in how English-language learning and socializing is clearly tied to how the white gaze looks to and systemically valorizes citizenship or a migratory immigrant status that conforms:

> SARA: How did English come into your life?
>
> JUNG: So, I learned English a little bit through school, and then also I took ESL classes when I first came here, because I came on a student visa, and in order to maintain the visa you had to take—well, not take—but you have to go to these language schools. So, I went there for several months until my visa expired; so that is how I learned English. And also, when I went to high school here.

In relating his learning of Englishes, Jung quickly ties documentation, and the walls of *nation*, to his vision of how this language practice has played a role in his life. As Jung notes, he had to "go to these language schools" to keep his student visa. Here, Jung offers several layers of critique. He does not call "these language schools" *college*. This resonates with Lorimer Leonard's (2017) analysis of how immigrant women view and value their own multilingual practices in segmented ways. Jung presents his experiences of becoming multilingual as an occurrence, but also critically links how the languages and literacies that he has become immersed and authorial in operate in particular ways in relationship with how the white gaze looks toward citizenship. Jung contests "these language schools," and rejects what the white gaze deems as the "safe" minority thread, which attempts to place him within the framework of the model minority he refuses. In other words, for Jung his multilingual practice has everything to do with his lived experience as an undocumented immigrant and the walls that this experience presents to his schooling, activism, and livelihood in the US context. For Jung, English is tainted with feelings of exclusion as well as pressures to assimilate to a national context that is monolingually-oriented and often denies his involvement in immigrant rights' advocacy as someone who is a "Korean and speaks French."

This personalized viewpoint about "the" English language and its acquisition stands in sharp contrast with his coming-into-Spanish and seems to carry an important intellectual pursuit and social aspect to his becoming-an-American (by culture).

> SARA: Spanish was something that came with friends?
>
> JUNG: So, I can read Spanish because I learned French. It's a very similar language. But also, even though I never took any classes in school, I actually learned it through books on my own. That helped a little bit. And hanging out with friends. I had Spanish friends growing up, so learning words and their context with them. And after I came to New York City, I see a lot of signs on the train that are bilingual, so I am constantly learning from that as well. I mean it's New York City.
>
> S: That's interesting that you said that the signs are bilingual. And that, for you, seeing two languages—in this case, English and Spanish—together, side by side, would be a sight of New York City.
>
> J: Yeah. I mean before, I did not know how to say *tarjeta* (MetroCard), but now I know.

Jung's relationship to Spanish is more about his socialization with and in metropolitan sites. He first meets friends with Spanish-speaking backgrounds through seasonal labor as well as schooling in the US South, but then Spanish becomes a more normed language in New York, where, as he explains, he sees bilingual signs on an everyday basis. That Jung is interested in reading and understanding these signs, and that he has gained access to new terms, like "MetroCard" in Spanish, is a telling sign of his rich and critical language architecture. This Jung confirms when he tells me that learning Spanish has been beneficial to his work related to immigration. It has given him a window into how his Korean culture is similar to Latinx/e cultures and has opened an avenue of communication for immigration-related discussions and events. For instance, because of his Spanish practice, on a number of occasions Jung was able to assist Spanish-speaking immigrants, who entered the office of the nonprofit where he worked. Moreover, in my long-term work with immigrant activists, I have observed something that Jung as well as other Asian participants in the project reported: engagement with Spanishes is common in many immigrant-based rallies. "Asians are the minority," as Jung has jokingly, but fiercely, put it. However, it is important to note that the Englishes that Jung has acquired by virtue of his American socialization have also shaped much of his multilingualism—though they are constantly tainted with his relation to being undocumented in the US.

Jung's relationship with writing in many ways mirrors his language architecture (Flores 2020). He does not claim it as extraordinary, but it exists beyond most people's everyday practice of writing. Like most participants in this study (n=12), Jung claims that college or writing in college interrupted his desire to write. That is, this wall that many immigrant and racialized students report about the US writing classroom is a real barrier extended by a white-gazed structure and system. Writing as presented in US classrooms extends a discourse that seeks to "discipline" and assimilate students into academic literacies as a supposed form of entry into schooling and "appropriateness," but this is inconsistent with the lived realities of racialized immigrant students. It is unrealistic in light of the actual ways that they will seek participation as workers and professionals in multilingual and global communities. Scholars at the intersections of immigration and education have long shown that these forms of systematic categorization cannot only be detrimental to the lifelong literacy experiences of immigrant-generation students, but also work to downplay students' agency, labor, and view of their own schooling experiences (Brooks 2020; Kleyn and Stern 2018; Turner and Mangual Figueroa 2019; Valenzuela 1999).

In the segment below, Jung shared his take on college writing when I asked about his writing at the Korean nonprofit immigrant organization he had worked for:

> I hated writing in college. I was writing about topics that I did not like. It was just very restrictive. It was not about any topic I want. It had to be about what they wanted, no matter how mundane. There is a lot more freedom and leeway that I like [in order to write]. Of course, at work [at the immigration nonprofit that Jung worked for three years] I had to write professional pieces that were restrictive, that were not the most enjoyable, like press releases. But that writing was not as restrictive as it used to be in college—no professor checking this, marking this and that. [And the writings for work] were pieces that had an impact. We wrote about housing issues, immigration, things that mattered to our communities and [neighborhood].

Here, Jung offers a strong critique of his experience writing in college. Jung notes the feeling of confinement in writing, the walling of writing, about topics that in his experience had small to any relevance. This sharply contrasts with the writing he did on his own and at work. That writing was purposeful and meaningful to Jung. It was not just about applying for the fellowship, but expressing a sense of self, advocacy, and work in something that greatly impacted his life and affected his everyday interactions.

Jung's reflection above also highlights how he understood the engagement of his professors with writing as more dedicated to "checking this, marking this and that," rather than perhaps offering commentary on how to develop his pieces and grow with his writing. This was different from how he described working on documents at the nonprofit, where he often had to move across languages and mainly compose in English.

In describing his writing in that multilingually-attuned professional space, and surrounded by emergent bilingual colleagues, Jung reported that "the thing is, my grammar is not that good. But I get comments and ideas from [American-born Korean colleague] and I learn. I help him with Korean, and he helps me with English. There is a balance of ideas and languages." Jung's experience with college writing courses has highly undermined and undervalued Jung's language labor and his architecting of it. As Jung explains, it is not just that the topics he had to write about were rather irrelevant to the many topics he was interested in, but that the feedback he received was poor, focusing solely on conceptualizations of grammar as an error "to fix." And while much can be said about Jung's interpretation of such feedback, the approach of being "marked" on a paper, as opposed to being engaged and responded to for his ideas, is one that multilingual and racialized writers often report as a feature of the white-gazed walling of their schooling experiences (Brooks 2020; Rosa and Flores 2017).

Jung's implicit critique of college writing in English confronts white-gazed constructions of language and argumentation. Jung's expressed relationship with college writing in the English language also speaks to having to write in a way that restricts and polices his dynamic ways of moving across and within languages, literacies, and subject-based knowledges. This further demonstrates how Jung's dynamic and critical multilingual literacies have been undermined via deficiency lenses that sought to (and did) categorize him as an English Language Learner (ELL), as an English as a Second Language (ESL) or L2 writer, and as a "basic writer"—categorizations which could not capture the richness of his embodied multilingual practice. Jung's experience with English writing in the college setting proved insufficient to his dynamic language and literacy practices. Jung's writing in English outside of academia, however, shows the richness of his language architecture.

Jung, English, and Nation

In the beginning of 2016, preparing for an open mic in New York, in which the nonprofit Jung worked for sought connection with other organizations and ways to raise funds for and celebrate Immigrant Heritage Month, Jung chose to write in English as he evaluated that a great part of the audience would be English-speaking. For Immigrant Heritage Month, Jung chose to draw on the richness of his English-language practice to convey to his audience how this issue was one that he embodied; Jung designed, constructed, and delivered "11 years a prisoner" (fig. 7.2).

"11 years a prisoner" opens up with "incarceration and limitation," directly addressing the white-gazed walls of *nation*, "forced, imposed, to limit my potentials." In these words, Jung labors and architects an important critique that specifically ties his undocumented immigrant status and Asian identity to experiences of racialization and imposed borders through schooling. What is more, Jung contends with how these white-gazed walls attempt to place him, as an Asian student, in a category "separate" from his migrant and American peers, a category that seeks in him a "model minority." Jung discusses the temptation and privileges granted by aligning with this myth of the model minority, which grants racialized access via the trope of meritocracy. As Jung explains, "I felt obliged to make it a reality, 90% grade point average, Student Council, French honor society." Of course, Jung writes about this high school experience in retrospect, and perhaps for this very reason, the poem also highlights how such an approximation to the model minority myth cannot (and did not) protect him.

In confronting the white-gazed walls of nation, Jung also contests with how these walls have manifested in his secondary school experience, where he wants "to explain [to his teachers] why he never sent [the college applications], but [Jung's] too afraid they cannot relate." That is, Jung has an understanding that his writing educators cannot understand the lived realities of his immigrant experience. And, yet, in the "bilingual city," "in the Big Apple," where he learned how to say *tarjeta* for *metrocard*, there is some hope, as Jung is now enrolled in college at the public university of New York and has an Employment Authorization Document (EAD). And yet, "dar[ing] to dream" has not been extended to his undocumented family members and communities. His mother, for instance, will likely "never get to reap what she sow." There is so much that can be said about this "English"-language poem, including the complex rhythm to his verse, the rhymes of the *-ion* words, and the poem's multimodality, but what is really powerful is how Jung is able to return to this piece a year later with pride and acknowledge that the vectors that impact his writing and self-advocacy are well represented. For instance, the only terms that get noted in capital letters are those that could with all deserved reason receive anger, "ICE RAIDS," and "EAD," and which Jung received with his DACA temporary relief from deportation (not status). This piece of writing is testament to Jung's politicized language and literacy practices, and it is for this reason that returning to this spoken-word poem is such a rich opportunity for Jung, and for me as a writing educator, to reflect on.

It is now the beginning of summer 2017, and I ask Jung to annotate "11 years a prisoner" and tell me what he remembers about this piece and what he wants me to know about it. Jung notes that he remembers this writing as one that made him feel "impressed [that he] could write like this," as shown in the handwritten marginalia he offered for context (see fig. 2). Of course, implicit in Jung's comment is that "writing like this"—so effectively, to the extent of moving a large audience to tears and joy—was done by moving through various forms of English, offering his story of being undocumented, and critiquing the system that operates and benefits from the criminalization of vulnerable human beings.

"11 years a prisoner," like "dream haiku," is a poem that can easily be classified and confined to the white-gazed elements of "craft," "creativity," and "artistry," and to the walls that seek to separate art from critical and "academic" argumentation, but it is crucial to distinguish the extraordinary language and literacy labor that Jung performs in constructing these works. It is crucial to make visible how his language architecture captures not only the full range of his rich language and literacy experiences as well as their relationship to citizenship, but also Jung's method for consistently contesting the walls of nation, state, and monolingual conceptualizations of English.

IMPLICATIONS

The undocumented immigrant young adults I have worked with and learned with, like Jung, surpass many of the goals and expectations set for courses designed to "teach" students how to write academically, as the careful and critical movements needed in the "rise of writing" are already embedded in their practice. These young adults "read as writers," as Brandt (2015, 14; 117) reports from her seven-year project examining how writing—as mass literacy practice—grows in different work and professional contexts, specifically for youth. Brandt (2015) explains that what youth do differently than older generation adults, amidst the rise of writing, is engaging in the many social aspects of doing writing. Youth are much more immersed in the laboring of writing, as Brandt describes, by "sitting for interviews, making videos, competing for performance titles . . . all of these are ways by which contemporary career writers promote themselves, cultivate followings, and expand readerships" (109). But in the case of immigrant and racialized writers, like Jung, these young adults also contest the white-gazed walls of education and citizenship. These immigrant young adults are carefully laboring vectors of identity into writing. In fact, their rich practices testify to how their politicized and fierce linguistic practices are a mechanism to defy nation and monolingual walls.

Many of the implications of this work move beyond the scope of simply doing things differently in writing classrooms. These implications call scholars and writing educators to continue thinking about the very definitions and premises we have set for writing amidst the global turn. In fact, these implications, too, remind us that writing education is also a dynamic mass literacy that happens beyond school-like settings, and to which multilingual immigrant students like Jung have long contributed.

The language practices and multilingual theories of transnational students like Jung subvert and transform monolingualized and racialized conceptions of writing. These practices ask that writing educators better understand how the exclusionary function of citizenship—in this case US citizenship—impacts the language and literacy practices of multilingual immigrant students in ways that enable learning that challenges fixed linguistic, ethnic, and racial categories and labors in the production of life literacies. These fierce language practices and theorizations of language—from the margins—generously open up opportunities for writing educators to take up new writing education practices that are more conscientious of lived experience.

Below I outline a few of these practices for writing scholars and educators to consider:

- Delve into so-called academic writing in ways that engage with the political, structural, and racial walls of this highly valued form of literacy. Specifically, presenting writing as a practice that is informed by lived experience and reflection and is often already ongoing outside of schooling settings and *en confianza* (Alvarez 2017). This is also about reconsidering assumptions about citizenship as the norm in writing classrooms, linking "standard" language ideologies to nationalistic and anti-immigrant ideologies. In this manner, writing educators are called to reflect on questions such as: Is my evaluation of this seemingly "standard" practice one that takes root in raciolinguistic ideology? Am I focusing on intent and not impact when I assume that multilingual students are "in need" of monolingual ideology for "professional" and "academic" writing purposes? Am I operating on the assumption that the global aspect of multilingualism is color-blind—and that it is not systematized through laws enforced by the state?
- Investigate further into what makes writing meaningful, impactful, and more purposeful for students in our classrooms. We ought to be more purposeful about how we centralize students' lived experiences, in ways that promote equity and humanization in writing education. Such promotion of a more equitable writing education

should make explicit the extraordinary labor that racialized immigrant students and writers (in general) contribute to writing and writing education (Alvarez and Lee 2019). For instance, we could begin by simply asking: What are some things that are happening in your neighborhood and that you wish to discuss with a larger audience? What should people know about your everyday experiences that impact your schooling practices?

- Create more opportunities for students to "cycle" into their writing. This means generating opportunities for students to review their work, not only for revision and "standardization," but for *self* and reflection. This is a consideration for more spaces that allow students moments to pause, revisit their writing, and better understand what feelings writing evokes in them, and how it does so.

CONCLUSION

In this chapter, I forward a call for rethinking conceptualizations of "academic" writing and writing education as they pertain to multilingual language theories and the communities and bodies of knowledge that produce them in their everyday experiences. I map a language architecture framework that carefully answers to how racialization and immigrants' lived experiences impact, intersect, and shape multilingual and academic practices. In particular, I draw attention to how Jung, an undocumented college-age adult and immigrant rights activist, continuously architects and labors against these monolingual and monocultural walls, and simultaneously cultivates critical writing practices that sustain his livelihood. Jung's lived experience and rich contributions to so-called academic writing not only reaffirm the demand and potential for more critical and humanizing pedagogies in writing education (Alim and Paris 2017; Kinloch 2017) but also demonstrate how such lived experiences are critical, valuable, and meaningful for *being*—being as a state of existing, moving, and doing in life.

As Jung shows in "dream haiku," his poetics are critically informed by and for his political statement and activism. His "dar[ing] to dream" testifies to Jung's committed activism for changing the legal system through proposed policies such as the DREAM Act. Jung's critical and activist poetry dynamically confronts the walls of *nation* as it also calls to the larger Asian immigrant community, who may be "dar[ing] to dream" and facing these same walls. In confronting the walls separating nations, Jung also conscientiously rejects links to the white gaze via the model minority myth, which places Asian communities as though they were in opposition to other language-minoritized and racialized communities. I emphasize that students like Jung consistently face the monolingual and monocultural walls of writing education, as they are not only confronted with state policies that deter them from attaining higher education but also face the uncritical global turn that ignores their lived realities.

Jung cultivates a form of visibility for Asian undocumented immigrant communities, without relying on white-gazed tropes that, ultimately, racialize all non-white imagined subjects. In fact, Jung's rich practices make it all the more imperative to (re)think the role of writing as a set of practices shaping and impacting life beyond the classroom setting while also posing implications for writing education sites, especially in postsecondary settings.

NOTES

1. The larger study traced the texts that these young adults produced in relation to immigrant rights advocacy, predominantly in the form of alphabetic-based writing, but also including media and artwork, such as that found in Jung's poem in figure 7.1.
2. The term *language architecture* is adopted from Flores (2020) and discussed in the following section.

REFERENCES

Alim, H. Samy, and Django Paris. 2017. "What Is Culturally Sustaining Pedagogy and Why Does It Matter?" In Paris and Alim, *Culturally Sustaining Pedagogies*, 1–21.

Alvarez, Sara P. 2018. "Multilingual Writers in College Contexts." *Journal of Adolescent & Adult Literacy* 62 (3): 342–45. doi.org/10.1002/jaal.903.

Alvarez, Sara P., and Eunjeong Lee. 2019. "Ordinary Difference, Extraordinary Dispositions: Sustaining Multilingualism in the Writing Classroom." In *Translinguistics: Negotiating Innovation and Ordinariness*, edited by Jerry Won Lee and Sender Dovchin, 1–16. New York: Routledge.

Alvarez, Sara P., and Amy J. Wan. 2019. "Global Citizenship as Literacy: A Critical Reflection for Teaching Multilingual Writers." *Journal of Adolescent and Adult Literacy* 62 (2): 213–16. doi.org/10.1002/jaal.1000.

Alvarez, Steven. 2017. *Community Literacies en Confianza: Learning from Bilingual After-School Programs*. Urbana, IL: National Council of Teachers of English.

Baker-Bell, April. 2017. "'I Can Switch My Language, but I Cannot Switch My Skin': What Teachers Must Understand about the Relationship between Black Language and Race." In *The Guide for White Women Who Teach Black Boys*, edited by Eddie Moore Jr., Ali Michael, and Marguerite W. Penick-Parks, 97–107. Thousand Oaks, CA: Corwin.

Baker-Bell, April. 2020. *Linguistic Justice: Black Language, Literacy, Identity, and Pedagogy*. New York: Routledge.

Brandt, Deborah. 2015. *The Rise of Writing: Redefining Mass Literacy*. London: Cambridge University Press.

Brooks, Maneka Deanna. 2017. "How and When Did You Learn Your Languages? Bilingual Students' Linguistic Experiences and Literacy Instruction." *Journal of Adolescent and Adult Literacy* 60 (4): 383–93. doi.org/10.1002/jaal.573.

Brooks, Maneka Deanna. 2020. *Transforming Literacy Education for Long-Term English Learners: Recognizing Brilliance in the Undervalued.* Urbana, IL: National Council of Teachers of English.

Camela, Vianey. 2019. "Sustaining Multilingual Literacies: Looking through an Immigrant Lens to Inform Practice." *Journal of Adolescent & Adult Literacy* 62 (5): 565–67. doi.org/10.1002/jaal.930.

Dovchin, Sender, and Jerry Won Lee. 2019. "Introduction to Special Issue: 'The Ordinariness of Translinguistics.'" *International Journal of Multilingualism* 16 (2) 1–6. doi.org/10.1080/14790718.2019.1575831.

Flores, Nelson. 2020. "From Academic Language to Language Architecture: Challenging Raciolinguistic Ideologies in Research and Practice." *Theory into Practice* 59 (1): 22–31. doi.org/10.1080/00405841.2019.1665411.

Flores, Nelson, and Jonathan Rosa. 2015. "Undoing Appropriateness: Raciolinguistic Ideologies and Language Diversity in Education." *Harvard Educational Review* 85 (2): 149–71. doi.org/10.17763/0017-8055.85.2.149.

Flores, Tracey. 2018. "Breaking Silence and Amplifying Voices: Youths Writing and Performing Their Worlds." *Journal of Adolescent and Adult Literacy* 61 (6): 653–60. doi.org/10.1002/jaal.733.

García, Ofelia, and Li Wei. 2014. *Translanguaging: Language, Bilingualism and Education.* New York: Palgrave Macmillan.

Gonzales, Laura. 2018. *Sites of Translation: What Multilinguals Can Teach Us about Digital Writing and Rhetoric.* Ann Arbor: University of Michigan Press.

Gonzales, Roberto G. 2008. "Left Out but Not Shut Down: Political Activism and the Undocumented Student Movement." *Northwestern Journal of Law and Social Policy*, no. 3, 1–22.

Gonzales, Roberto G. 2016. *Lives in Limbo: Undocumented and Coming of Age in America.* Berkeley: University of California Press.

Green, David F., Jr. 2016. "Expanding the Dialogue on Writing Assessment at HBCUs: Foundational Assessment Concepts and Legacies of Historically Black Colleges and Universities." *College English* 79 (2): 152–73.

Hall, Jonathan. 2014. "Multilinguality Is the Mainstream." In *Reworking English in Rhetoric and Composition*, edited by Bruce Horner and Karen Kopelson, 31–48. Carbondale: Southern Illinois University.

Horner, Bruce, and Sara P. Alvarez. 2019. "Defining Translinguality." *Literacies in Composition Studies* 7 (2): 1–30. doi: 10.21623%2F1.7.2.2.

Horner, Bruce, Min Zhan Lu, Jacqueline Jones Royster, and John Trimbur. 2011. "Language Differences in Writing: Toward a Translingual Approach." *College English* 73 (3): 299–317.

Iyer, Deepa. 2015. *We Too Sing America: South Asian, Arab, Muslim, and Sikh Immigrants Shape Our Multiracial Future.* New York: The New Press.

Kinloch, Valerie. 2017. "'You Ain't Making Me Write': Culturally Sustaining Pedagogies and Black Youth's Performances of Resistance." In Paris and Alim, *Culturally Sustaining Pedagogies*, 25–41.

Kinloch, Valerie, Tanja Burkhard, and Carlotta Penn. 2020. "Race, Justice, and Activism in Literacy Instruction." In *Race, Justice, and Activism in Literacy Instruction*, edited by Valerie Kinloch, Tanja Burkhard, and Carlotta Penn, 1–9. New York: Teachers College Press.

Kleyn, Tatyana, director. 2018. *Still Living Undocumented: Five Years Later* (documentary film). Living Undocumented. https://livingundocumented.com/.

Kleyn, Tatyana, and Nancy Stern. 2018. "Labels as Limitations." *MinneTESOL Journal* 34, no. 1 (Spring): 1–9.

Kynard, Carmen. 2013. *Vernacular Insurrections: Race, Black Protest, and the New Century in Composition-Literacies Studies.* Albany: State University of New York Press.

Lee, Erika. 2015. *The Making of Asian America: A History*. New York: Simon & Schuster.
Lee, Eunjeong, and Sara P. Alvarez. 2020. "World Englishes, Translingualism, and Racialization in the US College Composition Classroom." *World Englishes* 39 (1): 263–74.
Lee, Eunjeong, and A. Suresh Canagarajah. 2019. "Beyond Native and Nonnative: Translingual Dispositions for More Inclusive Teacher Identity in Language and Literacy Education." *Journal of Language, Identity & Education* 18 (6): 352–63.
Lee, Eunjeong, Sara P. Alvarez, and Amy J. Wan. 2021. "Cultivating Multimodality from the Multilingual Epicenter: Queens, 'The Next America.' " *Journal of Global Literacies, Technologies, and Emerging Pedagogies (JGLTEP)* 7 (1): 1256–81.
Lillis, Theresa, and Mary Jane Curry. 2010. *Academic Writing in a Global Context: The Politics and Practices of Publishing in English*. New York: Routledge.
Lorimer Leonard, Rebecca. 2014. "Multilingual Writing as Rhetorical Attunement." *College English* 76 (3): 227–47.
Lorimer Leonard, Rebecca. 2017. *Writing on the Move: Migrant Women and the Value of Literacy*. Pittsburgh, PA: University of Pittsburgh Press.
Menjívar, Cecilia, Leisy J. Abrego, and Leah C. Schmalzbauer. 2016. *Immigrant Families*. Cambridge, UK: Polity Press.
Muñoz, Susana M. 2015. *Identity, Social Activism, and the Pursuit of Higher Education: The Journey Stories of Undocumented and Unafraid Community Activists*. New York: Peter Lang.
Nicholls, Walter J. 2013. *The DREAMers: How the Undocumented Youth Movement Transformed the Immigrant Rights Debate*. Palo Alto, CA: Stanford University Press.
Paris, Django, and H. Samy Alim, eds. 2017. *Culturally Sustaining Pedagogies: Teaching and Learning for Justice in a Changing World*. New York: Teachers College Press.
Patel, Leigh. 2013. *Youth Held at the Border: Immigration, Education, and the Politics of Inclusion*. New York: Teachers College Press.
Pila, Daniela, and Kevin Escudero, organizers. 2018. Liminally Legal Asians: Consciousness Raising, Political Activism and (Re)articulations of Belonging in the United States Conference, Brown University, Providence, RI, September 28, 2018. https://liminallylegalasians.weebly.com/.
Ray, Brian, and Connie Kendall Theado. 2016. "Composition's 'Global Turn': Writing Instruction in Multilingual/Translingual and Transnational Contexts." *Composition Studies* 44 (1): 10–12.
Reyes, Y. 2020. *We Never Needed Papers to Thrive* (video and powerpoint). SpeakOut Ed Talks. April 16, 2020. https://www.speakoutnow.org/content/speakout-ed-talks-we-never-needed-papers-thrive.
Rosa, Jonathan, and Nelson Flores. 2017. "Do You Hear What I Hear: Raciolinguistic Ideologies and Culturally Sustaining Pedagogies." In Paris and Alim, *Culturally Sustaining Pedagogies*, 175–90.
Saldaña, Johnny. 2015. *The Coding Manual for Qualitative Researchers*. Thousand Oaks, CA: Sage Publications.
San Pedro, Timothy. 2017. " 'This Stuff Interests Me': Re-centering Indigenous Paradigms in Colonizing Schooling Spaces." In Paris and Alim, *Culturally Sustaining Pedagogies*, 99–116.
Santa Ana, Otto. 2002. *Brown Tide Rising: Metaphors of Latinos in Contemporary American Public Discourse*. Austin: University of Texas Press.
Turner, Erica O., and Ariana Mangual Figueroa. 2019. "Immigration Policy and Education in Lived Reality: A Framework for Researchers and Educators." *Educational Researcher* 20 (10): 1–9.
Trivette, Michael J., and David J. English. 2017. "Finding Freedom: Facilitating Postsecondary Pathways for Undocumented Students." *Educational Policy* 31 (6): 858–94.
Valenzuela, Angela. 1999. *Subtractive Schooling: U.S.-Mexican Youth and the Politics of Caring*. Albany: State University of New York Press.

Wan, Amy J., Eunjeong Lee, and Sara P. Alvarez. Forthcoming. "'Queens Is the Future': WPA Horizons for Transnational Spaces." In *Teaching and Studying Transnational Composition*, edited by Christiane Donahue and Bruce Horner. New York: Modern Language Association.

Wang, Xiqiao. 2019. "Observing Literacy Learning across WeChat and First-Year Writing: A Scalar Analysis of One Transnational Student's Multilingualism." *Computers and Composition* 52 (1): 253–71.

You, Xiaoye. 2016. *Cosmopolitan English and Transliteracy*. Carbondale: Southern Illinois University Press.

8
PUBLIC PEDAGOGY AND MULTIMODAL LEARNING ON THE US-MEXICO BORDER

Layli Maria Miron

A wall, built of steel bollards that soar above the dry earth of the Sonoran Desert, splits the city of Nogales into Arizonan and Mexican sides. As I walk along the Mexican side of the wall, I can see that it has been adorned with pictures and messages protesting division and policing: a boy shot to death by the Border Patrol gazes from a portrait; tiny crucifix memorials sprout from the earth in their dozens; and painted slogans shout from the wall's bollards—for instance, "Nuestros sueños de justicia no los detiene ningún muro" ("Our dreams of justice won't be stopped by any wall"). I have come here to Nogales, a hub of border-crossing and deportation, to learn how migrant advocates articulate their dreams of justice—how they seek to rewrite the civic discourse that birthed this border wall and that demonizes undocumented immigrants.

Over the past few decades, the federal policy called "Prevention through Deterrence" has pushed undocumented immigrants away from urban crossings into the Sonoran Desert. With its long stretch of border running through this desert, Arizona has experienced a huge influx of migrants, which has aroused the ire of many residents (De León 2015). Yet, some have responded to this migrant flow by creating organizations dedicated to upholding migrants' rights through efforts that include public pedagogy. The concept of "public pedagogy" recognizes that teaching and learning occur in many sites outside formal educational institutions, ranging from museums to streets to online media (Springgay and Truman 2019, 4). Public pedagogues may share many goals with college writing educators, including the objective of questioning the walls—physical and ideological—that divide nations and fracture societies.

As educators grapple with the resurgence of nationalism, we can find innovative teaching models in public pedagogy. I present one such model, drawn from my research on the Kino Border Initiative, a Nogales-based Catholic organization dedicated to the rights of undocumented immigrants. I will address the strategies Kino employs to enact its tripartite pedagogy of *humanizing, accompanying,* and *complicating* undocumented immigration for US audiences; these strategies show how multimodality can promote embodied learning and lead to new understandings.[1] After summarizing Kino's background, this chapter analyzes two examples of its educational materials (a comic book and an immersion program) and considers takeaways for college writing education.

INTRODUCING THE KINO BORDER INITIATIVE

The Catholic Church's stance on migration deprioritizes national sovereignty in favor of human dignity: that is, every human has a right to a dignified life, and if that dignity cannot be obtained where a person is from, then they have a right to seek it elsewhere (Demo 2015). It was within this ideological framework that, in 2009, a group of Catholic and Jesuit organizations founded the Kino Border Initiative to serve deported migrants along the Arizona-Mexico border (Kino Border Initiative 2020).[2] Kino has several objectives, one of which is to engage in public pedagogy, which will be my focus. Its other objectives are to provide humanitarian aid by giving food and other services to deportees and to advocate for policy change by composing white papers aimed at legislators in the United States and Mexico.

In terms of public pedagogy, Kino's efforts take a number of forms, including a comic book and an immersion program that brings participants to the border to hear from various groups affected by undocumented immigration. Its pedagogy, as I learned from interviewing staff members, rests on a three-pronged approach termed "humanize, accompany, complicate." As the staff members explained, "humanizing" means replacing abstract notions of border conflict with a focus on the people involved; it also means respecting all these people's human dignity, regardless of their views. "Accompanying" means getting to know migrants and learning their stories. "Complicating" means realizing that there are no easy solutions to undocumented immigration, as it is a complex international phenomenon. To see how these principles translate into Kino's educational materials, I will present two examples: the comic book and one session of the immersion program.

But first, a word about my methods of collecting data from these two examples is in order. The comic book I found online in 2017, the year of its publication, through web searches for a project on migration and comics that I was conducting (see Miron 2019, 2020). Through it, I became interested in visiting Kino, which I did in December 2017, accompanied by my colleague Mehr Mumtaz. My fieldwork during the visit involved participant observation and interviews. The participant observation entailed Mehr and me participating in an immersion program and taking fieldnotes. Individual interviews were conducted with five staff members, most of whom held leadership positions, using a semi-structured format in which Mehr and I posed various questions about Kino's programs. As my experience demonstrates, Kino's comic book provides inducement to engage in more immersive learning about the border.

MULTIMODAL EDUCATION THROUGH THE COMIC *MIGRANT*

Comics have a special form of multimodality that lends them to educational purposes. In her book about comics in technical communication, Han Yu (2015) shows how they may more effectively communicate instructions, health literacy, and academic topics than can traditional mediums. For one, they offer access for diverse users: the combination of words and images makes them good at reaching audiences with various levels of linguistic literacy. In addition, they have strong affective appeal: associated with stories and humor, they tend not to intimidate readers, even when dealing with sensitive or difficult topics. While we are only just beginning to see comics designed for formal education (e.g., Losh and Alexander's *Understanding Rhetoric* for writing instruction), they have long been used in public pedagogy.

Migrant: Stories of Hope and Resilience, which Kino co-published with the Hope Border Institute in 2017, is one such example of a comic aiming to educate the public, primarily targeting English- and Spanish-speaking Americans interested in learning about undocumented immigration. It is available for free online, as well as in print for a few dollars.[3] Kino's staff told me they hope that educators around the United States will incorporate the comic into their curriculum as an introduction to immigration policy. The comic takes a personal approach to this topic, using stories drawn from interviews with migrants served by Kino and Hope to contextualize—and *humanize*—the information it provides on the factors driving migration from Latin America and on the US government's responses.

Figure 8.1. Page 8 of Migrant: Stories of Hope and Resilience (Hope Border Institute and Kino Border Initiative 2017).

To take one example, the comic relates a story of three migrants who travel through the Sonoran Desert, giving each member of the trio a name and background information. Jose Leonardo, for instance, hails from El Salvador and is "married with three children he cannot feed on the money he makes" (Korgen and Pyle 2017, 7). Soon, the migrants encounter a big problem: they are subjected to the Border Patrol's "Chase and Scatter" technique, an apprehension strategy that "is especially dangerous to migrants at night," as it can disorient them in the desert (8). The "Chase and Scatter" page, seen in figure 8.1,[4] combines facts about the apprehension strategy with emotive drawings that contrast the agents' high-tech helicopter with the migrants' panicked stumbling through the darkness. After this episode, one of the characters gets lost and dies of exposure. The human consequences of border policy thus come to the fore, *complicating* the concept of security measures—after all, who is being protected by such lethal surveillance practices? While Jose Leonardo survives, he eventually gets apprehended at a checkpoint near Tucson.

Continuing in the vein of *humanizing* and *complicating* immigration policy, Jose Leonardo's apprehension sets up a personal context for the information that follows: a two-page flowchart of the complex pathways through which migrants like him are shuttled after apprehension, seen in figure 8.2. The graphic explains the possible next steps for arrested migrants like him, stating that "Border Patrol decides their fate based on a metric called a Consequence Delivery System the details of which are not public" (10). Orange arrows lead the viewer into a flowchart tracing the options for detention or imprisonment depending on various factors. The chart is busy, crowded with text and images. The tiny text relates facts such as "in 2015 the average Border Patrol agent caught twenty crossers" (10). The images provide a humanizing counterpart to these blunt facts, portraying snapshots of misery in a courtroom (upper left) and detention center (lower right). In the courtroom, a crowd of migrants' hands and feet are chained together. In the detention center, migrants walk into an ominous black floor plan, where detainees are imprisoned in bare rooms, a dollar sign symbolizing their profitability for the companies that manage detention centers.

It is hard to come away from the flowchart with a clear understanding of the policies it introduces; indeed, it could be critiqued for failing to clearly describe migrant processing. Yet, as Lee E. Brasseur (2003) has argued, the logic and clarity that viewers expect from technical visualizations can obscure the emotions and convolutions of reality. Neatly ordered charts and diagrams can lull us into forgetting that things are seldom *that* simple. So, the messiness of this flowchart makes a point. The pathways a migrant might be sent down look random and confusing. But is that not the reality of the Consequence Delivery System? Again, no one outside Border Patrol knows the details of this system (10). If the process of hearings, detention, and deportation is difficult for us to understand as we read about it at leisure, how much more so for someone going through it? Thus, the complexity of this graphic serves a purpose: *complicating* the issues of deportation and detention.

What *is* clear in this flowchart is that most apprehended migrants get incarcerated. Since the reader has gotten to know Jose Leonardo over the past few pages of narration, this fate might seem incongruous with his selfless desire to get work to feed his kids. The reader is thus encouraged not only to recognize the immigration system's complexity but

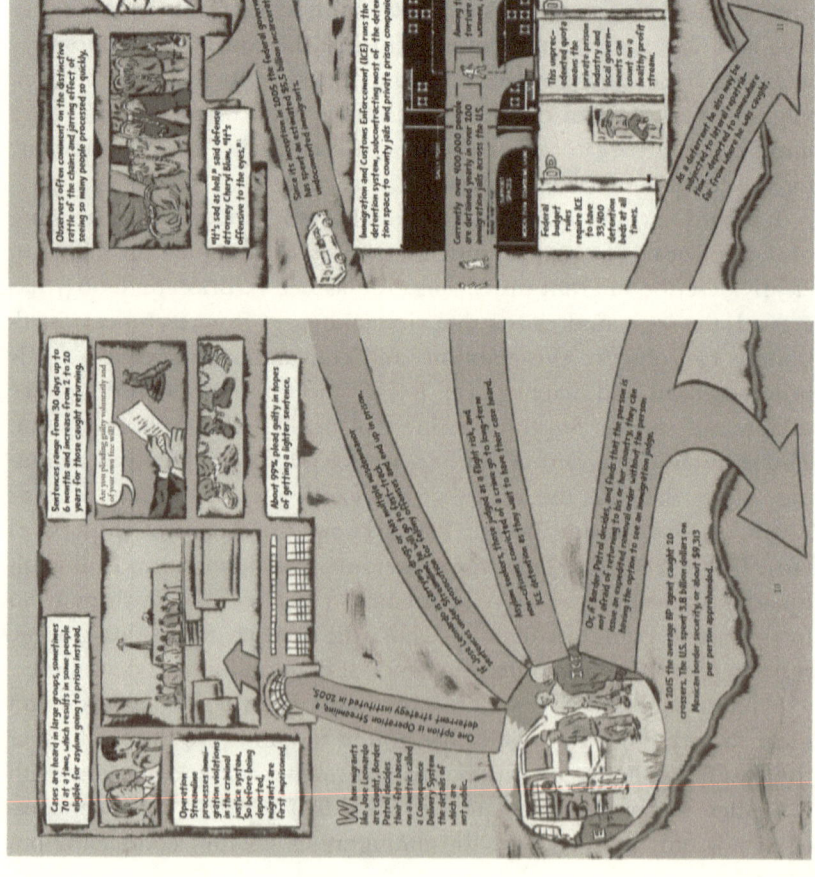

Figure 8.2. Pages 10 and 11 of Migrant: Stories of Hope and Resilience (Hope Border Institute and Kino Border Initiative 2017).

also to question its righteousness, harkening back to Kino's pedagogical goals of *complicating* and *humanizing* migration. Indeed, the flowchart communicates technical information and human emotion together. Information is explicit in the text, while the images implicitly convey migrants' distress.

Beyond linguistic and visual modes, comics also employ audio through speech and sound effects, gesture through facial expressions and body language, and space through portrayals of the environment (Yu 2015). In the detention center graphic, the gestural mode is employed in the distressed body language of the migrants curled up in their bare rooms, and the spatial mode comes across in the crowded, bleak floor plan. The comic thus encourages readers to feel the discomfort of the detained migrants and to envision themselves caged in a detention center—to engage in a form of embodied learning. In so doing, it potentially enrolls readers in any location, even thousands of miles from the US-Mexico border, in Kino's public pedagogy.

Indeed, recognizing its affordances for virtually transporting readers to the border, I assigned this comic book in a first-year writing class I taught at Penn State with a theme of "(Re)Writing US Immigration." In a reflection paper written near the end of the semester, one of my students, Geneva Flarend, identified it as our most noteworthy reading. She wrote,

> Struck by its strong emotional appeals, I found the comic *Migrant* to be incredibly troubling. It exposed me to many perspectives I was somewhat familiar with, but it did so in a much more humanizing way. For example, I am familiar with the policy of chase and scatter, but I had never seen it described in such a visual situation involving people with names and stories. . . . Reading this comic made me want to do more to help migrants reach their families in the States.[5]

Flarend testifies to the effectiveness of how the comic takes facts and personalizes them with "names and stories." The comic made her want to *act*.

The concept of acting takes us back to the pedagogy of accompaniment. In this section, I have noted where the comic *humanizes* and *complicates* the US immigration system, but the third prong of Kino's public pedagogy, *accompanying* migrants, is admittedly harder to implement through a two-dimensional text. Indeed, accompaniment entails physical togetherness, embodied fellowship, direct outreach. The last page of the comic points out the importance of this tenet, asking the reader, "What will you say to the migrant at your door? Will you give them shelter? Will you give them your heart?" (24). To jumpstart such a personal connection, Kino hosts immersion programs, which are arguably the crux of their public pedagogy.

IMMERSION EXPERIENCES: HUMANIZING, ACCOMPANYING, COMPLICATING

Kino's immersions unfold in the context of Catholic secondary and postsecondary education. Other Catholic institutions in the Southwest offer similar programs, bringing students to the border to learn about migration, according to my interviews with organizers of border immersions at Loyola Marymount University and the University of San Diego. Kino, I discovered, is well known in these circles, and its immersions are in high demand. In the year I visited, it hosted more than fifty immersion groups, in addition to over one hundred shorter retreats (Kino 2018). In general, border immersion programs share a goal of *humanizing* undocumented immigrants in participants' minds. Direct encounters between participants and migrants—*accompanying*—are key to such humanization. Kino also aims for participants to *complicate* their understanding of immigration by listening to divergent perspectives. Participants come from Catholic high schools and colleges; most are students, but some, like the group Mehr and I joined, are faculty and staff.

During their stay in Nogales, immersion groups participate in some or all of the following activities, interspersed with debriefing sessions and concluding with a goal-setting exit interview: walking in the desert wilderness near Arivaca, a US border town; attending Mass at a church in Arivaca and listening to talks by local ranchers there; helping at Kino's deportee aid center and talking to migrants there; participating in a visa application simulation; attending a presentation on immigration law and policy; visiting a migrant women's shelter; attending deportation hearings in Tucson; touring the Nogales Border Patrol facilities; and having dinner with a migrant family in Tucson. Mehr and I participated in all but the last two activities. In the next sections, I narrate one day of the immersion program, featuring the desert walk and the rancher talk, which together help to illustrate how embodied learning and the humanize-accompany-complicate pedagogy permeate Kino's immersion program. In these sections, I intentionally diverge from the analytical approach that typifies academic writing, instead using narrative to convey to the reader as much of the embodied experience as possible. Following the narrative, I reflect on how these activities demonstrate the potential of public pedagogy around migration.

Glimpsing the Traces of Migrants, Hearing the Fears of Ranchers: A Day in Arivaca

Sunday, December 10, 2017, dawns sunny and cool as Mehr and I prepare for the day's activities: a ninety-minute drive from Nogales to Buenos Aires National Wildlife Refuge, a hike of over an hour, and a three-hour visit to Arivaca's Catholic church, where Sunday Mass is celebrated, lunch is served, and several locals address the group. The group we will accompany comprises some ten employees of a Jesuit university. We have also already met the day's guide, Gillian.[6] With Gillian and the immersion group, we will travel to Arivaca.

This desert town surrounded by vast ranches is a hub of undocumented migration. After Prevention through Deterrence pushed migrants into the Sonoran Desert, Arivaca became a nexus in the journey north because its small highway, Arivaca Road, intersects with I-19. Countless migrants have hiked through the scrubland of the Wildlife Refuge to reach vehicles waiting on Arivaca Road. Border Patrol crackdowns and US economic recession have reduced migrant traffic here, but some still pass through. Because of Arivaca's recent history as a migrant corridor, Kino takes immersion groups there to experience the terrain and to hear from locals.

Desert Walk

The group drives to the Wildlife Refuge, breezing through a Border Patrol checkpoint on I-19. After arriving, we congregate around a picnic table near the trailhead, where Gillian has placed a backpack. She says the backpack holds items dropped by migrants in this area. She takes them out—there are maybe twenty objects, including baby bottles, a Bible, family photos, food packages, identity documents, and toiletries—while explaining them. For example, about a black water jug, she says that migrants sometimes buy these—a hot commodity in Mexican border towns—instead of typical transparent bottles because they believe the dark surface is less visible to Border Patrol agents. Nevertheless, the black jugs pose their own risks, as they heat up fast, fostering bacteria. She asks us to pass the objects around and to keep in mind that many of them were not abandoned freely; some migrants might become too exhausted to carry all their items, drop them to run from danger, or lose them when arrested. Later, in an interview, Gillian speculates that seeing these belongings "makes people realize how much about migration in this area or policy creation or . . . human rights violations happen out of sight"; making visible the traces of migrants has a "humanizing" effect, she says.

We now assemble at the trailhead, where some participants are reading a sign about the birds that migrate through the Wildlife Refuge; they comment that the sign fails to mention migratory humans. This park provides migrants a sort of sanctuary. Refuge paradoxically comes from the terrain's difficulty: its brambles and arroyos obscure migrants but make the walk more arduous, as Gillian explains. She announces that she will take us off-trail, into these very brambles and arroyos. She says she does this *not* to simulate a migrant's experience,[7] which we cannot comprehend, but to convey some physical realities of migration; to that end, she will set a fast pace, since migrants do not stroll. As we begin to walk, Gillian points out belongings on the ground, such as a black water jug and backpacks. Occupying the same space that many migrants have passed through on their northward journey strikes me as complementing the interactions with deportees that immersion participants have, fleshing out the "accompaniment" of hearing migrants' stories with seeing and feeling the environment through which they have passed.

It is hard for me to push through the thorny brambles and still walk fast. The thorns catch my clothing and scratch my hands. As I get tired, I find it harder to keep up. I am worried about an injury, a sprained knee that is mostly healed; will the pain return, forcing me to limp through the desert? I'm already feeling warm; I cannot imagine doing this hike in the sweltering summer. The desert seems to exacerbate every bodily disorder. We do, however, make several stops, permitting some recuperation. On the stops, which I order according to my recollection, Gillian talks about challenges migrants might confront in this terrain.

Stop 1. Gillian has us discuss the various health threats migrants face in this remote area, where even minor injuries could become life-threatening. She says that when she leads student groups, she asks them to think about how their common athletic injuries could, for a migrant, prove deadly.

Stop 2. Gillian asks us to consider how a migrant would feel walking through this area. Whereas we are taking care of each other, warning about thorns and holding back branches, migrants are often traveling with strangers who might lack such a caring bond. We also have the privilege of communicating loudly, while migrants would need to stay quiet. If they are traveling at night to avoid surveillance, it is hard to see obstacles; if walking in summertime, the grasses grow to eye level, obscuring hazards like huge ant nests. With risks abounding, every rustling bush could provoke anxiety.

Stop 3. Gillian leads a discussion of regional animals. We don't encounter any wildlife, aside from some insects, but biting ants, bees, tarantula hawks (wasps), rattlesnakes, javelinas (peccaries), deer, coyotes, cougars, and jaguars live here, any of which could injure migrants. The predators are the most dangerous, but javelinas can be aggressive, cattle might charge when startled, and tarantula hawks can inject excruciating venom.

Stop 4. Gillian has us talk about other humans in the area: beyond birdwatchers, there are Border Patrol agents, vigilante militias, hunters, and humanitarians. She belongs to the last group as a member of No More Deaths, which tries to prevent migrant fatalities by depositing water canisters and managing a first-aid camp. Both these projects have been threatened by militias and Border Patrol agents.

Stop 5. At another stop, Gillian describes how bodies decompose in the desert. Citing a forensic study conducted by an anthropologist (De León 2015), she informs us that animals quickly find the bodies, skeletonizing them and scattering their belongings. Identifying the remains, if they are found at all, is a challenge. She mentions the Colibrí Center, which works to match remains with missing migrants.

Stop 6. Gillian shows us a "drop site." When Arivaca was a popular thoroughfare for migrants, they would meet vehicles around here, first dropping their spare belongings. There used to be a sea of backpacks here. Now there are a few objects, including a lonely backpack; I wonder about its owner's fate.

Throughout Gillian's talks, she reminds us that she has a humanitarian's perspective. She encourages us to listen for differences between her views and those of the ranchers we'll hear later. For example, regarding drug trafficking, she notes that some smugglers are impoverished migrants who carry drugs to earn their passage; the ranchers would categorize these migrants as criminals, notwithstanding their desperate circumstances. With this kind of guidance, priming us to recognize discordant viewpoints, Gillian imparts rhetorical savvy for parsing—and complicating—immigration discourse.

Finally, we finish the loop. In a clearing, we can see a mountain, Baboquivari Peak, which Gillian has told us is sacred to the indigenous Tohono O'odham people. We stop to take photos. The landscape is beautiful yet hostile: visually, it is striking; physically, it is exhausting. Of course, what I considered a challenging hike, even a health risk, would be a small segment of a migrant's journey. Later, Gillian tells us that for students, the hike furnishes an opportunity to "recognize the privileges that they have in interacting with that environment in a recreational way versus when they think about people doing it out of desperation and having spent several thousand dollars to attempt crossing through it." Indeed, I had access to resources—a van, my water and food, a first aid-trained guide, a companionable group—that many migrants lack. Recognizing inequalities in privilege is a first step in understanding why undocumented immigration happens. Deliberating on what should be done about it is a subsequent, and likely more contentious, step—one that begins unfolding in the talks by local ranchers we will listen to that afternoon.

Rancher Talk

We clamber into the van and drive to noontime Mass in Arivaca's chapel, led by Kino's director, Father John. After Mass, the small congregation welcomes us to their potluck lunch. Mehr and I sit with Jimmy, who owns a ranch that extends to the border. We chat about cattle. After lunch, we return to the pews to listen to local ranchers, including Jimmy and his wife. On the one hand, the ranchers express sympathy for non-drug-carrying migrants and understanding about the socioeconomic factors driving them. On the other hand, they express frustration at the violence unleashed in their area by drug cartels. To protect their community from gangsters, they advocate for reinforcing the border with a wall and more Border Patrol infrastructure.

The first rancher to speak, Beatrice, describes how unsafe she feels walking around her ranch because of the cartel presence; she carries a gun outside. She sees the effects of the cartels on migrants she finds on her land: a dead woman, visibly raped, by her cow pond; a weeping woman who "jumped" into her arms, having been attacked by her *coyotes*. In each wounded migrant, Beatrice sees Jesus, so she ministers to them—until entrusting them to the police (who, one hopes, take them to a hospital). Beatrice's harrowing anecdotes testify both to the brutal fates of some migrant women and the daily anxiety experienced by rural borderlands residents.

While Beatrice's narrative strikes an emotional chord, the next presentation, by Jimmy and his wife, Trudy, hits an intellectual one; they submit a plenitude of firsthand evidence for their policy proposals. Visuals, large photographs displaying the ease of crossing the wire fence that separates their ranch from Mexico, underscore their message. Like Beatrice, they express sympathy for "good" migrants but fear the "drug packers," who have caused the murders of some friends. They see their ranch as a no-man's-land; Border Patrol is unwilling to police it due to the cartel's power and the terrain's difficulty. To address this dearth of protection, they endorse completing the wall and enhancing the Patrol's infrastructure. As public advocates for the wall, they know they are often portrayed as racists, xenophobes, and "deplorables." (I feel chagrined—I do tend to categorize all wall-boosters as nativists.) But they are not anti-immigrant, they explain; rather, they seek immigration reform via amnesty and a guest-worker program. After their presentation, I thank Trudy for sharing her perspective; she says, "Yes, well, it's the perspective of the people who *live* here." This firsthand testimony was persuasive; it made me question whether, stationed in an ivory tower in Pennsylvania, I had any right to opine about the border.

Gillian sees the rancher talks as playing a significant role in the immersion program. When we interview her, she remarks that the ranchers "bring the unique perspective of being concerned for the safety and security of their community and for themselves, and I think that's a great opportunity to ask students, 'What [do] safety and security mean to you?'" The presentations are "a moment for introducing new language and kind of raising students' skepticism of all border analyses," encouraging "nuance"—for instance, probing good guy/bad guy dichotomies, since some migrants are forced to serve cartels. On the drive back to Nogales, Gillian helps us reflect on the presentations, which she says challenge students who are unused to listening to perspectives they disagree with.

Learning Embodied Lessons from the Immersion

Like those students, I found the day's activities challenging. Our hike was taxing, both physically and emotionally. It made me speculate that I probably would not survive a desert migration. Would I even have the stamina to get through a daylong walk? Thus, the hike made me identify with undocumented migrants, *humanizing* migration by feeling a bit of it in my own body. Walking is a familiar element in public pedagogies, so by hosting a guided walk, Kino is tapping into a strong tradition.

Indeed, today, walking as a teaching and research method is attracting a great deal of attention (on top of its increased popularity as one of the few forms of exercise and outdoor enjoyment possible during pandemic-era lockdowns). As the directors of a public pedagogy project titled "WalkingLab" explain, "the sense of urgency and expediency surrounding walking is entangled with the desire to generate research and knowledge in situ, that is community-based, and that is attuned to more-than-human entanglements and encounters" (Springgay and Truman 2019, 2). Theorists of walking also recognize that ideologies such as ableism, racism, and settler colonialism influence who gets to move where (4); like any educational tool, walking comes with baggage.

But it also comes with a lot of potential. In the words of the Arizona-based Museum of Walking (2020), "Whether alone or with a group, moving through space creates connections between people and the environment, as it promotes well-being and enhances creative divergent thinking." As the organizers of WalkingLab and the Museum of Walking contend, walking in public pedagogy promotes embodied learning by attuning people to the larger ecosystems in which they operate. The inherent multimodality of walking plays a key role in such learning.

Returning to Kino's public pedagogy, multimodality exists in both the comic (*Migrant*) and the immersion program. But in the desert walk phase of the immersion, gestural and spatial modes come to the fore, as the entire body is in motion and in intimate contact with the landscape: with the brambles and thorns, the sand and dirt, the sun and wind. Numerous bodily sensations combine with the brief talks delivered by Gillian. As evident in my narrative, in my case, those sensations fused with my anxiety, making me empathize on a bodily level with her descriptions of migrants' experiences. The walk had a similar effect on Mehr:

> I was embarrassed, and humbled by my experience. I was reminded of my privilege again and again. And I was sorry for the thousands of people who either lose their lives, or the lives of loved ones, in their efforts to find a better future for themselves and for their families. (Mumtaz 2017)

Mind, body, and environment merged in the walk and brought us to an embodied understanding of national security's human consequences that we could not have gained simply by reading about it (even in the comic). This embodied learning may also have spiritual resonances, as participants might draw connections between the walk and ritual processions like posadas.[8] As Sara P. Alvarez points out in chapter 7 of this volume, embodied ways of knowing, especially as they pertain to migration, can profoundly contest nationalism and isolationism.

At least for myself as a participant—and, based on Mehr's fieldnotes, also for her—Kino made a successful intervention into immigration discourse through the desert walk, making us feel national security's human consequences. Going from the hike to the presentations by the ranchers *complicated* my empathy, because I also empathized with the fear they expressed as they recounted stories of friends murdered by a Mexican cartel. Moreover, the ranchers defied my stereotype of ignorant nativists; they seemed to know the transnational context of Latinx migration, and they advocated for a blend of conservative border securitization and liberal immigration reform. As they said, they are not mere "deplorables." I could hardly dismiss their wish for a wall, since it is grounded in their daily fears. For me, the Arivaca day both *humanized* and *complicated* undocumented migration, setting me up to continue thinking hard about my perceptions over the immersion's remaining days. My own experience can be taken as a sample of the personal transformation of immersion participants anticipated by Kino, which the staff explained in interviews.

Our interviewees expressed hope that participants transform their understanding of the immigration crisis. Gillian stated, "We're trying to move people to feel kind of a sense of . . . outrage at injustices and recognition that laws and policies can violate universal human rights." She encourages visitors to sit "next to someone who has had a very different set of opportunities than you," an encounter—and an act of accompaniment—that is "really important to growing that sense of rage at those realities." Kino's director, Father John, echoes Gillian's point: "What has the biggest impact is the direct contact with the people we serve." Both Father John and Gillian envision participants having strong affective responses to the immersion activities and thus becoming conscious of injustice.

While, as a participant, I didn't need much persuading to consider immigration in terms of social justice, some participants arrive seeing migrants as the problem and law enforcement as the solution. For many groups, realizing that "this is really my country that's creating the suffering" of migrants is "a really challenging space," Jody, the director of education and advocacy, explained. Not all visitors come ready to sympathize with migrants. Especially in the case of high school students, some might come because "their friend said it was cool, they go because their other friend is going on the immersion, they go because they want to go on an international trip." But Jody sees change even in politically conservative visitors who initially perceive migrants as "criminals"; "after two days here they say, 'wow, you know, I'm really learning that these are, they're humans.'" She recalled one very conservative participant who acknowledged, "You know, I believe in borders, and I believe in controlling who can come in and out, but also today I was talking to this guy from Honduras, and I could really understand why he wanted to cross the border. I know why he wants to cross the desert, and I want him to make it." She reflects that it is having "the chance to sit down with migrants and talk to them" that can change minds. Through direct encounters facilitated by public pedagogy, it seems immigration opponents can be persuaded to reframe their perspective.

After participants depart, they are expected to channel their newfound awareness into action. As Jody said, "It's not just a matter of understanding it, or seeing it, or being moved by it. But it's a matter of actually making life decisions on the basis of this reality that you're seeing." Similarly, Gillian tells students, "I encourage you all not to go away and say, 'Oh that was sad, or that was tragic, or it's really disgusting what's happening at the border and what's happening to these people'—to not have pity or hopelessness, but to turn that into growing their own activism and advocacy." Kino asks groups to take steps toward activism and keeps records of school's reports on groups' follow-up activities. These activities include sharing the immersion experience through publications or presentations, reaching out "to the local immigrant population," and getting "involved in advocacy." As a first step, participants may teach their classmates about immigration, evoking an approach to community literacy that Rebecca Lorimer Leonard describes in chapter 6 of this volume. Immersion participants, by bringing their newfound border literacies *into* their schools, unsettle the assumption that knowledge unidirectionally flows *out of* educational institutions. Beyond the short term of a student's time in school, Kino expects the effects of the immersion to unfold over the long term in their adult life. By stimulating personal engagement with migration and critical reflection on discourse, Kino's curriculum could germinate young cohorts of rhetorically savvy migrant advocates. These activists could influence people in their hometowns and thus disseminate Kino's challenge to dominant immigration discourse.

While the number of participants Kino can enroll in its immersion program is limited, its public pedagogy seems to offer an ideal way to learn about border issues. Not only do participants get access to the perspectives of stakeholders ranging from immigration judges to deportees, but they also enjoy a highly embodied learning experience thanks to the multimodal affordances of place-based education. Indeed, Kino's public pedagogy uses multimodality to create embodied learning. By uniting mind, body, and—especially in the case of the immersion program—the environment, learners move toward understanding undocumented immigration as a highly complex, deeply human issue. Such a recognition of complexity is undoubtedly similar to what college writing instructors aim toward.

FROM PUBLIC PEDAGOGY TO THE WRITING CLASSROOM

Kino, by sensitizing participants to multiple perspectives and asking them to think critically about each, demonstrates how embodied person-to-person interactions constitute a powerful form of rhetorical training. As Gillian said regarding the activities in Arivaca, "I appreciate it as a moment for introducing new language and kind of raising students' skepticism of all border analyses." Writing educators similarly aim to instill rhetorical "skepticism" or awareness. This awareness entails the metacognitive capacity to recognize one's own assumptions and those of one's audiences, a capacity requisite for making persuasive arguments and also for ethical behavior. Ethics is about how one receives others—as Jacques Derrida (2001) argues, it is synonymous with hospitality. So, rhetorical training in learning to comprehend one's stance and that of interlocutors instills a form of ethics, of hospitality. This connection between rhetoric and hospitality harkens back to Kino's "humanize, accompany, complicate" pedagogy. They help participants complicate immigration discourse primarily through direct, humanizing encounters with the Other, whether that Other is migrants or those who police migrants (Border Patrol agents, immigration judges, even ranchers).

To bring the productive encounters enabled by public pedagogy into the college writing classroom, instructors can arrange collaborative projects, ranging from online, transnational connections to local community partnerships. The internet is making intercultural encounters relatively easy to arrange without travel (and without virus exposure), as instructors use online resources to connect students in different countries, with the potential effect of eroding xenophobia (see Wu 2018; You 2016; Zhang 2018). In fact, in the next two chapters of this volume, Olga Aksakalova, Tuli Chatterji, and Joleen Hanson exhibit how online exchanges can promote cosmopolitan dispositions. In the local sphere, in community-engaged or service-learning projects, students conduct a project for an organization (there have been extensive studies on community-engaged writing instruction; see Kankiewicz 2018 for a useful overview, as well as Lorimer Leonard, this volume, for a case study). This is a strategy I tried when teaching my "(Re)Writing US Immigration" course. Working with a local literacy organization that primarily serves immigrants, I assigned the students—most of whom were white and nonimmigrants—a project in which they wrote posts that the organization could use for its blog. To design the project, I had worked with the organization's leaders to develop some broad topics for students to write about: ESOL education, immigrants' contributions to US literacies, challenges experienced by immigrants, language diversity in Pennsylvania, and World Englishes.

Interestingly, while I believe the project did have the effect of *humanizing* immigration to some extent for the students, it seemed to fall short in terms of *complicating* it and *accompanying* immigrants. Most of the students' posts fell into the common argument that, because immigrants contribute economically to the United States, they should be appreciated. While there is nothing inherently wrong with this argument, it doesn't *complicate* the capitalistic assumption that only people who provide labor and skills should be allowed into the nation. Also, most students—perhaps because of time constraints—did not take the organization up on its offer to set up interviews with its clients, so only a few based their posts on direct encounters with local immigrants. Perhaps the imperfections in this project demonstrate how, while public pedagogy benefits from not being constrained by semester timelines, grading requirements, and the other pressures of college life, instructors seeking to facilitate direct encounters do encounter these barriers.

But it is still worth trying. As Sara P. Alvarez asserts in the previous chapter of this volume, writing educators need to think about how to make writing more meaningful and purposeful for our students. She advances this call in the context of immigrant students, who, because they straddle ethnolinguistic, national, and racial borders, can enrich academic writing with their multilayered community literacies. Yet, many students at predominantly white institutions (like mine, or like the one Joleen Hanson describes later in this volume) lack ready access to such literacies, as they are ensconced in homogenous social contexts. Writing instructors can therefore make a real difference in their students' lives by introducing them to intercultural communication through community-engaged or online exchange projects. Even if humanizing a social Other is the only outcome of such a writing project, that certainly makes it worthwhile, for it could influence how our students apply their literacy in the long term—whether they use their skills in persuasion to build up or to tear down walls.

NOTES

1. A note about terms: I use "multimodality" to refer to communication that occurs through various channels, including audio, gestural, linguistic, spatial, and visual design (New London Group 1996). "Embodied learning" means that learners are not just walking brains. Rather, our minds, bodies, and environments come together when we achieve a meaningful understanding of a given topic (Stolz 2015, 174). Finally, I use "migrant" in place of "immigrant" when I am emphasizing a person's in-transit status.
2. The organization is named after a Jesuit missionary, Eusebio Kino. His work in Spanish colonial times spanned the Sonoran region (now divided into Sonora, Mexico, and Arizona, United States), representing Kino's goal of fostering binational solidarity.
3. As of this writing, the English version of the comic can be accessed at issuu.com /migrantstories/docs/migrant.eng.fin.lr.

4. Excerpts and images from the comic are reproduced here with the permission of the publishers, Kino Border Initiative and Hope Border Institute.
5. Quotation used with permission.
6. All names of Kino staff members and affiliates are pseudonyms.
7. A comparison could be drawn between Kino's desert walk and the "Caminata Nocturna," an unauthorized border crossing simulation held in central Mexico, which has been critiqued by Hasian, Maldonado, and Ono (2015). As they explain, in the Caminata, the organizers—an Indigenous community drained by emigration—create a nighttime crossing experience for tourists, complete with pretend traffickers, thugs, and Border Patrol agents. The stated aim is to discourage border crossing. Both Kino's walk and the Caminata instill some embodied understanding of the physical difficulties of crossing the border, but Kino rejects the notion that this act, with its attendant desperation and potential lethality, can be simulated.
8. A posada is a Christmastime reenactment of Mary and Joseph's search for shelter in Bethlehem. Each year, Kino holds a Bi-National Posada that remixes this Mexican Catholic tradition, comparing the forced movements of the Holy Family of Christianity to the treatment of migrants today as the procession wends along the border wall in Nogales. (The Bi-National Posada is featured in the comic *Migrant*.) When Mehr and I visited Kino, we participated in the 2017 Bi-National Posada the day before we joined the immersion group and went on the desert walk. With these communal walks serendipitously occurring on consecutive days, we were attuned to the role bodily movement plays in Kino's public pedagogy.

REFERENCES

Brasseur, Lee E. 2003. *Visualizing Technical Information: A Cultural Critique*. Amityville, NY: Baywood.

De León, Jason. 2015. *The Land of Open Graves: Living and Dying on the Migrant Trail*. Oakland: University of California Press.

Demo, Anne Teresa. 2015. "Faithful Sovereignty: Denationalizing Immigration Policy in the 2003 Pastoral Letter on Migration." In *The Rhetorics of US Immigration: Identity, Community, Otherness*, edited by E. Johanna Hartelius, 50–69. University Park: Pennsylvania State University Press.

Derrida, Jacques. 2001. *On Cosmopolitanism and Forgiveness*. London: Routledge.

Hasian, Marouf A., Jr., José Ángel Maldonado, and Kent A. Ono. 2015. "Thanatourism, Caminata Nocturna, and the Complex Geopolitics of Mexico's Parque EcoAlberto." *Southern Communication Journal* 80 (4): 311–30. doi:10.1080/1041794X.2015.1043138.

Kankiewicz, Kim. 2018. "Using Service-Learning in Writing Courses." The WAC Clearinghouse. https://wac.colostate.edu/resources/teaching/guides/sl/.

Kino Border Initiative. 2018. *Sharing the Journey (Compartiendo el Viaje): 2017 Annual Report*. https://www.kinoborderinitiative.org/wp-content/uploads/2018/08/KBI_Annual Report_2017_FINAL_Web.pdf.

Kino Border Initiative. 2020. "Who We Are." https://www.kinoborderinitiative.org/who-we-are/.

Korgen, Jeffrey Odell, and Kevin C. Pyle. 2017. *Migrant: Stories of Hope and Resilience*. Nogales, AZ: Kino Border Initiative; El Paso, TX: Hope Border Institute.

Losh, Elizabeth, Jonathan Alexander, Kevin Cannon, and Zander Cannon. 2014. *Understanding Rhetoric: A Graphic Guide to Writing*. Boston: Bedford/St. Martin's.

Miron, Layli Maria. 2019. "Making Visible the Nativism-Ableism Matrix: The Rhetoric of Immigrants' Comics." *Rhetoric Review* 38 (4): 445–63. doi:10.1080/07350198.2019.1655307.

Miron, Layli Maria. 2020. "No Reclaimed Homeland: Thi Bui's Postcolonial Historiography in *The Best We Could Do*." *INKS: The Journal of the Comics Studies Society* 4 (1): 44–65. doi:10.1353/ink.2020.0008.

Mumtaz, Mehr. 2017. "Report on Arivaca Desert Hike—Sunday, December 10, 2017." Unpublished fieldnotes.

Museum of Walking. 2020. "About." http://www.museumofwalking.org/about.

New London Group. 1996. "A Pedagogy of Multiliteracies: Designing Social Futures." *Harvard Educational Review* 66 (1): 60–92.

Springgay, Stephanie, and Sarah E. Truman. 2019. "Walking in/as Publics: Editors Introduction." *Journal of Public Pedagogies*, no. 4, 1–12. doi:10.15209/jpp.1170.

Stolz, Steven A. 2015. "Embodied Learning." *Educational Philosophy and Theory* 47 (5): 474–87. doi:10.1080/00131857.2013.879694.

Wu, Zhiwei. 2018. "Technology-Mediated Transnational Writing Education: An Overview of Research and Practice." In *Transnational Writing Education*, edited by Xiaoye You, 70–86. New York: Routledge.

You, Xiaoye. 2016. *Cosmopolitan English and Transliteracy*. Carbondale: Southern Illinois University Press.

Yu, Han. 2015. *The Other Kind of Funnies: Comics in Technical Communication*. Amityville, NY: Baywood.

Zhang, Yufeng. 2018. "English Teacher Development through a Cross-Border Writing Activity." In *Transnational Writing Education*, edited by Xiaoye You, 187–202. New York: Routledge.

Part III

Building Transnational Connections

Partnerships and Cosmopolitan Dispositions

9
COMBATING ISOLATIONISM THROUGH COIL VIRTUAL EXCHANGE
Programmatic and Pedagogical Perspectives

Olga Aksakalova and Tuli Chatterji

INTRODUCTION

Widely recognized as a multi-literacy transborder pedagogy, Virtual Exchange (VE) enables students residing in geographically and culturally remote settings to collaborate on thematically linked activities via digital platforms. During the pandemic, this practice has gained prominence in higher education across the world (Hauck 2020), yet its proliferation should not be attributed purely to the hiatus with study abroad programs. A form of Internationalization at Home, which is defined as "the purposeful integration of international and intercultural dimensions into the formal and informal curriculum for all students within domestic learning environments" (Beelen and Jones 2015), VE is grounded in the principles of diversity, equity, and inclusion. Central scholarly forums in the field reveal critical approaches. For example, a keynote at a recent International Virtual Exchange Conference was "Towards Global Fairness in the Digital Space through VE" (Hauck 2020), which corresponded to the justice-related conference theme "Towards Digital Equity in Internationalization." Similarly, the theme of the 2020 biennial L2 Digital Literacies Symposium held at the University of Arizona was "Critical Transnational Dialogue and Virtual Exchange." In practice, students participating in virtual exchange often engage with contemporary global issues through United Nations Sustainable Development Goals (see for instance recent grantees at the Stevens Initiative ["Projects" n.d.], which supports virtual exchanges between young people residing in the US and the Middle East / North Africa region). Additionally, State University of New York (SUNY) has developed an approach that synthesizes the threads of social justice, global engagement, experiential learning, and professional development

https://doi.org/10.7330/9781646423248.c009

through their program SUNY COIL Global Commons, whereby student groups virtually engage with international community-based organizations to "apply [their] skills and knowledge to helping this organization craft the story of their work" (SUNY COIL Global Commons). Such civically oriented programs and scholarly preoccupations create a fertile space for literacy practices that defy isolation.

The virtual exchange practice emerged in the mid-1990s in the fields of foreign language education and business communication (Lewis and O'Dowd 2016, 21; Wu 2018, 171). Termed "telecollaboration," it has sought to "develop learners' multiliteracies or translingual and transcultural competence" (Wu 2018, 170–71). At the heart of these language-centered exchanges is access to the global experience, collaborative knowledge creation, and engagement with "a larger education agenda in the New Literacies Movement" that emphasizes "digital literacy in meaning making, communication, and negotiation and the participatory nature of literacy practices in glocal communities" (Wu 2018, 171). These allegiances, Zhiwei Wu argues, infuse virtual exchange with transnational ethos "because when participants are engaged in virtual communication, their identities projected, relations forged, and languages practiced all emerge from the context, defying any static or discrete nation-based grouping" (171). Wu introduces the term "transnational" into the name of this practice to highlight its ability to "develop [learners'] cosmopolitan disposition and communicative repertoire in and across various discourse communities"; he calls the practice Technology-Mediated Transnational Writing Education (TTWE) (Wu 2018, 171). Originating at SUNY, Collaborative Online International Learning (COIL) broadens the practice to include multiple disciplines. Still promoting intercultural communication and language learning, COIL activities emerge from a shared-content syllabus (O'Dowd 2018, 14–15) and emphasize active collaboration.

Currently, the umbrella term that describes international virtual collaborations is "virtual exchange," and this practice is recognized as crucial in "a world increasingly characterised by the rise of right-wing extremism, religious fanaticism, and populist political movements" (O'Dowd 2018, 21). In this chapter, we use the term "virtual exchange" in reference to the general practice and the term "COIL" to describe class-to-class exchanges.

As evident above, Wu (2018) and O'Dowd (2018) point to the potentiality of COIL to counter isolationist and xenophobic mindsets, and their line of thought is grounded in the numerous case studies as well as theoretical and methodological scholarship on virtual exchange pedagogy that have emerged in the last decade. These works distill facets of intercultural learning in virtual exchange pedagogy that are responsible for disrupting hegemonic and nationalistic thinking, such as "challenging the 'common sense' of each national group within the international project" (Byram 2016, 258); designing activities to "denaturalize assumptions regarding fixed cultural identities" (Moore and Simon 2015, 93); interrogating "U.S.-centric priorities" (Runyan, Marchand, and Stoll 2015, 110); modeling through methodological choices the process of decentering hierarchical processes of knowledge construction (Moore and Simon 2015, 93). Our chapter builds on these principles to formulate targeted programmatic and pedagogical virtual exchange actions aimed at dismantling isolationist dispositions fueled by nationalistic and xenophobic thinking. We analyze the adaptation of COIL at an urban community college as a program that, to use the words of the COIL founder, Jon Rubin, "draws attention to the specific national and cultural approach to a subject as well as to the way it is taught and learnt" (Rubin 2016, 266), opening opportunities for deep critical evaluation of nation-state mentality, cultural norms, and stereotypes. In addition, our institutional and classroom perspectives on COIL illuminate the capability of this transnational pedagogy to counter xenophobic perceptions and portrayals of geopolitical spaces, such as state borders, as firm entities separating homogenous, inherently antagonistic groups of people. We argue that while the political discourse on borders employs spatial rhetoric to isolate and antagonize groups, COIL can offer a way of conceptualizing border space and "space-making" (Yang 2018, 115) as empathetic, transformative, and collaborative community-building.

We illustrate that to achieve these goals, as a program COIL must be integrated in the institutional fabric where global learning is targeted or can be fruitfully facilitated, and it must serve and be recognized as an instrument to foster transcultural literacies and cosmopolitan dispositions. It should also emphasize a critical internationalization approach toward both professional development and literacy pedagogy, one that shows how to strive for equity, diversity, social and linguistic justice, and respect between the groups participating in the exchange ("About" n.d.). We suggest that these programmatic orientations can bring pedagogical success when COIL projects, such as the one described in this study, seek to

- address a global issue about the political and oppressive forces responsible for border construction and the impact on communities and individual lives; this enriching transborder engagement provides

students with an opportunity to develop a critical lens when navigating across diverse spaces (digital and sociocultural) and to defy sociopolitical construction of borders;
- decenter US experience while illuminating the United States' role in global injustice, thereby enabling students to delve into topics rarely taught in US academia; this practice sensitizes students to the colonial practices of the US educational system;
- introduce an experiential dimension to averting xenophobia and division by fostering literacy practices that legitimize and prioritize the primacy of biographical and transgenerational knowledge of the subject matter as a site of literacy production;
- promote literacy activities by utilizing multiple digital platforms that enable students to serve as mediators of difficult dialogues and to critically reflect on their own attitudes and perspective on the Other.

Our goal in this chapter is to examine practical implementations and implications of these pedagogical features through a case study of a COIL project on the theme of the partition of India in a capstone English course at LaGuardia Community College of the City University of New York. First, Olga Aksakalova will briefly describe the infrastructure and context of the COIL program at LaGuardia. Second, Tuli Chatterji will narrate in the first person the case study of her course project, "Partition of India." The case study will be followed by project analysis, as well as pedagogical and programmatic recommendations for facilitating cosmopolitan dispositions through COIL.

COIL AT LAGUARDIA COMMUNITY COLLEGE, CUNY

LaGuardia Community College is a leading community college in the nation, serving over 20,000 degree students who hail from 150 countries and speak 98 languages ("Fast Facts" n.d.). It is a member of the CUNY system, which is the largest urban public university in the country with six other community colleges, eleven senior colleges, and seven institutions that grant graduate or professional degrees. Close to 60 percent of LaGuardia students are born in countries other than the United States. Numerous obligations and financial challenges prevent many from performing physical mobility, and COIL serves as an important access point to global experience. The so-called digital divide (Ragnedda and Muschert 2013), or unequal access to the internet based on the intersection of class, race, and ethnicity (Perez 2018), can further complicate our students' participation in the global culture. Therefore, COIL is envisioned as an opportunity to cross socioeconomic borders that limit student engagement in global learning.

Table 9.1. Strong and weak approaches to telecollaborative task design

Strong Approaches to Telecollaborative Task Design	Weak Approaches to Telecollaborative Task Design
Tasks reflect themes of social justice and intercultural citizenship	Tasks focus on superficial communicative themes
Tasks engage students in active collaboration together	Tasks only require learners to present and report information
Tasks include reflection on the role of the medium in online communication	The role of the technology in the communication is taken for granted
Tasks include stages of cultural self-reflection and critical evaluation	No critical self-reflection is involved
Tasks avoid stereotyping and forced culture clash	Tasks often involve a focus on stereotyping and forced culture clash

Since the program's inception in 2016, over one hundred courses have implemented COIL across disciplines. The program seeks to foster a cosmopolitan mindset, defined as shared global citizenship (Appiah 2007), and it emphasizes ethical responsibility, respect for difference and ambiguity, empathy, and pluralism (Appadurai 1996; Appiah 2007; Canagarajah 2018; Galinova 2015; Perez 2018). LaGuardia COIL projects usually center around global issues related to topics in social justice, such as migration, hegemony of the English language, racism, sexism, and religious extremism (see Baksh and Esprit 2018; Boumlik and Van Slyck 2019). In designing their tasks, faculty are guided to adapt approaches that fall under the recommendations of Robert O'Dowd (see table above from O'Dowd 2016, 287).

These approaches foster what Eunjeong Lee and Suresh Canagarajah (2019) call "transcultural dispositions": humanistic habits and attitudes that enable people to "negotiate diversity, embrace creativity, and co-construct meanings in contemporary contexts of superdiversity" (5). Therefore, professional development activities promote student practices that stimulate negotiation and collaborative production of content, and position each partner group as a primary source of cultural knowledge that cannot be otherwise located online or in literature (Helm and Guth 2010, 98). To ensure engagement and to model the virtual exchange methodology that leads to learner autonomy (Lewis and O'Dowd 2016, 50), faculty are guided to claim full agency over their COIL projects: they are encouraged to find their own partners, decide on the topics and tasks, and design their own assessment based on the learning objectives of the project, and they are able to adapt the COIL reflection prompt, a uniform qualitative assessment method, to the specifics of their projects. At the same time, faculty receive individualized assistance with curriculum design and technology tools, and they are also invited to professional development workshops and other forums to learn about best practices from each other, discuss COIL theory, and share their work with the college community.

COIL CASE STUDY: PARTITION OF INDIA

The COIL project "Partition of India" discussed in this case study took place in fall 2019 and involved four partner groups residing in New York, US; Pune, India; Dhaka, Bangladesh; and Lahore, Pakistan. The topic of partition and COIL methodology were well suited for the course "World Literatures in English," a capstone for English majors that explores postcolonial literature, focusing on the texts' historical and cultural contexts and often revolving around a specific region or ethnic group. First, the course targets the Global Learning Core Competency, as well as Digital and Written Abilities, LaGuardia's general education requirements. Second, students learn to compare and contrast historic and social periods across geopolitical boundaries, strengthening their knowledge and understanding of diverse global perspectives and pluralistic views. This learning objective in particular lends itself well to the partition theme. My project sought not only to expose students to the colonial forces behind, and repercussions of, border construction and division of people based on religion, nationality, ethnicity, or race, but also to engage them experientially in cross-border literacy practices to model the importance, the possibility, and the challenge of peace- and community-building.

Three hundred years of British rule in India ended in August 1947, with the nation being divided into two countries: Hindu-majority India and Muslim-majority Pakistan. As a result of three simultaneous partitions—of British India, of the province of Punjab, and of the province of Bengal—the partition produced the largest forced migrations of the twentieth century. Between 1946 and 1965, nearly nine million Hindus and Sikhs moved to India, and approximately five million Muslims moved to both parts of Pakistan, leading to unimaginably bloody forms of massacre and sectarian violence. It left almost fifteen million people uprooted, over two million dead, and around seventy-five thousand women raped (Dalrymple 2).

While the political situations have undoubtedly made any forms of collaboration both challenging and risky, recent times have seen an effort by scholars to engage in cross-border studies together that would initiate new discourses on the study of the partition, one that is grounded in "commonality and connection" rather than differences across international borders (Roy 8). These efforts are mostly in the form of scholarly writing, and to my knowledge no pedagogical endeavor heretofore has been made to connect students from these places, so that the future does not appear as bleak as the past. On those grounds, this project made history, as ninety-two students from both sides of the Atlantic formed a virtual community to engage with the literary histories of partition and discuss present politics in the region. As students from the Indian subcontinent shared family narratives to counter hate and isolationism, US students were in the position to serve as mediators of healing and critically reflect on their national history of xenophobia and isolation. In turn, LaGuardia students confronted the silencing of partition in the US secondary and postsecondary curricula.

PROJECT OVERVIEW

The genesis of this project stems from my experiences of growing up in India and later moving to the United States, a shift that was followed by yearly visits to India, where I started to witness a rising intolerance towards minorities shaping both the political and social landscape. These changes in the country that I grew up in prompted me to reflect on the patterns of similarity between partition and the contemporary anti-immigration and xenophobic attitudes that have been ripping apart both my country of origin and my new home. In my fall 2019 "World Literatures in English" course, I aimed to bring together students from both sides of the Atlantic with the primary intention that through readings of partition literature they could collaboratively combat isolationist political actions, develop tolerance towards other cultures and communities, learn about the silenced history, and collaboratively help each other heal from the hate that continues to follow from partition.

COIL provided me with the space and a unique opportunity to connect my LaGuardia fall 2019 capstone students with students from India, Pakistan, and Bangladesh so that they could share their perspectives on the subject as well as document their knowledge in diverse digital spaces such as WhatsApp, Facebook, and Google Docs. For students at LaGuardia Community College, this was an altogether new experience, having neither heard nor learned about the subcontinent's horrendous history of religious genocide, nor participated in COIL before. I turned to my professional network to find four faculty partners from India, Pakistan, and Bangladesh, and together we designed what for

LaGuardia students was a full-semester project, while international groups joined at different times and in different configurations. It's important to mention that none of the faculty partners had partition on their syllabi. That they accommodated my request shows that collegiality, courage, and commitment to cross-border pedagogy are key to creating a fruitful COIL collaboration. We chose a difficult topic, but it had a profound personal and civic value for each of the instructors, which in turn motivated us to overcome challenges with coordination and remain flexible in this multi-partner collaboration.

Selected texts represented Pakistani, Bangladeshi, and Indian authors to provide multiple regional perspectives on the partition. Each text was chosen after considerable planning and deliberation so that students of all levels of familiarity could enhance their knowledge of the subject as well as learn from each other. Since LaGuardia students had no knowledge about the partition, I started the semester with William Dalrymple's (2015) essay "The Great Divide," which provided an overview of the context and set the stage for a brief understanding of the history, politics, and geography of the region. The short reading also allowed students to draw connections with histories of forced displacement that they were already familiar with, such as America's history of slavery. I then paired the reading with the BBC documentary *The Day India Burned* (Pollack 2007), which students from India had already watched at the beginning of their semester. The short article and the documentary served as an apt segue to Bapsi Sidhwa's canonical novel, *Cracking India* (also called *Ice-Candy Man*), which was read by the students from India, the United States, and Pakistan. Narrated from the perspective of a disabled seven-year-old Parsi girl named Lenny, the novel's narrative technique, content, and style gave a comprehensive knowledge to the background and immediate effects of the partition. Once students were well settled into the history of the region, I led them through Khushwant Singh's intense novel *Train to Pakistan*, which offered a more gruesome narrative to the genocide than Sidhwa's novel. By this time of the semester, around early November, LaGuardia students were deeply immersed in the subject of partition. Taking advantage of students' newly acquired knowledge, I collaboratively designed with Suhaile Azavedo (St. Mira's, India) a high-stakes assignment on *Train to Pakistan* that involved a transnational peer-review experience between first-year students at St. Mira's and the capstone students of LaGuardia.

The high-stakes assignment, which was composed of three sections, was the culmination of the course. First, a 1,500–2,000-word essay was built on previously completed low-stakes close-reading exercises; it prompted students to analyze how their reading of the works by authors from diverse ethnic, cultural, and social environments enhanced their understanding of the effects of constructing borders and dividing people based on religion, nationality, ethnicity, or race. Second, a critical reflection on the COIL exchange aimed to give LaGuardia students metacognitive awareness of how virtual communication with ethnically, culturally, and linguistically diverse international peers from the Indian subcontinent affected their understanding of the partition and the region. Students were also asked to think about how this communication helped them understand their own views and attitudes about other cultures. Third, since English 295 is a capstone course, it was important to facilitate another level of reflection on the course theme and method to enable students to analyze the value of a civically engaged and cosmopolitan pedagogical approach to English studies. Students were asked to reflect on the ethical implications of studying the partition of India, the importance of including the history and literature of partition in school curricula in the US and around the world, and the ways in which the course material enhanced their understanding of contemporary global issues and events.

This sequence of steps follows the recommendation of telecollaboration scholars Francesca Helm and Sarah Guth, who insist on the value of "transformed practice" in virtual exchange (Helm and Guth 2010, 98). Having immersed themselves in the culture of the Other through online interactions and collaborative activities, learners are led on "one of two possible journeys: transfer of acquired knowledge and experience to an unfamiliar cultural context [. . .]; or return to the life-world of one's original experience with fresh perspectives and newly relevant knowledge of underlying processes [. . .] or other worlds" (Kalantzis and Cope 2000, 241, qtd. in Helm and Guth 2010, 98). Through scaffolded literary analysis and subsequent critical reflections, LaGuardia students completed this act of return with new knowledge about the ethical, cultural, local, and global value of cosmopolitan pedagogy.

To foster a meaningful collaboration, not only between US students and their international peers but also between Indian, Pakistani, and Bangladeshi students, digital tools were selected based on their capacity to enable patterns of productive social, personal, and academic negotiations and cross-cultural literacy-building. Striving for equity and the "collaborative, distributed, and participatory nature of new literacies" (Wu 2018, 179), we opted for a range of platforms with varying purposes: (a) a shared Google document to discuss literature through low-stake assignments and comment on each other's posts; (b) an informal WhatsApp group between Pakistan and the United States; and (c) a student-driven Facebook group where they shared narratives and photographs, with the purpose of connecting beyond academic discourse. This mixture of platforms for social networking and collaborative composing helped to disassociate the transnational exchange from the strictly academic environment and emphasize social connection.

My faculty partners and I were also mindful of what Jon Rubin calls "cultural bubbles." While the digital environment offers a variety of views, Rubin posits, users tend to seek out information and ways of communicating that are familiar to them and reaffirm their cultural beliefs and prejudices. Online interactions and spheres where these interactions occur do not automatically break these bubbles; rather, "because the internet largely obscures our embodied selves, we more easily attach ourselves to ideas and images sometimes intended to reinforce prior prejudices, without the caution or criticality we observe in the street. The seeming fluidity of the digital space thereby gradually encourages us into digitized cultural bubbles that then separate us" (Rubin 2020, 7). Addressing the theme of the partition and doing so in the online space was a new endeavor for all participating student groups, but the tools they used were familiar. Our goal was to defamiliarize students with the habitual online modes of meaning construction and illuminate the possibility of "digital diversity" (Rubin 2020, 7). Instead of submitting to popular social media practices of nurturing everyday biases against other communities, students exercised their agency in challenging those biases. By sharing family narratives, hobbies, and photographs, students collaboratively critiqued politically maneuvered creation of international borders based on religious differences.

PROJECT ANALYSIS

In selecting a global issue situated outside of the US, I aimed to decenter the US experience and perspective and locate the source of knowledge in a non-Western region. For example, students from both St. Mira's College in India and LaGuardia read *Train to Pakistan* in their respective classes. For LaGuardia students, the in-class discussions involved critical analysis of characters followed by low-stakes writing assignments about the contrast in the relationship between Sikhs and Muslims in Mano Majra before and after partition and the significant role of trains during partition. Discussion of these examples with their international peers on the shared Google document built a sense of community among students where US students specifically started to conceptualize the extent of hate and isolationism that the formation of Pakistan and the genocide had on human lives on both sides of the border. In many ways, St. Mira's students emerged as the mentors to LaGuardia capstone students and helped them understand both the setting of the novel and the historical context. As LaGuardia student Gabriel notes, "Mostly everything introduced to me by my international peers was new because I barely even knew anything about India, Pakistan or Bangladesh, let alone partition." Gabriel highlights here the US-centric tenor of American secondary and postsecondary curricula as well as his appreciation for the global literacy in history, religion, geography, literature, and culture that emerged from his St. Mira's peers: "I am so glad I now know much more about the topic and will be able to remember this perhaps forever." This form of mentorship continued in the Facebook group "Partition of India: A COIL Initiative." Upon learning that none of the LaGuardia students were familiar with the Parsi culture referred to by Sidhwa in *Cracking India*, Parsi students from St. Mira's started posting videos of their temples and religious practices. These informal but informative exchanges gave confidence to LaGuardia students when drafting their final research papers, which required them to navigate the works of diverse partition literature authors from the region, such as Saadat Hasan Manto, Bapsi Sidhwa, Khushwant Singh, and Ashraf Siddiqui, among others.

Importantly, having found themselves in the position of literacy sponsors, students from India, Pakistan, and Bangladesh reached into the realm of the personal and transgenerational experience, foregrounding community literacy as a legitimate and fruitful form of cross-cultural knowledge construction. Thus, Afridi from Pakistan retold the story of his professor, whose friend "had a huge scar on his forehead that made him look creepier irrespective of his elegant personality." In response to the professor's question about his scar, his friend "got furious and narrated the encounters of his past and how while migrating to Pakistan, a group of men hit him with an axe but he was lucky enough to be still alive. People killed each other with no interest of killing each other but only out of revenge." Naina from India shared the story of her grandmother, who was separated from her two sisters when they were forced to migrate to Pakistan from Mumbai: "They met each other only after 54 years, after a thread of failed visas and security concerns after the Partition." These personal accounts of transgenerational trauma exposed the impact of divisive policies on individual lives, highlighting the importance of resisting internal and external attempts at othering, and nurturing instead a cosmopolitan mindset.

Through their exchanges, students were able to see the value of such resistance, but first they had to confront their own stereotypes toward the people from the region. For instance, Zoe (US) revealed that the project helped her to overcome the misconceptions that she had about students from the region, a feeling that many LaGuardia students shared: "I remember when I first heard that we would be interacting with college students from India, I was expecting them to speak in very formal English, but . . . I didn't have to change the way I spoke at all for anyone to understand." Like Zoe, Yejin (US) openly admitted how this international educational partnership in fact helped her to overcome her prejudices about India, Bangladesh, and Pakistan, which she had assumed were much less developed than the United States. Eli, in Lorimer Leonard's chapter "Writing to Mend Literate Fragmentation" (chapter 6, this volume), speaks of how "community writing experiences" helped him explore the "impact of monolingual ideologies he saw circulating in the community space." Here too we see how the vital community literacy practices helped Yejin and Zoe reflect on their own misconceptions of the region and on their affiliation to monolingualism in the United States.

COIL interactions allowed students to confront these misconceptions, but also to develop ways of dismantling them. One literacy practice that occasioned moments of cultural disconnection based on assumptions was the peer-review assignment between Prof. Azavedo's class at St. Mira's and the LaGuardia students. Though the LaGuardia students were familiar with the peer-review experience, international peer-reviewing was new to all twenty-two of them. They assumed familiarity on the part of their international peers and expected to receive feedback on their writing in a direct manner. As LaGuardia student Kathryn reflects, "instead of focusing on the text itself, my peer primarily focused on the history of the Partition of India." However, St. Mira's students were new to the research essay genre and to peer review. In addition, their manner of engaging with strangers was to become culturally informed; they wished to get acquainted first and only then talk about the subject. Kathryn's response indicated her lack of awareness of the possible cultural difference in social behavior and literacy experience. She was also unable to transcend the immediate parameters of the peer-review genre and treat her peer's content-related input as an indirect suggestion to include the new information as primary source in her essay. Her expectation and disappointment reveal the assumption that the US literacy genre of peer review is by default universally recognized and practiced. Her response allowed no space for other ways of treating peer-to-peer learning.

However, having completed several critical reflections and engaged in varied and constant social interactions with her international peers on Facebook, by the end of the course Kathryn was able to critique the US educational system: "excluding partition history and literature from Western education is dangerous . . . and it is only through international partnerships such as these [that] people become more informed about past histories that directly relate to current global matters, such as the wars in the East and the rise of Islamophobia." By choosing the word "dangerous," she draws our attention to American curriculum's conscious silencing of non-Western histories and literatures, and thereby underscores the significance of community literacy practices that have the power to decenter borders and binaries.

Initially, Kathryn's LaGuardia peers were also reticent to revise their habits of interacting with peers. I observed that it was challenging for LaGuardia students to extend friendship, while it was very easy for the international students to engage socially on Facebook; in fact, the Facebook page was created by an Indian student. I made the effort to encourage my students to participate on Facebook and share videos. In the process of performing peer reviews, socializing online with the international group, and learning about the topic, LaGuardia students became more open to social interactions. WhatsApp exchanges helped them to develop friendships with their transnational peers, which many continued on their own Instagram or other platforms, beyond the prescribed spaces created by faculty from India (Sataravala) and Pakistan (Riaz). Moreover, they were able to adjust their expectations of immediate responses from peers (regardless of the twelve-hour difference) and develop a critical lens to view the established principles of US education. At the end of the project, they unanimously acknowledged that if they had not taken the course, they would not have known the histories of their Indian, Pakistani, and Bangladeshi peers, who at first they often reductively addressed as Indians, to be later corrected. Ignorance on topics such as partition that reshaped concepts of citizenship and altered international borders can have lasting impacts on how US-educated students might perceive the rest of the world and how they could be perceived by others.

The WhatsApp group in particular became a significant digital space for students to raise questions about each other's cultures, to dispel several myths perpetuated by the media about Pakistan and the United States, and especially in the case of the LaGuardia students to become both empathetic and actively interested in the social and political scenario in Pakistan. For example, Allison wrote in her essay that "after reading *The New York Times* article titled 'Panic in Pakistani City After 900 Children Test Positive for H.I.V.,' I could not stop crying as I learned that due to poverty and no access of clean medical supplies, children were being treated for illnesses with dirty syringes." A mother herself, she continued: "Immediately I reached out to my counterparts in Pakistan through our WhatsApp Platform and they too shared news of the catastrophe as published in their newspapers. It was devastating and heartbreaking to think about young children in those regions dying and made me wonder what the long-lasting effects of this devastation would be." In You's reference to study abroad programs, he mentions how such opportunities enhance "cultural adaptability" by offering students a scope to "communicate across linguistic and cultural borders" (Fraiberg, Wang, and You, 172). What we see here is that Allison's COIL exchange fulfills similar expectations entrenched in study-abroad programs, as she empathetically crosses over to the previously unfamiliar culture.

Similar to You's idea of cosmopolitan disposition, I too wanted my LaGuardia students to "move across the boundaries of nation . . . to [become] open to and tolerant of difference[s]" with their trans-Atlantic peers as well as their shared histories (Fraiberg, Wang, and You, 173). In other words, through this project I wanted my Capstone students to understand the complexity of the history of my country of origin. Clearly, COIL fostered these connections, which I argue would not have been possible otherwise. As another student, Jennifer (US), unhesitatingly admitted: "It is definitely meaningful to actually have conversations with people from these countries, even if it is through a Google doc or Facebook/WhatsApp group, because one gets a whole different perspective about the region, people, cultures, and politics from such interactions." Jennifer's reflection emphasizes the power of socially grounded and student-driven pedagogy to facilitate literacies from the ground up, forging values that are both impactful and self-transformative. LaGuardia students were able to bridge the gaps in their knowledge of the region, as well as become mindful of how the sociocultural and political landscape of the period described in the texts is not a thing of the past but is intricately woven into the identity of the present population.

Informal conversations and the common goal of mentoring US students also helped Bangladeshi, Pakistani, and Indian students to develop a friendship and perhaps overcome inherited hostility toward each other. At a time when the sudden repeal of Article 370 of the Indian Constitution by the Indian government triggered a situation of extreme tension between India and Pakistan (curfew, cutting off internet, closing schools in the Kashmir Valley), students from both sides of the borders responded to the situation with kindness and concern. It was one of the best moments in the COIL partnership when students of Sadia Riaz went of their own accord to visit museums in Lahore and then shared pictures of partition artifacts and stories on Facebook, extending love and friendship for their Indian peers on the other side of the border and also inviting them to visit Lahore. This experiential aspect of the class reinforced the ideas conveyed in the literary works the students studied. As Kathryn remarks, "I believe that reading the works of Khushwant Singh and Saadat Hasan Manto has allowed me to see how people are only engaged in prejudiced behavior when pushed by outside forces such as corrupt or opposing political leaders to divide a population." It was also an eye-opening moment for LaGuardia students to witness firsthand the pedagogical subversion of government policies that perpetuate hate and conflict. Idris (US) summed up the heartwarming attitude of his international peers: "Despite what happened during partition, it gives me great joy to see how students from all four nations (United States, India, Pakistan, Bangladesh) came together to discuss this issue, because it shows that even the worst of tragedies do not stand a chance against friendship and compassion. I just wished that at the time of partition, those politicians and men in power saw it the same way." By highlighting the power of community to counter nationalism, Idris also helped to see how an absence of such practices, or the silencing of non-Western histories and narratives within American academia, can also prevent developing "friendship and compassion" for others.

The value of transnational, student-driven, alternative, community-based practices exposes the need to challenge the isolationist pedagogy often perpetuated in American classrooms—where students, if not participating in study abroad programs to the non-West, seldom become acquainted with non-Western cultures, histories, and geographies. COIL exposed the gaps in the curriculum and prompted a conversation about the urgency of revising both curriculum and pedagogies that foster unethical and epistemological violence by silencing histories and narratives—such as those of the partition project—that permanently transformed the world map and the lives of people from both within the region and the diaspora.

CONCLUSION: PROGRAMMATIC AND PEDAGOGICAL IMPLICATIONS

Our study indicates that COIL can serve as a pedagogical tool in transnational community-building, creating a powerful critique of divisive sociopolitical actions. In closing, we offer a few programmatic, curricular, and methodological recommendations for implementing this model of cross-cultural online teaching.

First, if practitioners of COIL or other forms of virtual exchange aim to grow the program as a civically engaged educational practice that produces impact, its socially significant goals should underlie the program's institutional positionality, professional development activities, project curriculum, and methodology. This effort should start with concrete steps to legitimize and prioritize virtual exchange institutionally and within individual courses. It is common for virtual exchange to develop from the ground up through faculty efforts; as such it might easily be perceived as a marginal pet project. To avoid such positionality, on the programmatic level virtual exchange should be aligned with institutional priorities and other global learning activities (curricular or co-curricular). For example, at LaGuardia we are scoring COIL artifacts on the institution's Global Learning rubric to show that it can serve as an effective tool to facilitate one of the core competencies contained in the general education requirements. Furthermore, Tuli Chatterji's course was on the curricular map to fulfill Global Learning Competency and Digital Ability. The same principle of centrality should operate in a class where virtual exchange is implemented: the project can contain a high-stakes course assignment and/or be included in the course grade breakdown.

Second, faculty development activities should model practices that facilitate the same dispositions of flexibility, openness, and empathy that we wish to see in cross-cultural student exchanges. This can be achieved by respecting faculty's academic freedom in task design and offering different ways to engage in faculty development (seminars, workshops, individualized mentorship). It's crucial to create a vibrant community of practitioners, decenter program leadership, enable peer-to-peer mentorship, and promote exchange of ideas. For instance, LaGuardia faculty development workshops are often co-led by COIL practitioners, so new COIL faculty learn from not only the program coordinator but also their peers; in fact, the program coordinator (Olga Aksakalova) is a fellow COIL faculty member rather than an administrator. Faculty participants offer each other feedback at different stages of their projects. They also help to cultivate this culture of sharing and co-mentoring; for instance, one faculty member invited the LaGuardia COIL community to hear and provide feedback on her experiment with a mini-COIL project. This level of engagement is also a result of faculty's agency and intellectual investment in a project.

At the same time, professional development activities should illuminate a critical approach to virtual exchange by drawing attention to issues of equity, privilege, and power in transnational partnerships and by disrupting patterns of dominance. As Chatterji's case study illustrates, virtual exchange can serve as a strong platform to de-emphasize US approaches to literacy pedagogy (Donahue 2009) by stepping away from Western academic genres and mechanisms of knowledge production (she legitimized personal and transgenerational experience as knowledge sources). At the level of faculty partners, openness to non-US writing genres, teaching methods, and choices of technology will help to destabilize US dominance. In the same way that COIL students are led to develop a critical lens on the established norms, faculty should critically evaluate their teaching practices.

Third, COIL's anti-isolationist ethos could prevail if the topic of the collaboration addresses borders—physical or metaphorical. As such, it will provide a metacognitive dimension to the collaboration, illustrating the importance of cross-border pedagogy. In turn, the use of technology can further reinforce the possibility of creating an even field between partnering groups. Especially when relying on digital tools not associated with institutional platforms, such as course management systems (see Wu 2018), COIL projects create a transnational space in which learners are neither hosts nor guests as in study-abroad contexts, but co-creators of the learning environment that exists "neither there nor here" and is "shared" (O'Rourke 2018, 28). As Chatterji's project illustrates, the agentive work students perform can be called "space-making": it is "essentially a matter of crossing artificially created boundaries. . . . As a result, individuals may take up an identity position as a hybrid, rather than purely as one or the other" (Yang 2018, 115). The liminal subject position empowers learners to initiate cross-border dialogue, as they draw on their personal and community resources to disrupt traditional modes of institutional knowledge production. Their continuous reflective activity further "disrupts the filters of authorized vision (critical literacy)" (Davidson 2018, 79) and allows for development of the "cosmopolitan perspective of the sojourner," which in turn depends on their ability to "recognize the identities and allegiances they already have even as we discuss with them the exciting and potentially transformative possibilities of connecting with people from diverse cultures, languages, and geographic locations through international people from diverse cultures, languages, and geographic locations through international educational partnerships" (Hanson, chapter 10).

In the current post-pandemic landscape of higher education, the trend of increased online international collaborations is likely to continue. In this unique moment lies a real possibility of change. As educators engage more deeply with online teaching, the considerations on cross-border pedagogies and programs presented in this chapter can assist in charting a trajectory for constructing anti-isolationist literacy projects.

Acknowledgment. I, Tuli Chatterji, am grateful to Dr. Snober Sataravala and Prof. Suhaile Azavedo from St. Mira's College, Pune, India, Dr. Sohana Manzoor from University of Liberal Arts, Dhaka, Bangladesh, and Prof. Sadia Riaz from University of Management and Technology, Lahore, Pakistan, who willingly supported my vision by opening their classrooms for the above COIL project.

REFERENCES

"About." n.d. Critical Internationalization Studies Network. https://criticalinternationalization.net.

Appadurai, Arjun. 1996. *Modernity at Large: Cultural Dimensions of Globalization*. Minneapolis: University of Minnesota Press.

Appiah, Anthony K. 2007. *Cosmopolitanism: Ethics in a World of Strangers*. New York: W. W. Norton.

Baksh, Anita, and Schuyler Esprit. 2018. "Teaching Edwidge Danticat's *Krik?Krak!* through Global Learning Classrooms." In *Approaches to Teaching the Works of Edwidge Danticat*, edited by Joseph Celucien, Suschi Banerjee, Danny Hoey, and Marvin Hobson, 167–79. New York: Routledge.

Beelen, J., and E. Jones. 2015. "Redefining Internationalization at Home." In *The European Higher Education Area*, edited by A. Curaj, L. Matei, R. Pricopie, J. Salmi, and P. Scott. Cham, Switzerland: Springer.

Boumlik, Habiba, and Phyllis Van Slyck. 2019. "Addressing Extremism through Literature: Mahi Binebine's *Horses of God* (*Les étoiles de Sidi Moumen*)." *Ikhtilaf: Journal of Critical Humanities and Social Studies* 1 (2): 34–56.

Byram, Michael. 2016. "The Cultnet Intercultural Citizenship Project." In *Online Intercultural Exchange: Policy, Pedagogy, Practice*, edited by Robert O'Dowd and Tim Lewis, 256–62. New York: Routledge.

Canagarajah, Suresh. 2018. "Transnationalism and Transculturalism: How They Are Connected." In *Transnational Writing Education: Theory, History, and Practice*, edited by Xiaoye You, 41–60. New York: Routledge.

Dalrymple, W. 2015. "The Great Divide: The Violent Legacy of Indian Partition." *The New Yorker*, June 22, 2015.

Davidson, Cynthia. 2018. "Reconstructing Ethos as Dwelling Place: On the Bridge of Twenty-First Century Writing Practices (ePortfolios and Blogfolios)." In *Thinking Globally, Composing Locally: Rethinking Online Writing in the Age of the Global Internet*, edited by Rich Rice and Kirk St. Amant, 72–92. Logan: Utah State University Press.

Donahue, Christiane. 2009. "'Internationalization' and Composition Studies: Reorienting the Discourse." *College Composition and Communication* 61 (2): 212–43.

"Fast Facts." n.d. LaGuardia Community College. Revised September 17, 2021. https://www.laguardia.edu/fast-facts/.

Fraiberg, Steve, Xiqiao Wang, and Xiaoye You. 2017. *Inventing the World Grant University: Chinese International Students' Mobilities, Literacies, and Identities*. Boulder: University Press of Colorado.

Galinova, Elena. 2015. "Promoting Holistic Global Citizenship in College." In *Internationalizing Higher Education: Critical Collaborations across the Curriculum*, edited by R. D. Williams and A. Lee, 17–34. Rotterdam, Netherlands: Sense Publishers.

Hauck, Mirjam. 2020. "Towards Global Fairness in the Digital Space through VE." International Virtual Exchange Conference, September 14–16, 2020 (virtual). https://iveconference.org/2020-conference/.

Helm, Francesca, and Sarah Guth. 2010. "The Multifarious Goals of Telecollaboration 2.0: Theoretical and Practical Implications." In *Telecollaboration 2.0: Language, Literacies and Intercultural Learning in the 21st Century*, edited by Sarah Guth and Francesca Helm, 69–106. Bern: Peter Lang.

Kalantzis, Mary, and Bill Cope. 2000. "A Multiliteracies Pedagogy: a Pedagogical Supplement." In *Multiliteracies: Literacy Learning and the Design of Social Futures*, edited by Bill Cope and Mary Kalantzis, 239–48. London: Routledge.

Lee, Eunjeong, and Suresh Canagarajah. 2019. "The Connection between Transcultural Dispositions and Translingual Practices in Academic Writing." *Journal of Multicultural Discourses* 14 (1): 14–28.

Lewis, Tim, and Robert O'Dowd. 2016. "Online Intercultural Exchange and Foreign Language Learning: A Systematic Review." In *Online Intercultural Exchange: Policy, Pedagogy, Practice*, edited by Robert O'Dowd and Tim Lewis, 21–66. New York: Routledge.

Moore, Alexandra Schultheis, and Sunka Simon. 2015. "Building a Borderless Class: Theories and Practices in the Humanities." In *Globally Networked Teaching in the Humanities*, edited by Alexandra Schultheis Moore and Sunka Simon, 93–95. New York: Routledge.

O'Dowd, Robert. 2016. "Learning from the Past and Looking to the Future of Online Intercultural Exchange." In *Online Intercultural Exchange: Policy, Pedagogy, Practice*, edited by Robert O'Dowd and Tim Lewis, 273–93. New York: Routledge.

O'Dowd, Robert. 2018. "From Telecollaboration to Virtual Exchange: State-of-the-Art and the Role of UNICollaboration in Moving Forward." *Journal of Virtual Exchange*, no. 1, 1–23.

O'Rourke, B. 2018. "Intercultural Encounters as Hospitality. An Interview with Richard Kearney." *Journal of Virtual Exchange*, no. 1, 25–39.

Perez, Annemarie. 2018. "Digital Divides." In *Digital Pedagogy in the Humanities: Concepts, Models, and Experiments*, edited by Rebecca Frost Davis, Matthew Gold, Kathy Harris, and Jentery Sayers. New York: Modern Language Association.

Pollack, R., director. 2007. *The Day India Burned*. BBC Two. Retrieved from www.bbc.co.uk/programmes/b007wv67.

"Projects." n.d. Stevens Initiative. Accessed on June 30, 2021. https://www.stevensinitiative.org/projects/.

Ragnedda, Massimo, and Glenn W. Muschert, eds. 2013. *The Digital Divide: The Internet and Social Inequality in International Perspective*. New York: Routledge.

Roy, Haimani. 2018. *The Partition of India*. New Delhi, India: Oxford University Press.

Rubin, Jon. 2016. "The Collaborative Online International Learning Network: Online Intercultural Exchange in the State University of New York Network of Universities." In *Online Intercultural Exchange: Policy, Pedagogy, Practice*, edited by Robert O'Dowd and Tim Lewis, 261–70. New York: Routledge.

Rubin, Jon. 2020. "Digital Internationalisation: A Look beneath the Surface." *Forum* (Spring): 6–8. Retrieved from https://www.eaie.org/our-resources/library/publication/Forum-Magazine/2020-spring-forum.html.

Runyan, A. S., M. H. Marchand, and C. Stoll. 2015. "Crossing Borders: Transnational Feminism and Transnationally Networked Learning." In *Globally Networked Teaching in the Humanities*, edited by Alexandra Schultheis Moore and Sunka Simon, 110–23. New York: Routledge.

Sidhwa, Bapsi. 1991. *Cracking India: A Novel*. Minneapolis, MN: Milkweed Editions.

Singh, Khushwant. 1956. *Train to Pakistan*. New York, NY: Grove Press.

SUNY COIL Global Commons, State University of New York. Accessed on June 30, 2021, https://system.suny.edu/global/coil-global-commons/.

Yang, Shizhou. 2018. "Potential Phases of Multilingual Writers' Identity Work." In *Transnational Writing Education: Theory, History, and Practice*, edited by Xiaoye You, 115–37. New York: Routledge.

Wu, Zhiwei. 2018. "Technology-Mediated Transnational Writing Education: An Overview of Research and Practice." In *Transnational Writing Education: Theory, History, and Practice*, edited by Xiaoye You, 170–86. New York: Routledge.

10
FOSTERING COSMOPOLITANISM
International Educational Partnerships in a Professional Communication Course

Joleen Hanson

In the field of technical communication, much has been written about the challenges of preparing students to participate effectively and ethically as members of a diverse, globalized professional community (Agboka and Mateeva 2018; Hunsinger 2006; St. Amant and Flammia 2016; Stark-Meyerring 2010; Thatcher et al. 2011; Yu 2012). In fact, Grady (2016) identifies no fewer than ten field-specific special journal issues related to this topic between 1997 and 2011. International educational partnerships are frequently highlighted as a particularly robust means of achieving this goal. As Starke-Meyerring (2010) explains, such partnerships provide learning environments that "systematically address globalization issues by integrating experiential learning opportunities for cross-boundary knowledge making" (261). Recently, scholars have begun to draw on the theoretical framework of cosmopolitanism to articulate key learning goals and outcomes for international educational partnerships (Palmer 2013, 2018; Verzella 2018). Fostering cosmopolitanism through international educational partnerships resists isolationism by bringing students into a relationship-building process that expands not only their perceptions of people outside their borders but also their perceptions of themselves.

In this chapter, I explore how international educational partnerships organized through the Trans-Atlantic and Pacific Project (TAPP) (NDSU n.d.) can contribute to the development of a cosmopolitan outlook among student participants. After establishing the benefits of such a point of view for professional communication students, I summarize current descriptions of a cosmopolitan outlook in technical communication and in writing studies and point out how closely these descriptions correspond to formulations of the nature of intercultural communicative competence (ICC) in the disciplines of Foreign Language Teaching (FLT) and Teaching English as a Second Language (TESOL). Drawing from this rich transdisciplinary perspective, I identify a set of attitudes and practices that characterize the cosmopolitan outlook that I seek to foster in students. I then describe four TAPP collaborations I have conducted in a professional communication course at a rural polytechnic university and examine students' written reflections about their collaboration experiences for evidence of attitudes and practices consistent with a cosmopolitan outlook.

COSMOPOLITANISM AND PROFESSIONAL COMMUNICATION

Palmer (2013) was one of the first to suggest cosmopolitanism as a useful framework for thinking about current research and teaching in professional and technical communication. Palmer's conception of cosmopolitanism is based primarily on Beck's 2006 cosmopolitan research framework and Canagarajah's 2010 formulation of *dialogical cosmopolitanism*. To explain the need for a cosmopolitan perspective, Palmer points out that traditional theorizing of culture as an array of dimensions that vary from one country to another provides an inadequate basis for understanding intercultural communication in today's globally interconnected communication environment. Indeed, a crucial disadvantage of traditional theory of cultural modeling is its potential to reinforce stereotypes and to promote isolationism by circumscribing individual identity within national boundaries. In applying cosmopolitan theory to technical communication pedagogy, Palmer explains that introducing students to a cosmopolitan outlook will better prepare them to interact effectively across differences in language and culture. In contrast to the traditional cultural dimensions approach, which alerts students to predict ways that a person from a different country will likely prefer to communicate based on the country's national culture, a cosmopolitan communication strategy "emphasizes the cooperative process of creating norms for each interaction by starting negotiations on equal terms and always being ready to re-evaluate previous assumptions and values through self-critique" (Palmer 2013, 395).

This approach to communication enacts the cosmopolitan outlook of openness to cultural difference and the understanding of cosmopolitanism as "universality plus difference" (Appiah 2006, 92). Palmer notes that the earlier theoretical emphasis on cultural dimensions "has been very much focused on cultural difference often ignoring commonalities: the universal part of the cosmopolitan equation" (Palmer 2013, 395).

Nevertheless, a cosmopolitan outlook does not erase a communicator's identification with a nation or with other social groups. Instead, cosmopolitanism offers a path to be both a citizen of a specific place as well as a "citizen of the world." You expresses the "fundamental meaning" of cosmopolitanism this way: "Though sometimes defined by kindred relations, ethnicity, nation, race, or class, all people are first and foremost members of the human race and as such are morally obligated to those outside their categories; further they have the agency to develop and sustain new allegiances across cultures, communities, and languages" (You 2016, 6). The cosmopolitan's identity is complex, inflected by a range of circumstances, interests, and allegiances. Verzella explains that a cosmopolitan outlook emphasizes "the coexistence of rival ways of life in the individual experience" (Verzella 2018, 694). It is this agency and outlook that Palmer (2013) and scholars in writing studies such as Verzella and You have sought to cultivate in students through a variety of pedagogical projects, including international educational partnerships.

The current discussion of cosmopolitanism in professional communication and writing studies has much in common with the theorizing of ICC in the disciplines of FLT and TESOL. For example, in a 2014 blog post about the nature of ICC, TESOL President Yilin Sun (2014) listed the following characteristics required for effective intercultural communication that could also describe a cosmopolitan outlook:

- **empathy**: an understanding of other people's behaviors and ways of thinking
- **respect**: genuine admiration and appreciation of different ways of thinking and communication
- **tolerance**: the ability and willingness to accept and acknowledge different behaviors and ways of thinking, the existence of opinions or behavior that one does not necessarily agree with
- **sensitivity**: the awareness and responsiveness to other people's behaviors and ways of thinking
- **flexibility**: willingness to adapt and open to change and different ways of thinking

Sun (2014) also cites the work of Lippi-Green (1997) regarding the imperative for members of the dominant language group to "share the communicative burden" when interacting with people from culturally and linguistically diverse backgrounds, a principle that resonates with Palmer's 2013 cosmopolitan communication strategy of negotiating meaning on equal terms.

In addition, FLT scholar Michael Byram's 1997 metaphor of the successful language learner as "sojourner" rather than "tourist" has much in common with a cosmopolitan outlook. Byram compares the sojourner and the tourist to illustrate two approaches to interaction across cultural difference. He distinguishes the tourist from the sojourner according to the impact of their travel on themselves and on the community they visit: "It is the sojourner who produces effects on a society which challenge its unquestioned and unconscious beliefs, behaviors, and meanings, and whose own beliefs, behaviors, and meanings are in turn challenged and expected to change" (Byram 1997, 1). In contrast, the tourist "hopes . . . first that what they have travelled to see will not change . . . and second that their own way of living will be enriched but not fundamentally changed by the experience of seeing others" (Byram 1997, 1). Byram explains that "the experience of the sojourner is potentially more valuable . . . both for societies and for individuals" because it entails "the opportunity to learn and be educated, acquiring the capacity to critique and improve their own and others' conditions" (Byram 1997, 2). This outcome of mutual benefit is the ultimate goal of a cosmopolitan outlook as expressed in the translation of the Greek word "cosmopolitan" as "citizen of the world."

Byram's 1997 ideas also correspond with cosmopolitanism when he describes the intercultural communicative competence represented by the sojourner as "the ability to decentre and take up the perspective of the listener or reader," and he explains that this competence is ultimately "focused on establishing and maintaining relationships" (Byram 1997, 3). Importantly, Byram points out that the qualities of the sojourner "are seldom acquired without help [and] seldom learnt without teaching" because they run counter to the socializing effects of social institutions which nurture "a sense of loyalty and group identity" (Byram 1997, 2). This observation is consistent with Brewer's warning that "merely having an international experience does not mean that intercultural learning goals and outcomes will be achieved" (Brewer 2016, 255). Like Byram and Brewer, Verzella also notes that a cosmopolitan outlook must be taught: "A cosmopolitan approach to the teaching of writing revolves around the goal of stimulating interest, attention, and recognition for unknown languages, unfamiliar rhetorical traditions, and different customs" (Verzella 2018, 696). Simply organizing an international educational partnership is not enough. To support students in gaining the cosmopolitan perspective of the sojourner, we must help students explicitly recognize the identities and allegiances they already have, even as we discuss with them the exciting and potentially transformative possibilities of connecting with people from diverse cultures, languages, and geographic locations through international educational partnerships.

Table 10.1. Attitudes and practices consistent with a cosmopolitan outlook

Category 1: Self-perception (identity)
As simultaneously members of a local community and a global community; a citizen of the world (You 2016, 7; Palmer 2013, 383)
As belonging to more than one cultural or linguistic group (You 2016, 6)
As having "a hybrid identity" (Palmer 2013, 385)
As having allegiances across cultures, communities, and languages (You 2016, 6)

Category 2: Attitudes towards linguistic and cultural difference
Openness toward and acceptance of cultural difference (Palmer 2013, 385)
Recognition and acceptance of linguistic diversity (Palmer 2013, 396)
Willingness to accept and acknowledge different behaviors and ways of thinking that one does not necessarily agree with (Sun 2014, "tolerance")
Genuine admiration and appreciation of different ways of thinking and communicating (Sun 2014, "respect")
Willingness to adapt and openness to change and different ways of thinking (Sun 2014, "flexibility")
Desire to establish or maintain a relationship with linguistically or culturally different people (Byram 1997, 3)

Category 3: Communication practices and strategies
Look for commonalities while accepting differences (Appiah 2006 as cited in Palmer 2013, 386)
Use verbal negotiation strategies such as more detailed double-checking of meaning, rephrasing, and repetition; overlooking unclear meanings that are nonessential (Canagarajah 2010 as cited in Palmer 2013, 388)
Take action to maintain relationships (Byram 1997, 3)
"Share the communicative burden" (Lippi-Green 1997 as cited in Sun 2014); approach verbal negotiation "on equal terms" (Palmer 2013, 395)
May reevaluate previous assumptions and values (Palmer 2013, 395)

The preceding discussion of the similarities between descriptions of cosmopolitanism and of intercultural communicative competence provides a range of specific attitudes and practices that international educational partnerships may foster and that we can look for when assessing student learning. I have drawn from Palmer (2013), You (2016), Sun (2014), and Byram (1997) to develop three categories of attributes that would indicate a move toward a cosmopolitan outlook, as shown in table 10.1.

TRANSATLANTIC AND PACIFIC PROJECT (TAPP) COLLABORATIONS

International educational partnerships have proliferated across the disciplines in response to globalization and the availability of easy-to-use online communication tools. The scale of such partnerships ranges from those developed through an individual instructor's network of contacts to those sponsored by governments, such as Movetia (2018) in Switzerland, or other national- or international-level organizations such as UNICollaboration (2020). In some cases, the international educational partnership is the course focus for an entire semester, but often the partnership functions as one project among others within a course.

International educational partnerships have developed in a range of disciplines, which have used different terms to refer to similar experiences. As noted by Aksakalova and Chatterji in this volume, Computer-Assisted Language Learning (CALL) practitioners and researchers were among the first to develop and report on the use of international educational partnerships. For example, Helm lists a 2003 journal special edition on the topic (Helm 2015, 198). CALL publications have used the terms "online intercultural exchange" (Dooley and O'Dowd 2012; Belz and Thorne 2006; O'Dowd 2007), "telecollaboration" (Guth and Helm 2010; Helm 2015; Kern 2014), and "virtual exchange" (Helm 2018). International educational partnerships have also been well documented in professional and technical communication using the terms "international collaboration" (Maylath et al. 2013; Paretti, McNair, and Holloway-Attaway 2007; St. Amant and Kelsey 2012; Vandepitte et al. 2016) and "global virtual teams" (Brewer 2016). International educational partnerships have also been reported in the humanities and social sciences using the terms "globally networked learning environments" (Craig 2014; Starke-Meyerring and Wilson 2008), and "cross-cultural collaboration" (Verzella and Tomaso 2015). As described by Aksakalova and Chatterji in this volume, the State University of New York (SUNY) has developed a system-wide process for creating transdisciplinary international educational partnerships using the term "Collaborative Online International Learning" (COIL).

My own experience with international educational partnerships began in fall 2016 when I joined a network of college instructors called the Trans-Atlantic and Pacific Project. Originating with two university faculty members in the 1999–2000 academic year, the TAPP network has connected forty-one universities in nineteen countries on five continents, most often linking writing classes to usability testing or translation studies courses (NDSU n.d.). Since its earliest days, the TAPP network has functioned as a wholly grassroots endeavor, without any institutional agreements or government support, which distinguishes it from COIL and larger international networks. TAPP collaborations have thrived and spread in part because their independence protects them from budget cuts and changes in institutional priorities. From fall 2016 to spring 2020, I have conducted thirteen TAPP collaborations in five different courses, ranging from first-year writing to a master's-level professional writing course. My various collaborators outside the US have taught courses in translation, research writing, English as a foreign language, and technical writing.

TAPP collaborations are a natural fit for Transnational Professional Communication, a required upper-level course for students majoring in Professional Communication and Emerging Media (PCEM) at the University of Wisconsin–Stout (UW-Stout). The course description promises that students will learn about "theories and practical approaches to the global aspects of professional communication, including translation and cross-cultural visual communication." TAPP collaborations that foster a cosmopolitan outlook provide students with coherent assumptions (theory) and practical approaches for effective transnational professional communication. The following discussion will present an analysis of student learning based on four TAPP collaborations completed in spring 2017 and spring 2018. This research was approved by UW-Stout's Institutional Review Board, and informed consent was obtained from students whose work is quoted here.

The Students

Students who choose to attend this institution in a small midwestern town tend to be attracted by its polytechnic identity, which emphasizes applied learning and a career focus. A project-based international educational partnership appeals to their preferred learning style and can provide a novel opportunity to experience linguistic and cultural diversity. Most of the students I have taught at this institution self-identify as monolingual English-users and have limited, if any, travel experience outside the US. The institution's foreign language department consists of one full-time faculty member who teaches Spanish, though courses in six other languages are available through an online consortium. Although study abroad is strongly encouraged across campus, many students perceive it as out of reach, not only due to the financial cost but also because they don't have space for electives in the program of specialized courses in their major. In the last five academic years (2015–2019) the ethnicity of the student body has been 86 percent White/Caucasian (UW-Stout 2020).

Students who take Transnational Professional Communication are almost exclusively PCEM majors, the only major on campus to require foreign-language study and one of the few that both encourages off-campus study and provides ample room for electives in student schedules. Nevertheless, survey data collected on the first day of the spring semester in 2017 and 2018 indicated that student language use and travel experience was similar to that of the overall student body. Among fifty-four students enrolled in 2017 and 2018, only three had studied abroad, and other international travel experiences were infrequent, consisting of—not surprisingly for these traditional-aged students from a cold climate—family vacation cruises in the Caribbean or short-term trips with school or church groups. Most students self-identified as monolingual English-users despite having studied one or two other languages. A total of fifty-two stated that they only used English, though half of these reported studying another language (most often Spanish) but said they did not use it outside of the classroom. Only two students reported that they regularly used a language other than English, and they used it with family members. Among all fifty-four students, twenty-six reported that their home was in a rural area or small town (comparable to the location of our campus), while only six were from a metropolitan area. In 2017, fourteen of the thirty-two students who participated in the TAPP collaborations were taking the class online.

International Collaborations and Supporting Activities

The major assignments in Transnational Professional Communication include readings and videos with discussion and reflection, online exploration of a target culture chosen by the student, and a localization project. In 2017 and 2018, the readings and videos presented traditional cultural model theory, principles of translation and localization, cultural differences in written and visual rhetoric, and workplace case studies. For the localization project, students revised three webpages related to on-campus summer housing at UW-Stout so that the content emphasis, visuals, and style of the pages would meet the needs and expectations of users from the target culture that each student had chosen to study. The English-language webpage text was edited to optimize it for efficient translation (Kohl 2008). Building on this foundational course content, specific preparation and guidance was provided for each TAPP collaboration project.

Activities Supporting All Collaborations

Two assignments supported all collaborations: the journal of reflections about culture and the multimedia self-introduction. The journal of reflections about culture was a key assignment throughout the semester, because developing a cosmopolitan outlook requires personal change, which can be facilitated by reflective writing. Weekly reflection assignments asked students to make personal connections to course content, to question it, and to revisit and reexamine beliefs, values, and experiences in light of new knowledge. While each journal prompt focused on a major assignment or theme being studied that week, it also invited students to "begin by noting what seemed most important to you this week . . . which might include: (1) Potential sources of misunderstanding in transnational professional communication, (2) Aspects of cultural difference, (3) Strategies for communicating effectively across cultural difference." With repeated practice, students became more adept at this valuable thinking skill, and their reflections also provided a record of their learning, which I asked them to review and comment on in a short essay as part of the final exam. Students' reflective journal entries also gave me insight about how students were understanding and responding to course content, including the TAPP collaborations.

The multimedia self-introduction was created early in the semester for students to share with each other and with future collaboration partners. The introduction had to include a visual—not necessarily a photo of the student—and a voice or video recording of no more than three minutes. Previously, I had used this assignment as a way for online students to get acquainted, but when I began conducting TAPP collaborations, I used it to prepare students to introduce themselves to their international partners, adding a requirement that students include a cross-cultural experience. One purpose of the assignment was to help build relationships with collaboration partners, but I also valued asking students to think about how they wanted to present themselves to someone from a different country, language, and culture. This small act of identity construction in preparation for working with an international partner reinforced a concept presented in other ways during the course: that awareness of one's own cultural perspective is essential to relating effectively to people who have different perspectives.

Belgium Collaboration

The Belgium collaboration offered US students the opportunity to participate on a translation team in the role of target culture informants. Their partners in a Belgian master's-level translation course were also learning the professional translation process and their roles as peer editors on the team. The translation instructor obtained a real-world text to translate from Dutch to English as a service-learning project and parceled it out to teams of translation students. In 2017 the text was a chapter about the US Civil War in a world history textbook, and in 2018 the text was a few chapters from a young adult novel. After two rounds of draft translation and feedback within the translation team, the translators shared the third draft with the US students, who provided feedback about clarity and readability from a target user perspective. To prepare for the task, my Belgian colleague had provided examples of informant feedback about different aspects of a translation (lexis, grammar, style, spelling), noting which were effective and which were not. We each discussed these examples with our students to raise their awareness of the appropriate style, tone, length, and content of effective feedback. In 2018, I used the draft translations from 2017 for practice. Students worked in two-person teams to provide feedback on the 2017 drafts, and then we compared their work to the actual 2017 feedback and the final versions of the translations. When doing the "live" feedback, the US students also worked in classmate teams to discuss their feedback ideas and to learn from each other's experiences and partner interactions. During the collaboration, a limited amount of class time was devoted to discussing translation issues and partner interaction. The collaborating international students in the US and Belgium were encouraged to contact each other with questions about the draft or the feedback, but unfortunately international partner interaction was infrequent. This collaboration was mainly text-focused and asynchronous.

China Collaboration

In the China collaboration, the partners practiced cross-cultural communication in English. The Chinese students were English majors in a course titled "Extensive Reading." All students read a US magazine article about gun violence published in 1999 in the wake of the Columbine, Colorado, school shooting. The collaboration task was to discuss asynchronously both the article and student reading practices through posts to a shared wiki page. Teams of assigned partners (two US students matched with two Chinese students) exchanged introductions and chatted on their shared wiki page, and then the Chinese student teams posted a brief summary of key ideas in the article and a few questions about the reading and its cultural context for their US partners to answer. The Chinese instructor also posted questions about reading practices for all students to answer and discuss. The US students responded to the summaries, posed questions, and answered questions on the shared wiki page. Preparation for the US students consisted of an in-class discussion of the expected communication norms that had been provided by the Chinese instructor; a written response to the reading, which included a summary of their reading practice; and an in-class discussion of the ideas in the article. Once a few summaries and questions were posted to the wiki by the Chinese students, a few were selected for in-class discussion, which included brainstorming ideas for how to respond to them. Both collaborating instructors also provided feedback to all students about their initial discussion posts to the wiki.

Thailand Collaboration

In the Thailand collaboration, the US students provided readability feedback on short paragraphs written by undergraduate science students enrolled in a beginning-level English course titled "Fundamental English for Reading and Writing." This opportunity to interact with beginning English-users was facilitated by using Facebook as the communication platform, which required less reading and writing than email would. Facebook was familiar to all because it was used routinely by the Thai instructor to communicate with her large class of approximately eighty-two students, and the US students also had experience with Facebook. After the US students introduced themselves by "friending" their assigned Thai partners on Facebook, the Thai students could send them photos of texts they had written. Each week for two weeks, each Thai student sent one handwritten paragraph using the Facebook message function, along with the instructor's writing prompt for the paragraph. The US students provided feedback each week about their understanding of the paragraph's message. To prepare for this task, we discussed strategies for providing limited but clear feedback using simple language. When the first paragraphs were posted, the US students discussed several examples during class time, working together to figure out the meaning and how to respond most helpfully. Informal interaction using Facebook was encouraged but not required. However, simply viewing their partner's Facebook pages provided all students the opportunity to learn about their partners and to see different ways of using language.

Italy Collaboration

The Italian collaboration was part of a larger project titled "Educational Biographies." This project was adapted from a model of intercultural education for teachers titled "The ABC's of Cultural Understanding and Communication" that was developed by Patricia Ruggiano Schmidt in the US and Claudia Finkbeiner in Germany. Schmidt and Finkbeiner (2006) explain that the key to their model is the adage "Know thyself and understand others," which students experience through the model's steps of autobiography, biography, and cross-cultural analysis of similarities and differences in the documents. The project sequence explicitly emphasizes the importance of being aware of one's own cultural perspective, and the culminating analysis highlights the value of reflection as a means of understanding and appreciating cultural similarities and differences. In my adaptation of Schmidt and Finkbeiner's model, students write two biographies instead of one, and the scope of the autobiography and biographies is narrowed to focus on K–12 educational experiences rather than on the subject's entire life. After writing an educational autobiography, students interview two people in order to write an educational biography of each one: a classmate who attended a much smaller or larger high school, and a person educated outside the United States.

In 2018, for the second, cross-cultural biography, I arranged for my students to interview Italian undergraduate students who were studying English for the professions (such as law) in a course titled "Applied Interlinguistic Communication." The US students emailed their assigned Italian partners to arrange the interview, conducted the interview using a video or audio chat platform, and then met online a second time to discuss the accuracy and completeness of the draft educational biography. Initiating contact with an unknown person was daunting for the US students, so to build their confidence I asked students to draft an initial email, which was discussed in small groups during class time. Students were well prepared to conduct the interviews, because they had already written about their own educational experiences and had interviewed and written about a classmate's experiences. To prepare for the cross-cultural interview, class time was devoted to discussing ideas for modifying both the interview questions used in the classmate interview and the practical aspects of determining a convenient interview time and suitable platform. Though the required interaction was only two meetings, the real-time, oral conversations about a significant experience common to both partners made this a high-impact collaboration, which was mentioned frequently in student reflections at the end of the semester.

STUDENT RESPONSES TO THE TAPP COLLABORATIONS

In order to investigate whether the TAPP collaborations described above fostered a cosmopolitan outlook among student participants, I compared what students wrote about their collaboration experiences in their journals of reflections about culture and in their final exam reflective essays, with attitudes and practices that scholars associate with a cosmopolitan outlook (shown in table 10.1) Although I have grouped these cosmopolitan attributes into three categories, the categories overlap when comparing them to student experiences. Certainly attitudes (category 2) influence practices (category 3). Likewise, category 1, which relates to identity, both influences and is influenced by the other categories. For example, if a student describes developing a friendship with a collaboration partner (category 3), that would surely influence the student's perceived allegiances (category 1). Having a friend in Italy or Thailand would be an allegiance that contributes to a perception of oneself as a "citizen of the world." As a result, though the following descriptions of how student reflections indicate movement toward a cosmopolitan identity are keyed to specific cosmopolitan attitudes or practices in table 10.1, the heading does not narrowly define the student's cosmopolitan outlook.

Building on Openness to Cultural Difference

In their final exam reflections, many students exhibited two of the cosmopolitan attitudes: openness to cultural difference, and desire to establish a relationship with linguistically or culturally different people. For example, online student Liam said, "I liked working with partners from three different cultures rather than just one, because it exposes me to more cultural differences, thus resulting in me learning more about different cultures." Overall, students were not only open to cultural difference but were eager to experience it. Their reflections indicated that they had had enough of talking about cultural difference and reading case studies about cross-cultural communication in the workplace; they wanted to take action! Kyle explained, "I think the projects are a good way to learn and get actual experience [rather] than having a professor just talk about 'this is how the experience could be like.'" However, student reflections also suggested that though they might be impatient with continual preparation for action, many students had had little or no experience of actually engaging in conversation with someone culturally or linguistically different from themselves, and they were nervous about trying it. Several students revealed an initial fear that they would not understand a partner's accent when they expressed relief that this turned out to not be a problem. Cassie gave a typical explanation: "At first, I was really nervous and scared of doing a Skype call with someone that I've only ever emailed with before. But . . . my partner . . . actually had a better English vocabulary than I was expecting; the accent wasn't very harsh at all."

Students appreciated the "push" of the TAPP collaborations to help them move beyond their fears. Hunter explained, "Normally I might be nervous about the cultural differences or language barrier but being pushed into it was very rewarding actually." The TAPP collaborations offered students a limited, safe way to step out of their comfort zone. They provided a reason to cross linguistic and cultural boundaries, a structure for interaction (the task), the support of classmates taking on the same challenge, and the instructor's guidance. As result, students could build on their nascent cosmopolitan outlook (their openness to cultural difference) and gain experience that increased their confidence and changed their self-perception. One of several students who expressed this transition was Julie, who mentioned the importance of "guidance" twice in a journal entry, concluding: "This was a great opportunity to get a hands-on experience with the guidance of a professor. I know that if I ever come across a transnational communication situation in the future, I will be prepared." For students like Julie, by applying what they had read about in textbooks and case studies through the TAPP collaborations, they came away with strategies and experience that gave them confidence as well as an openness for future cross-cultural interactions.

Taking Action to Maintain Relationships

Despite student enthusiasm for working with international partners, few reflections described interactions outside the required task, and most students indicated that they did not expect to stay in touch with their partners. However, some students did enact the cosmopolitan practice of taking action to maintain relationships. For example, though Kyle had never traveled outside the US, his Thai partner prompted him to envision himself visiting Thailand. He wrote, "after the Thailand collaboration, one of my collaborators and I talked back and forth on Facebook. It got to be very casual, and he thought I lived in Thailand which was the greatest thing that happened. He told me that if I were to ever visit Thailand to visit Phuket. . . . and I think I might have to visit Phuket now!" Whether Kyle makes that trip or not, he has developed a stronger cosmopolitan outlook by seeing himself as his Thai partner did—as a person who might travel to Thailand and fit in.

Other students also mentioned that they would likely stay in touch with their partners because they had connected on social media. For example, Chloe wrote about her Italian partner: "Claudia was also really happy to keep in touch after the interview. We text on WhatsApp occasionally, and she has sent me an adorable video of her grandpa saying 'Hi' and some other pictures of food or her friends in Italy. Getting to see her snippets of her daily life has been very exciting for me because I am curious about a lot of people that are different than me." Building a friendship with Claudia was a new experience for Chloe, who also wrote in her final exam reflection, "I was very shy to talk to people from different countries before these projects, but they gave me a chance to break out of my comfort zone and really enrich my almost non-existent knowledge of other countries." Chloe took action to maintain a relationship, not just by interacting on social media but, as she reported, she also "actively worked to make my emails and texts easy to understand for her. I also identified slang in my language . . . and tried to filter it out of our conversations in case [it was] . . . confusing." With the encouragement of an enthusiastic TAPP partner and her own openness to cultural difference, Chloe was motivated to build and maintain a relationship with her partner by trying new communication strategies and using social media.

Using Verbal Negotiation Strategies

Several students described how the real-time conversation required by the Italian collaboration caused them to listen carefully and use different strategies to communicate effectively. Cassie described how she used this cosmopolitan practice: "you have to . . . explain things so that everyone can understand. . . . I remember a couple times throughout my interview with my Italian partner where I had to rephrase, explain, or give an example before they could answer my questions correctly." Cassie went on to describe her surprise that phrases she thought would be "simple" to understand caused problems, and she expressed the expectation that she would draw on this experience when communicating across language difference in the future. In this way, the TAPP collaboration strengthened Cassie's cosmopolitan outlook.

In contrast to Cassie's successful negotiation, Mao explained how he learned a similar lesson "the hard way." Due to miscommunication with his Italian partner during the interview, he wrote an educational biography of his partner that "was incorrect." Mao evidently discovered this when he checked the draft in his second meeting with his partner. In the following passage from his journal, Mao struggles to express his ideas about how the misunderstanding occurred, but he concludes by describing a verbal negotiation strategy he will use in the future, showing that confronting difficulty in the TAPP collaboration led to a stronger cosmopolitan outlook for Mao:

> sometimes just conversation was difficult back and forth. I didn't know what she meant sometimes, and she didn't know what I meant sometimes. Because of this, some of the info on my report was incorrect. . . . I tried my best to understand her, but it was mostly like I just interpreted what she said a different way than what she meant. I don't think her accent played that much of a role. It may just be because her grasp of English is different than mine and maybe English is interpreted/used differently over there,

> ... [This] will also play a role into my future career. I think whenever I interact with someone in another country, I will confirm some facts or ask them to repeat what they said in a different way, so I completely understand what they are saying to me.

The Italian collaboration caused Mao some discomfort, but the requirement that he meet a second time with his partner to check the accuracy of the draft biography shed light on how to relieve the discomfort. As a result, the discomfort was productive, preparing Mao to communicate more effectively in the future.

Recognizing and Accepting Linguistic Diversity

In the text-based collaborations with translation students in Belgium and with beginning English language learners in Thailand, the US students encountered different varieties of English. Their reflections about this experience often showed movement toward a cosmopolitan outlook that recognizes and accepts linguistic diversity. For example, Lisa recognized that her Belgian translation partners were using British English, "so the way some phrases were written is different than what I may write." She also used her own experience of learning Spanish to understand her Thai partners' use of English and to avoid assuming it was simply an error. She wrote, "I learned that the language of that culture can play a role in how they write English. For example, each of my partners said that the place they were writing about 'lives in' a certain area. This is also reflected in the Spanish language because instead of saying, 'I am cold,' you would say, 'I have cold' when translated. It shows that the native language makes the learner perceive text in different ways."

Similarly, John's reflection about working with his Thai partners shows his effort to move away from expecting all English-language users to follow a native-speaker norm, and towards a cosmopolitan expectation of collaboratively negotiating meaning without making judgments about "correct" or "incorrect" language use. John does not fully avoid making value judgments about language use, but he clearly desires collaborative communication that positions all interlocutors as "peers" on equal terms when he writes: "The collaborations . . . have shown me that you need to be somewhat sensitive and tentative in conversations that take place with non-native speakers of your language. This is to not only make sure you're using language that they can understand, but to also help them ease into the language and to not feel uncomfortable or embarrassed. . . . And this would especially be true in a more professional environment where everyone is supposed to be peers: sensitivity to accents, mispronunciations and grammatical mistakes are important to reduce frustrations." To clarify, by "*sensitivity to* accents" I believe John means "*lack of judgment regarding* accents." He seems to be taking the cosmopolitan stance that collaborative communication and respect for one's peers has higher priority than linguistic correctness.

Reevaluating Previous Assumptions and Values

In their final exam reflections, some students described how their collaboration experiences led them to reevaluate previous assumptions and values and to take on cosmopolitan attitudes and values instead. For example, Lexi described how she had previously avoided cultural difference without consciously deciding to do so. This led to unawareness of her own culture and a complete absence of a cosmopolitan outlook. However, her experiences and reflections throughout the semester caused her to recognize what she had been missing and motivated her to embrace a more cosmopolitan outlook:

> I'd never thought too much about my own culture before because I've never had to. I've always been fairly sheltered and have only been around people from similar cultures to me. I grew up in a town where nearly everyone was from the same culture as me, and now I go to a school where nearly everyone is from the same culture as me. This was a very interesting observation I hadn't thought much about prior to taking this class. I rarely go outside of my personal circle of friends and talk to someone new and different from me. I remember reading a piece for this class that talked about how we are more likely to be friends with people who are similar to us, and I've found that this has been true in my life. I would like to go beyond this, though. I would like to branch out more and make it a point to talk to more people with different perspectives than me.

Lexi's description of her lack of cultural awareness was similar to reflections from a number of other students from small rural towns, though few articulated their previous assumptions as clearly. Duke's reflection adds to the picture Lexi sketched out by giving a brief explanation of how a TAPP collaboration contributed to his turn toward a more cosmopolitan outlook. He explained that his online conversations with his Italian collaboration partner raised his awareness of his own cultural perspective and had a greater impact on his cosmopolitan transformation than international travel had. Finally, Duke envisioned the beneficial impact his cosmopolitan outlook would have for his future employer and its clients:

> Elena also had questions for me, questions that I had never had to answer while just being present in my own culture. Her questions helped me see

my own culture from an outside perspective that I rarely experience. . . . Growing up in Midwest Wisconsin hasn't exactly given me many diverse experiences. I have traveled abroad, but I didn't really get that involved with the cultures. I have also been prone to subconsciously jumping to biases and stereotypes that I have learned from being in my own culture. . . . I plan to get a community management position in the entertainment industry. The entertainment industry isn't known for being the most inclusive or open to other cultural experiences. As a community manager, I would expect that I would be interacting with lots of different people from lots of different cultures. They might be coming to me with issues or problems that they have with a particular media. Instead of saying "too bad" and telling them that this is the way things are going to be, I will be able to listen to them, ask them questions, and do my best to figure out how to help.

The reflections of Lexi and Duke present a strong argument for the potential of TAPP collaborations to foster a cosmopolitan outlook, especially for students who have reached college without engaging with people outside their familiar linguistic, cultural, and geographic borders.

The excerpts from student reflections discussed above illustrate how TAPP collaborations can help students begin to develop a cosmopolitan perspective, and many more examples from other students could have been presented also. Nevertheless, some collaborations were more effective at cultivating a cosmopolitan outlook than others. Among the four TAPP collaborations described here, the Belgium collaboration had the least potential for cultivating a cosmopolitan outlook, though it was effective as a professionalizing experience and for raising language awareness as students encountered varieties of English, made decisions about the meanings of words, and were impressed by their Belgian partners' multilingualism. For most students, the Belgian collaboration task was completed successfully without any conversation, written or oral, with their Belgian partners. Alex noted, "it didn't really matter who the people we were editing for were. The documents themselves were the focus, and we did not ever speak to the Belgium students concurrently."

As a result, what students learned about their Belgian partners' language use and ways of thinking about the text was perceived indirectly and without the need to negotiate meaning or make a personal connection. And students wanted that kind of interaction, as Choua explained: "My only suggestion [for improving the TAPP collaborations] . . . is to be able to communicate directly with one another whether it is through e-mail or Facebook, Skype or any other forms of communication . . . This will help you understand the way they write and help you try to see why they wrote it the way they did." The more interaction students have with their international partners, the more likely it is that they will move towards a cosmopolitan outlook, because only interaction can reveal the cultural assumptions and values behind textual choices and behaviors. Synchronous interaction will likely have the greatest impact.

Student motivation and availability also affect the success of any collaboration. A student who drops out after the collaboration begins or who simply fails to respond to a partner's communication will cause disappointment and frustration, and every collaboration I have conducted has included a few such cases. However, students who begin with low expectations of the collaboration but participate consistently tend to show greater openness to cultural difference at the end of the semester. On the other hand, the written reflections of Laura, Sarah, and Angelica suggest an opposite pattern. These three students participated fully in the collaborations, but their reflections showed no development in their cosmopolitan attitudes or practices. They all began and ended the collaboration with an openness to cultural difference and a desire to establish a relationship with linguistically or culturally different people. These students had two other noteworthy similarities. First, all three were dissatisfied with the collaborations due to the limited nature of their interactions with their international partners. Laura expressed their common view: "I personally really enjoy interacting with people of different cultures so . . . I was dismayed not to have the level of interaction I was expecting." Second, all three entered the course with extensive experience interacting with people from other parts of the world, which set them apart from most of their classmates. This experience, along with their initial enthusiasm, suggests that the limited TAPP collaborations that I conducted in 2017 and 2018 were not sufficient for them. Such students may need the challenge of a larger, student-directed collaborative task to continue to build on their existing cosmopolitan attitudes and practices. Examples of more intensive transnational educational experiences include the COIL virtual exchange described by Aksakalova and Chatterji and the joint-degree program discussed by Schreiber and Bluemel, both in this volume.

PEDAGOGICAL IMPLICATIONS

To foster a cosmopolitan outlook that resists isolationism among students in professional and technical communication courses, where most assignments tend to focus on both product and process, the process aspects of the TAPP collaboration must be emphasized. Ideally the collaboration tasks will require direct communication between partners—synchronous if possible—and preparation for this will include a discussion of communication strategies and expectations for language use. The practice-based approaches of a cosmopolitan outlook can be introduced explicitly in these discussions. Communication strategies can include everything from choosing an appropriate time of day for synchronous communication to brainstorming ideas for handling miscommunication. Expectations of language use can include learning about partners' language preferences, discussing the role or relevance of correctness for the project, and identifying the appropriate tone for feedback. Even if the course is taught exclusively in English, students can be encouraged to learn greetings or short phrases in the language(s) used in the collaborating classroom. Finally, the regular practice of both open-ended and guided reflection throughout the collaboration will provide a space for students to articulate and interrogate their own identities and allegiances as they discover differences and similarities between themselves and their international partners. This concomitant increase in self-awareness while engaging with someone who is culturally and linguistically different can then lead to the development of cosmopolitan attitudes, practices, and self-perception.

CONCLUSION

Student reflections about their TAPP collaboration experiences in a professional communication course were replete with evidence supporting the hypothesis that TAPP collaborations can foster a cosmopolitan outlook. These findings suggest that international educational partnerships will become an increasingly valuable pedagogical tool for teachers of technical and professional communication should the field embrace a cosmopolitan theoretical framework to more adequately describe the effects of globalization on communication products and processes, as Palmer (2013) recommends. The results of this analysis may apply most strongly to students from small rural towns who have had limited direct exposure to linguistic or cultural diversity. However, this does not exclude the possibility that international educational partnerships can promote a cosmopolitan outlook among other types of students in other academic settings. Further research is needed to investigate the impact of students' prior experiences on their response to international educational partnerships. In addition, follow-up surveys or interviews with collaboration participants a year or more after the experience would indicate the extent to which a cosmopolitan outlook and its potential to push back against nationalist and isolationist tendencies has taken root and continued to grow in the lives of these students. Likewise, comparing long-term attitudes, practices, and self-perception of collaboration participants with those of similar students who did not participate in an international educational partnership would provide further insight into the impact of these collaborations.

REFERENCES

Agboka, Godwin Y., and Natalia Matveeva, eds. 2018. *Citizenship and Advocacy in Technical Communication: Scholarly and Pedagogical Perspectives*. New York: Routledge.

Appiah, Kwame Anthony. 2006. *Cosmopolitanism: Ethics in a World of Strangers*. New York: W. W. Norton.

Beck, Ulrich. 2006. *Cosmopolitan Vision*. Translated by Ciaran Cronin. Cambridge, UK: Polity Press.

Belz, Julie A., and Steven L. Thorne. 2006. *Internet-Mediated Intercultural Foreign Language Education*. Boston, MA: Thomson Heinle.

Brewer, Pam Estes. 2016. "Teaching and Training with a Flexible Module for Global Virtual Teams." In *Teaching and Training for Global Engineering*, edited by Kirk St. Amant and Madelyn Flammia, 173–97. Hoboken, NJ: IEEE Press.

Byram, Michael. 1997. *Teaching and Assessing Intercultural Communicative Competence*. Bristol, PA: Multilingual Matters.

Canagarajah, A. Suresh. 2010. "From Intercultural Rhetoric to Cosmopolitan Practice." Plenary speech given at the 6th Annual Conference on Intercultural Rhetoric and Discourse, Atlanta, GA, June 2010.

Craig, Jennifer Lynn. 2014. "Teaching Writing in a Globally Networked Learning Environment (GNLE): Diverse Students at a Distance." In *WAC and Second-Language Writers*, edited by Terry Myers Zawacki and Michelle Cox, 369–86. Anderson, SC: Parlor Press.

Dooley, Melinda, and Robert O'Dowd, eds. 2012. *Researching Online Foreign Language Interaction and Exchange: Theories, Methods and Challenges*. New York: Peter Lang.

Grady, Helen M. 2016. "Strategies for Developing International Professional Communication Products." In *Teaching and Training for Global Engineering*, edited by Kirk St. Amant and Madelyn Flammia, 201–18. Hoboken, NJ: IEEE Press.

Guth, Sarah, and Francesca Helm, eds. 2010. *Telecollaboration 2.0: Language, Literacies and Intercultural Learning in the 21st Century*. New York: Peter Lang.

Helm, Francesca. 2015. "The Practices and Challenges of Telecollaboration in Higher Education in Europe." *Language Learning and Technology* 19 (2): 197–217.

Helm, Francesca. 2018. "The Long and Winding Road . . ." *Journal of Virtual Exchange*, no. 1, 41–63.

Hunsinger, R. Peter. 2006. "Culture and Cultural Identity in Intercultural Technical Communication." *Technical Communication Quarterly* 15 (1): 31–48.

Kern, Richard. 2014. "Technology as Pharmakon: The Promise and Perils of the Internet for Foreign Language Education." *The Modern Language Journal* 98 (1): 340–57.

Kohl, John. 2008. *The Global English Style Guide*. Cary, NC: SAS Institute.

Lippi-Green, Rosina. 1997. *English with an Accent: Language, Ideology and Discrimination in the United States*. New York: Routledge.

Maylath, Bruce, Sonia Vandepitte, Patricia Minacori, Suvi Isohella, Birthe Mousten, and John Humbley. 2013. "Managing Complexity: A Technical Communication Translation Case Study in Multilateral International Collaboration." *Technical Communication Quarterly*, no. 22, 67–84.

Movetia. 2018. "About Us." Accessed June 10, 2020. https://www.movetia.ch/en/about.

North Dakota State University (NDSU). n.d. "Transatlantic and Pacific Project." Accessed June 10, 2020. https://www.ndsu.edu/english/transatlantic_and_pacific_translations/.

O'Dowd, Robert. 2007. *Online Intercultural Exchange*. Bristol, PA: Multilingual Matters.

Palmer, Zsuzsanna Bacsa. 2013. "Cosmopolitanism: Extending Our Theoretical Framework for Transcultural Technical Communication Research and Teaching." *Journal of Technical Writing and Communication* 43 (4): 381–401.

Palmer, Zsuzsanna Bacsa. 2018. "Enabling Global Citizenship in Intercultural Collaboration: Cosmopolitan Potential in Online Identity Representation." In *Citizenship and Advocacy in Technical Communication: Scholarly and Pedagogical Perspectives*, edited by Godwin Y. Agboka and Natalia Matveeva, 39–60. New York: Routledge.

Paretti, Marie C., Lisa D. McNair, and Lissa Holloway-Attaway. 2007. "Teaching Technical Communication in an Era of Distributed Work: A Case Study of Collaboration Between U.S. and Swedish Students." *Technical Communication Quarterly* 16 (3): 327–52.

Schmidt, Patricia Ruggiano, and Claudia Finkbeiner, eds. 2006. *ABC's of Cultural Understanding and Communication: National and International Adaptations*. Greenwich, CT: Information Age Publishing.

Starke-Meyerring, Doreen. 2010. "Globally Networked Learning Environments in Professional Communication: Challenging Normalized Ways of Learning, Teaching and Knowing." *Journal of Business and Technical Communication* 24 (3): 259–66.

Starke-Meyerring, Doreen, and Melanie Wilson, eds. 2008. *Designing Global Learning Environments: Visionary Partnerships, Policies, and Pedagogies*. Rotterdam, Netherlands: Sense Publishers.

St. Amant, Kirk, and Madelyn Flammia, eds. 2016. *Teaching and Training for Global Engineering*. Hoboken, NJ: IEEE Press.

St. Amant, Kirk, and Sigrid Kelsey, eds. 2012. *Computer Mediated Communication across Cultures: International Interactions in Online Environments*. Hershey, PA: IGI Global.

Sun, Yilin. 2014. "What Is Intercultural Communicative Competence?" TESOL (blog). Dec. 15, 2014. http://blog.tesol.org/what-is-intercultural-communicative-competence/.

Thatcher, Barry, Kirk St. Amant, and Charles H. Sides, eds. 2011. *Teaching Intercultural Rhetoric and Technical Communication: Theories, Curriculum, Pedagogies, and Practice*. New York: Routledge.

UNICollaboration. 2020. "Home." June 8, 2020. Accessed June 10, 2020. https://www.unicollaboration.org/.

University of Wisconsin–Stout (UW-Stout). 2020. "FactBook." Accessed June 10, 2020. https://www.uwstout.edu/about-us/meet-our-leadership/institutional-accreditation/fact-book.

Vandepitte, Sonia, Bruce Maylath, Birthe Mousten, Suvi Isohella, and Patricia Minacori. 2016. "Multilateral Collaboration between Technical Communicators and Translators: A Case Study of New Technologies and Processes." *The Journal of Specialized Translation*, no. 26, 3–19.

Verzella, Massimo. 2018. "Inviting the Stranger: Building Pedagogical Practice on the Foundations of Cosmopolitan Thought." *Journal of Global Literacies, Technologies, and Emerging Pedagogies* 4 (3): 693–713.

Verzella, Massimo, and Laura Tommaso. 2015. "Learning to Write for an International Audience through Cross-Cultural Collaboration and Text-Negotiation." *Changing English* 21 (4): 310–21.

You, Xiaoye. 2016. *Cosmopolitan English and Transliteracy*. Carbondale: Southern Illinois University Press.

Yu, Han. 2012. "Intercultural Competence in Technical Communication: A Working Definition and Review of Assessment Methods." *Technical Communication Quarterly* 21 (2): 168–86.

11
SMOOTHING THE PATH
Chinese-American Joint-Degree Programs as Resistance to Nationalism

Brooke R. Schreiber and Brody Bluemel

INTRODUCTION

The past several years have seen a sharp increase in anti-Asian rhetoric and policy in the US, beginning even before the rise in violent attacks influenced by racist rhetoric around the COVID-19 pandemic (Tessler, Choi, and Kao 2020). Throughout 2019, headlines such as "Colleges Face Growing International Student-Visa Issues," "Tensions between U.S. and China Hitting Campus Quads," and "U.S. Trying to Slam Door on 350,000 Chinese Students?" attested to a growing crisis in the movement of international students across borders, one born of xenophobic and isolationist actions at the national level that particularly targeted students from the Middle East and China. The crisis stemmed from restrictions on Chinese student visas put in place in 2018 amid national rhetoric in the US around China's "economic aggression" and the portrayal of Chinese students and scholars as stealing US technology (Yoon-Hendricks 2018). As visas for Chinese students and scholars came under greater scrutiny, the Chinese Ministry of Education began warning students to be cautious about committing to study in the US (Redden 2019); Chinese students already in the US began to feel threatened and marginalized by the American government's monitoring and anti-Chinese rhetoric (Feng 2020). In this atmosphere of increasing nationalism, trade wars, and political antagonism between the two countries, together with travel restrictions and health concerns related to the pandemic, the continued enrollment of Chinese students at American universities has been thrown into deep uncertainty.

These strains and limitations on Chinese students entering the US came at a time in which US institutions of higher education (IHEs) had been increasingly turning toward a range of strategies for international recruitment, both as a way to make up for fiscal shortfalls created by less federal funding (DeJoy and Smith 2017) and as part of a rush to embrace globalization, regularly featured as a key element of mission statements and in other forms of academic discourse. As Tardy (2015) points out, diversity and internationalization are "touted in US education in an almost obligatory way" (253); partnerships across borders are often promoted as evidence of universities' prestige and as a sign of desirable diversity in the student body, operating "under the assumption that simply having a more global student body will result in a transformative educational experience" (Shapiro and Siczek 2017, 168). The emphasis on international recruitment—and the use made of the presence of international students in universities' marketing materials—has come to sit in uneasy tension with the visibly elevated nationalism within the US and other countries. This tension is especially striking in regards to Chinese students, who make up the largest percentage of international students recruited to the United States each year (Open Doors 2020) but, as described above, whose future in the US has been thrown into uncertainty by xenophobic national policies and rhetoric.

In the face of these ongoing, serious challenges to international enrollment, especially international enrollment from China, we believe that joint-degree programs can present an important way forward, as the world begins to reopen following the isolation of the pandemic, and provide a future for international studies and programming. Joint-degree programs, in which students typically complete their first two or three years of coursework at their home university and then finish their studies at an international university, are only possible when partnerships are negotiated and formalized between international institutions. Because these partnerships represent significant investment from both institutions, they have the potential to smooth the path for Chinese students entering the US, even in the face of evolving political barriers. As a result, joint-degree programs have the capacity to work against nationalist and isolationist policies and practices, opening up opportunities for faculty and students in both countries for rich cross-cultural experiences—yet in practice, such programs are often fraught with practical and ethical difficulties which diminish this potential.

The goal of this chapter is to consider what role Chinese-American joint-degree programs have been playing in keeping educational pathways open for Chinese students in the US, and how that role could be bolstered by improving the practical implementation of the programs at the administrative level. We argue that these programs can serve as a potential point of resistance to both anti-Chinese policies within the

US and anti-American sentiment in China—but only if implemented with an eye towards ethics and with thoughtful attention to a range of issues such as assessment, placement, curriculum equivalency, and cultural difference. We begin by defining joint-degree programs in the context of other international collaborations. Then, based on a survey of public-facing university websites, we present a snapshot of the state of Chinese-US joint-degree programs at the time of data collection, the summer of 2019. Next, we draw on data from interviews with administrators and faculty across the US, to explore a few of the many practical concerns which arise in implementing such programs: accreditation and articulation agreements and how to assess language proficiency across institutions. This is followed by a discussion of how joint-degree programs can best be sustained to push back against nationalist and isolationist policies that impact students' ability to move across borders.

TRANSNATIONALITY AND WRITING PROGRAMS

Scholarship within writing studies has recently begun to examine how various types of cross-border partnerships affect the work of both writing instructors and writing program administrators—in particular, the establishment of international branch campuses, especially in the Middle East (e.g., Weber et al. 2015; Wetzel and Reynolds 2015), and the increasing use of international recruitment agencies (e.g., Jordan and Jensen 2017). These partnerships constitute an expanding "variety of avenues for entrance" for international students that have broken down traditional boundaries within institutions—for example, blurring lines between admissions, orientation, and academic support (DeJoy and Smith 2017, 3). WPAs are increasingly responsible for organizing, staffing, and administering courses for new populations of students, both on their own campuses and in new and unfamiliar locations and cultures, as writing programs now "are increasingly entangled with other near and far-flung institutional practices and spaces" (Fraiberg, Wang, and You 2017, 11).

Because these programs are typically implemented quickly and at high levels of administration, there is often a lack of consultation with faculty, especially faculty involved with language and writing instruction. As Jordan and Jensen point out, "institutions are entering lucrative agreements with international recruitment agencies but failing to inform or prepare academic programs" (2017, 41). Language diversity is often not considered in the early planning of such collaborations, which leads to reinforcement of the harmful perceptions that multilingualism is a problem (Smith and DeJoy 2017; Jordan and Jensen 2017) and that such programs are creating a "back door" for students who don't meet the usual academic or language standards (Ehlers-Zavala, Didier, and Berry 2017). It also means that US institutions may not be prepared to support the influx of international students, either academically or socially: with only "haphazard" planning, students are "[propelled] into a competitive environment of academic life with little or no English language support" (Gass and Walters 2017, 67) and may remain in enclaves, rather than being integrated into the social life of the campus (Ehlers-Zavala, Didier, and Berry 2017). None of this serves the goal of creating meaningful globalized educational experiences—the kind that truly work to build transnational and cosmopolitan dispositions (You 2016) and push back on xenophobic ideologies—neither for the international students themselves, nor for domestic students or the university community as a whole.

This lack of planning has an especially strong impact on writing instructors, who may have extensive teaching experience but no formal training in L2 composition (Meier, Choi, and Cushman 2017; Pelaez-Morales 2018). As a result, feeling underprepared and overwhelmed, they may default to views defined by monolingualism and notions of deficiency (i.e., that language issues should be "taken care of" before students arrive in writing classes) and to English-only policies, believing that any change to pedagogy is equated to lowered standards (Haan 2018). Because "faculty members as well as writing program administrators are key players in the sustainability of internationalization efforts" (Pelaez-Morales 2018, 238), for partnerships like joint-degree programs to succeed, not only financially but pedagogically, it is crucial that both writing faculty and WPAs are involved—and supported—from the outset (Jordan and Jensen 2017).

It is clear that, as Rose and Weiser argue, "the dramatic increase in international undergraduate students in US universities is changing—or should be changing—college writing programs" as a whole, creating a valuable opportunity and impetus to revise curriculum and pedagogy with an eye both towards accessibility (2018, 6–7) and towards the creation of student pedagogical experiences that live up to the "rhetoric of a global education" (Shapiro and Siczek 2017, 168), changes which will ultimately benefit all students (Donahue 2018; Haan 2018). Joint-degree programs, particularly those between the US and East Asia, constitute an important part of international recruitment efforts and thus an opportunity for this sort of impactful change. Yet while joint-degree programs have been studied fairly robustly in fields such as education policy and education management (e.g., Asgaray and Robbert 2010; Culver et al. 2012; Obst and Kuder 2012), they remain relatively unknown in writing studies.

This chapter aims to partially fill that gap by providing an overview of the scope of these programs and an introduction to broader questions related to the establishment and management of the programs. Joint-degree programs are far from novel, but our findings suggest that there has been an increased shift toward developing such programs in recent years. As a result, joint-degree programs will increasingly impact the work of writing instructors and writing program administrators. It is imperative that second-language writing educators are informed about the unique challenges and parameters of joint-degree programs in order to support effective management from a language and writing perspective.

CHINESE STUDENTS IN US INSTITUTIONS

According to the 2020 Open Doors Report, Chinese students continue to comprise approximately a third of all international students in the US. More than 370,000 Chinese students were enrolled in classes in US universities in 2019–2020, a number which has been rising steadily since 2012. In particular, across the US, institutions had (until very recently) been making efforts to attract a new, upwardly mobile Chinese middle class, for whom America has been the favored option. Economically elite Chinese students have been drawn to the US, both to escape "domestic constraints" like high tuition and low acceptance at highly-ranked Chinese institutions, and to pursue "overseas enticements" like control over the selection of courses and American schools' reputation for incubating creativity and innovative pedagogy (Yang 2016, 4–5).

In turn, American institutions have welcomed the new source of students paying international tuition, though, as with all international recruitment, often without putting into place effective support systems for either the students themselves or the faculty who teach them (Gass and Walters 2017; Jorden and Jensen 2017; Weiser and Rose 2018). As Fraiberg, Wang, and You (2017) note, IHEs in the US "have been unequipped to absorb such a large contingent of students from a single region or to accommodate sometimes wide cultural and linguistic differences" (5). As a result, even as universities have taken advantage of their presence to promote "narratives of inclusivity and diversity," students regularly experience conflict with unprepared faculty and administrators, demonstrating the stark contrast between "institutional rhetorics of diversity and the more messy and complex realities on the ground" (32–33).

Along with the influx of Chinese students has come a growing distrust of Chinese influence on US higher education, visible in incidents like the one at Duke University (see Wan, this collection) and in the shuttering of Chinese-sponsored Confucius Institutes at many institutions (Critchfield 2019). The tension between the two nations, as mentioned earlier, has only been exacerbated as a result of the COVID-19 pandemic, which has resulted in sinophobic rhetoric and outright racist attacks in the US (Yang 2020), and rising anti-American sentiments and general nationalism within China (Wang and Qin 2020). In 2020, according to a Gallup poll, Americans' opinion of China had sunk to an all-time low, and vice versa (Jones 2020). In short, the relationship between the US and China, in and outside of higher education, has been under threat, creating ever more uncertainty and ambivalence for Chinese students hoping to study abroad.

Thus, this chapter focuses on the following questions: how can joint-degree programs between the US and China be most ethically managed in order to smooth the path of students across borders, enable IHEs to pursue truly globalized experiences for students, and ultimately push back against nationalist tendencies? What do writing faculty and writing program administrators need to know about these programs in order to participate fully in creating ethical, sustainable policies and practices?

DEFINING JOINT-DEGREE PROGRAMS

The term "joint-degree program" has been used broadly and somewhat confusingly to describe a wide range of collaborative program models, including dual-degree / double-degree programs and combined-degree programs (Obst and Kuder 2012, Michael and Balraj 2003). Dual-degree or double-degree programs refer to models wherein an individual earns two separate degrees at equivalent levels (e.g., two BS degrees in physics from two separate institutions). Combined-degree programs, which are also often offered intra-institutionally, refer to models in which two degrees at consecutive levels are earned (e.g., a 3+2 model resulting in a BS in physics and an MS in physics). Joint-degree programs more specifically refer to models in which students typically complete their first two or three years of coursework at their home university and then finish their studies at an international university; they result in one *joint* degree that is endorsed by both partnering institutions, and it is this type of program which is the focus of our analysis.

As described above, as with other types of international recruitment, joint-degree programs are regularly founded on financial motives and agreed upon quickly by high-level administrators without input from faculty, which can result in a variety of administrative and pedagogical challenges. As Martins observes, "in the global expansion of higher education, the tension between economic and pedagogical interests strongly influences decisions made about what kinds of programs to offer and how to offer them" (2015, p.1). For joint-degree programs in particular, there is a lack of established procedures for developing, managing, and evaluating joint-degree initiatives (Michael and Balraj 2003). As a result, the programs have something of a mixed reputation: they are perceived by some as a natural and welcome development in the field of international exchanges and by others as a potential for double-counting of credits: "the thin edge of academic fraud" (Knight 2009, p.12).

Given this less than ideal perception, it is worth asking what benefit joint-degree programs have for students, above and beyond traditional degree programs. Joint-degree programs are often marketed as ways to prepare graduates for the global job market, given that students should theoretically gain experience and social connections in a second cultural context. This has had mixed support in the literature: when Culver and colleagues (2012) studied graduate-level joint-degree programs via a series of surveys administered to students, faculty, and employers, the employers reported not having a clear understanding of what the programs were, and so did not view the graduates as being especially any more marketable. In China specifically, employers have become increasingly suspicious of foreign degrees, viewing them as easier to obtain than those from prestigious domestic schools (Yang 2016). In other words, despite the greater financial investment required on the part of the student (and their parents), and the perceived prestige of US degrees, there is no clear financial advantage for joint-degree program graduates—as is true for Chinese students who choose any pathway to studying in the US (Yang 2016).

In Culver's study, students did report personal gains, such as having developed greater capacity for self-reliance, flexibility, problem-solving, and open-mindedness. They also reported that their primary motivations for enrolling in the program were social and cultural rather than economic: a desire to travel, to experience other cultures, and to develop language skills. This suggests that for at least some students, both the motivation for enrollment and their experiences during the program open up the possibility for developing the sort of cosmopolitan attitudes which counterbalance nationalist and isolationist ideologies (You 2016).

The potential of joint-degree programs as a possible pushback against nationalist policy is tempered by practical and ideological challenges. As with any transnational educational efforts, it is important to consider who is privileged by the exchanges, at both the individual and institutional level; how English is taught and assessed, and by whose norms; whose labor supports the programs, and how that labor is compensated; and what pedagogical choices will support students' development of cosmopolitan attitudes (Martins 2015a; You 2016).

METHODS

One of the initial goals of our project was to determine how many joint-degree programs exist between US and Chinese IHEs. Our team, including the authors and two graduate research assistants, conducted a national survey of public-facing university websites during the summer and fall of 2019. However, as we began to survey websites, important complications emerged: what counts as a joint-degree program? How do we distinguish these programs from other related international partnerships? Do these programs provide increased access to international students? In order to address these questions, our team selected a working definition of joint-degree programs and developed a model for how international collaborations are arrayed on a spectrum, both presented below. We also created a heuristic for determining the reliability of the data presented on university websites, looking for the level of detail in information and consistency between American and Chinese sites, as well as additional corroborating sources such as press releases and reports. Using this model (figure 11.1), we were then able to return to our data and explore the driving questions on "writing education across borders" that emerged.

The survey of program websites collected available data regarding program existence, names and locations of partner institutions, dates of inception, field of study, and credit arrangement, on a total of 494 programs, as summarized below. In addition to this survey, the authors also conducted individual interviews with administrators involved with joint-degree programs at institutions nationwide. These semi-structured interviews took place via phone and lasted between one and two hours, covering topics such as the administrator's role and responsibilities, the scope of the program, language testing and admissions policies, labor practices, course equivalencies, and problems experienced (appendix

11.A). In total, six interviews were conducted, transcribed, and then coded for emerging themes. In the section that follows, we present findings from both the survey of program websites and the semi-structured interviews. These findings address our stated questions of how joint-degree programs (1) facilitate international student mobility, (2) increase and improve the globalization of IHEs, and (3) ultimately push back against nationalist tendencies.

A SPECTRUM OF CROSS-BORDER PARTNERSHIPS

In the course of our data collection, we came to see joint-degree programs as one option in a spectrum of international partnerships, which vary in how tightly interconnected the two institutions are—or in other words, how much control the delivering institution (in these partnerships, the US institution) has over the flow of students. As Martins (2015) notes, it is the delivering institution which occupies the privileged position, and whose "pedagogical and curricular ideologies, administrative structures, and often labor and workplace practices" are the ones typically adhered to in the partnership (4).

Figure 11.1 represents the range of pathways for Chinese students entering US institutions that emerged in our survey. On one end is the branch campus, in which US institutions establish a satellite campus in China, and at the other end of the spectrum, third-party recruitment firms assist students in identifying international programs on an individual or group basis, sometimes under contract with US institutions. In the middle, the consortium model represents formal agreements among multiple IHEs, which allow students to select from a variety of partners to complete courses within their program of study. Each of these arrangements presents unique practical and ideological challenges, raising complex issues around admission standards, language testing, curricular adaptations, allocation of resources, and academic support for international students once they arrive on campus (see, for example, Ehlers-Zavala, Didier, and Berry 2017; Jordan and Jensen 2017). Our emphasis in this chapter is on the middle range of this spectrum: joint-degree programs often referred to as 4+0, 3+1, or 2+2 programs. These numbers represent the years of study completed at each institution. In the 4+0 model, all four years of study are completed in China, typically with upper-level courses taught by visiting faculty from the US institution. In the more common 3+1 and 2+2 models, students complete the first two or three years of study in China and finish their studies in their senior year (or junior and senior years) at the US institution.

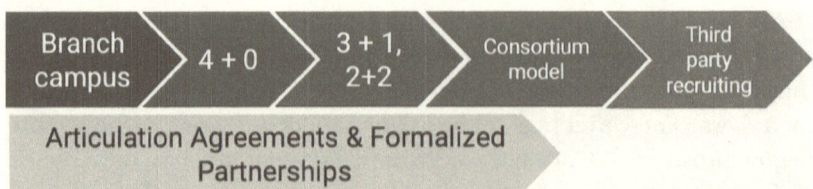

Figure 11.1. Spectrum of Joint-Degree Program Models.

JOINT-DEGREE PROGRAMS: A RECENT SNAPSHOT

As part of our research, we conducted a survey of joint-degree program information published on IHE websites. While it is impossible to determine the exact number of existing programs, in part due to diversity of program types and frequent cancellation (Obst and Kuder 2012), we aimed to capture a reasonable "snapshot" of the landscape of joint-degree programs available in the summer of 2019.

Although these data points are limited to institutionally self-advertised programs, the findings are informative in providing a general understanding of the number of programs, their recent growth trends, and the primary disciplines of focus. In total, 494 individual Chinese-US joint-degree programs were identified, with some institutions involved in multiple separate programs and partnerships. There were 72 identified as belonging to consortiums, and the remaining 422 that were identified as institutional partnership joint-degree programs (i.e., 3+1, 2+2, etc.) were the focus of our analysis.[1] There was a wide range of program arrangements identified, with some iterations that go beyond four or five years of study and include graduate degree programs. The most frequent construction is the 2+2 model (two years in China, then two years in the US); we identified 164 programs following this curriculum design. Other common models include 3+1 (69 programs), 1+2+1 (58 programs), 3+2 (50 programs), 2+2+1 (40 programs), and 3+1+1 (24 programs). Figure 11.2 provides a geographical breakdown of where these programs (including those in the consortiums) are concentrated. As depicted, there are programs represented across the continental US, with noted concentrations in both the Northeast and Midwest. Of the programs identified, 250 reported the date or year of program inception. Figure 11.3 presents this data, and clearly shows an upward growth trend with a significant increase in the number of new programs forged in the last four years. Analysis of the academic disciplines of these programs identified the five top area disciplines: (1) business/finance, (2) engineering, (3) physical and life sciences, (4) humanities and social

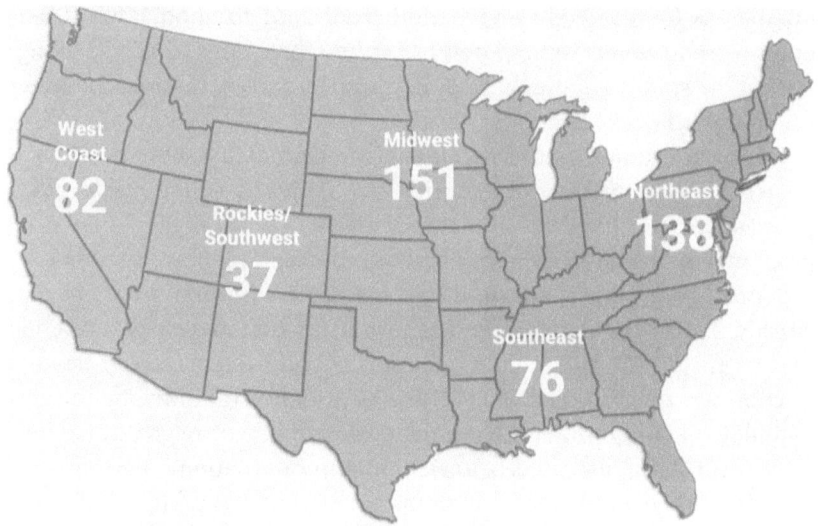

Figure 11.2. Distribution of Joint-Degree Programs in US.

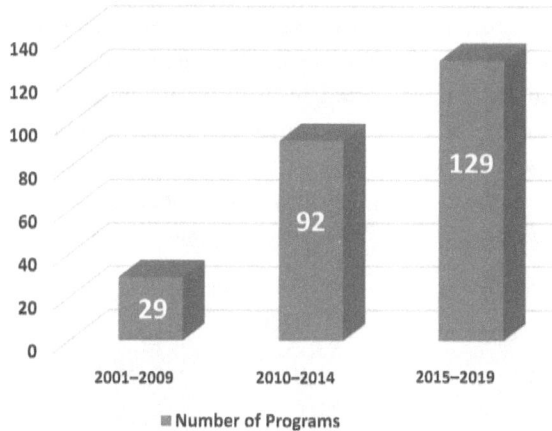

Figure 11.3. Reported Joint-Degree Program Inception by Year.

sciences, and (5) computer and data sciences. Business and finance programs were by far the most numerous, with 143 programs of study identified.

These data depict overall trends in joint-degree program development and growth. In particular, figure 11.3 demonstrates that joint-degree programs experienced significant growth from 2016 to 2019. We identified twenty-nine new programs that began in 2019—the same number as for the eight-year period from 2001 to 2009. This recent upward trend suggests the potential of these programs to persist alongside or in spite of nationalist policy and increased tensions between China and the US.

A further example of this potential has emerged in light of pandemic-related restrictions on travel worldwide. Typically, Chinese education policy does not allow for the US instruction portion of joint-degree programs to be conducted online, yet according to follow-up interviews with two of our participants in the spring of 2020, several programs had already obtained exception and approval for the 2021–2022 academic year to ensure the programs would persist and students would be able to continue their studies. We see this as evidence that investment in a joint-degree program, and the relationships built in negotiating their terms (as will be discussed below), can help international partnerships to withstand changing global circumstances as well as political fallout.

PRACTICAL CONCERNS

While this data is cause for hope, the existence of a program on a university's website does not necessarily indicate that the program has either been successful in moving students physically across borders, has been sustained over time, or has accomplished its stated goals: more globalized experiences for students or expanded international connections and presence. In the following section, we turn to data from qualitative interviews to explore a few of the key challenges that emerged as considerations in effective implementation and fulfilment of program objectives: accreditation, articulation agreements, and language assessment.

Accreditation and articulation agreements

China has a national educational system; the state-run Chinese Ministry of Education evaluates, regulates, and approves all joint-degree programs associated with a Chinese institution ("What We Do" 2018). However, their oversight is restricted to the regulation of the Chinese institution alone and not the US partner. In contrast, IHEs in the US are accredited through regional accreditation agencies (e.g., Middle State Commission on Higher Education in the eastern US). The US IHEs must also account for the standards of joint-degree program implementation and administration, yet again, the oversight only applies to the one partner school, with no jurisdiction over the partnering Chinese institution. As Hou and coauthors (2016) found between IHEs in Europe and East

Asia as well as between the US and China, there are three key challenges in engaging international institutions with different accreditation procedures: (1) like many East Asian countries, China stipulates national regulations for joint-degree programs, yet (2) there are no accreditation agencies mediating between the government and individual institutions, and thus (3) the adoption of international accreditation raises the complex issue of national jurisdiction over higher education.

A primary challenge of assuring quality implementation is that national and regional oversight is conducted independently within each nation. Academic programs in the United States must adhere to stringent accreditation guidelines. The same is true of programs within China that are overseen by the PRC Ministry of Education. However, joint-degree programs exist in a challenging in-between space where the two regulatory systems may be at odds with one another, and there is not an international accreditation or oversight body. It is left up to the institutions and the program directors to navigate this in-between space. Finding a successful balance in between these two systems has become even more challenging as measures put in place by the PRC Ministry of Education to tighten academic censorship directly impact how joint-degree programs teach about China and address specific topics within their curriculum (Gueorguiev et al. 2020).

One scenario reported in the semi-structured interviews provides an example of the challenges faced by institutions as they navigate this in-between space and have to take on the added responsibility of ensuring their programs adhere to both Chinese and US standards. In one case, a program amendment was developed and fully vetted by the Chinese Ministry of Education but did not comply with the US accreditation agency standards. More specifically, this amendment would have allowed students to matriculate into their senior year at the US institution without demonstrating English-language proficiency, as long as the students had maintained a 3.0 GPA in years one through three of their Chinese coursework. The amendment was made in year four of an extant 3+1 program prior to the first cohort of students arriving at the US school. This amendment was approved by the Chinese Ministry of Education and then a new Memorandum of Understanding (MOU) was signed into practice by both partnering institutions—without consulting the ESL specialists or accreditation officers at the US institution (as regularly happens with such programs; see Jordan and Jenson 2017). However, the details of the amendment were in conflict with several requirements of the US institution's accrediting body, including the standard on recruitment that stipulates admission criteria be established between partnering institutions prior to student enrollment. When seven students from the cohort arrived at the US institution unprepared to successfully study in English, creating an administrative mess, ultimately multiple accommodations had to be made to assist them.

This example illustrates both the challenges and importance of articulation agreements or MOUs in these formalized joint-degree partnerships. Chinese national education policy, as well as most US accreditation boards, requires written agreements in order to create and implement joint-degree programs. These MOUs serve an important role in not just formalizing partnerships but also outlining the specific practices or policies each institution must follow to adhere to national accreditation or education policy. In addition to the example above, there were multiple accounts in the interview data of problems that could have easily been avoided if written agreements had been carefully crafted in consultation with all parties. Several participants specifically emphasized the necessity of consulting ESL faculty or professionals in the development of the agreement.

One rich potential of the process of developing MOUs is that as representatives from international institutions work together toward common program goals and outcomes, they learn from each other. Administrators setting up and managing joint-degree programs must navigate two very different educational systems and unique accreditation requirements, articulate the differences and commonalities of the two systems, and then weave them together into one coherent program. In the process, the US IHE leaders and faculty working in these programs gain a more in-depth understanding of Chinese educational policy, how the Ministry of Education operates, and many of the key differences between the Chinese and US higher education systems (and the inverse may be true for faculty and administrators on the Chinese side). It is precisely this need to negotiate two dueling independent-oversight systems, which represent nationally articulated ideas and values, that generates the potential for joint-degree programs to counter traditional nationalist practices and policies. As administrators must learn to recognize and articulate differences and commonalities, they forge new understandings of each other. As one of our participants noted, "I think . . . it's not just what you've written in the contract, it's the relationship you have and how well you're really understanding each other on both ends."

However, much of this learning occurs through trial and error without explicit training in intercultural communication or multilingual pedagogy prior to involvement and engagement in the program. In particular, as the literature on cross-border partnerships suggests, the preparation of writing faculty to teach multilingual students, especially international students, is left out entirely of the planning and MOUs (see, for example, Jordan and Jensen 2017; Smith and DeJoy 2017). One of our participants commented that "there hasn't been enough training of 'normal' faculty for how to deal with these increased numbers of international students at the institution." Both our own data and the literature point to the necessity for building faculty development into the MOU itself, ideally before or at least co-occurring with the program's implementation. To sustain a cross-border partnership that promotes truly global education, "student recruitment and faculty support should go hand in hand," and that support should come directly from the increased revenue international students provide (Pelaez-Morales 2017, 245).

Language Assessment

Language is an obvious hinge point in the successful implementation of joint-degree programs, because Chinese students enrolled in these programs learn through their first language (Chinese) as well as their second, or tertiary, language (English). Yet challenges associated with language assessment, placement, and curriculum are frequently overlooked when partnerships are formed. As observed by one participant, "ESL is largely unthought of when the higher administrators are putting these programs together . . . had I not asserted myself in the beginning and got involved with some of this, I don't think we'd be looking at the ESL component so carefully." Even among administrators who are well-intentioned and reasonably informed, there may be a somewhat less than nuanced understanding of the complex linguistic and cultural issues involved in crossing between borders (Fraiberg, Wang, and You 2017), as the use of the term *ESL component* here suggests.

In our interview data, language assessment emerged as a consistent concern across contexts. A common theme that arose affirmed that programs must have measures in place to ensure students have the language skills necessary to be successful in their program of study and appropriate support to navigate both the Chinese and US educational systems. In many cases, language assessment and support resources were adopted as afterthoughts and not part of the initial joint-degree program design. In other instances, where language proficiency was addressed in the program design, ESL experts were not consulted, or exceptional policies were implemented to accommodate students in the program without evident consideration of how English-language proficiency impacts student success as they transition to the US institution.

In the example given above, the amendment made to the 3+1 program waived any English-language assessment requirement for students with a 3.0 GPA at the end of their junior year. On the surface, from an administrative perspective, this seemed a viable policy, as GPA is indicative of successful student performance; however, as the first three years of coursework are exclusively in Chinese, hypothetically this policy would allow a Chinese monolingual student to matriculate into the fourth year of the program at the US institution. While this is an extreme example, it highlights the recurring theme of many institutions not consulting or considering the impact of English-language training and support on the success of students' academic achievement as they transition to the US.

Interview participants reported that although the typical practice of most programs is to require either an in-house language assessment or third-party test as a measure of proficiency, there is great variance in how this is done. There is a tendency for institutions to find alternatives to the traditional IELTS or TOEFL exams and to instead either implement individual in-house assessments or alternative evaluations. Another participant highlighted a key challenge with one of the program administrator–designated assessments, a commercial language instruction program called Duolingo:

> I do know from colleagues [who] . . . adopted Duolingo without speaking with the ESL specialists on the campus . . . there's some false positives, in the sense of students seem to be English-ready and they get to campus: Whoa. It's really different from what the campus had expected [. . .] we have found no correlation between their Duolingo scores and their scores on the Michigan or other proficiency test . . . It's all over the place.

In other words, Duolingo as an assessment instrument provides a score, but often with minimal equivalency to actual student performance or skill level in the classroom. Multiple participants suggested that a best practice for language assessment in joint-degree programs is to implement a combination of in-house classroom-related outcome-based assessments and to establish benchmarking or language-proficiency measures, indicating that the US institution also needs to be closely involved in the administration of the in-house assessment.

DISCUSSION

The steady increase in the number of international joint-degree programs over the past decade, and the many complex challenges that accompany them, make it imperative that writing and language educators understand the scope and nature of these programs in order to become effectively involved early on in their implementation. By facilitating student mobility, these programs can (but do not always) serve the institutional goals of increased globalization on domestic campuses and expanded international presence.

We argue that joint-degree programs therefore have the potential to push back against isolationist tendencies in higher education in at least three key ways. First, the formation of these programs requires the development of formalized partnerships and agreements between US and Chinese institutions, which may withstand nationalistic political trends. Second, negotiating these formalized agreements requires senior leadership to understand the partnering institution's educational system, beliefs, and practices, building cross-cultural awareness. When faculty and staff are integrated in the development and implementation of such programs, as is vital to effective management (Jordan and Jensen 2017), this effect has the potential to permeate all levels. Third, the purpose of these programs is to create an academic environment that prepares students for success in their profession in two cultures. The students graduate with a degree from both institutions, an in-depth understanding of their area of study in two separate cultural contexts, and the credentials and expertise to function professionally in both societies—all opportunities for (though not a guarantee of) cosmopolitan perspectives (You 2016). For joint-degree programs to sustain over time and be successful in navigating a fraught political climate, IHEs, administrators, and language educators have to fully understand the key challenges and pitfalls so they can implement these programs effectively.

In contrast to other forms of study abroad or international recruitment programming, joint-degree programs require representatives from both institutions to collaborate in outlining objectives, designing curriculum, training and managing program faculty, and administering the programs overall. Because such partnerships rarely form without the direct leadership of a dean, provost, or president at the US institution and the equivalent leadership at the Chinese institution, these programs necessitate cooperation and communication from key faculty in the program discipline as well as senior leadership. The relationship-building and effort required from upper administration can promote a deeper institutional commitment to supporting these programs and adapting to ensure their success.

Effective implementation demands that institutions navigate differences in educational culture and expectations between the US and China broadly, as well as set up specific, clearly defined plans for administrative processes around admission, language testing, curricular equivalencies, and teacher training. If that is done, these partnerships have deep potential to counteract nationalist and isolationist policies by providing a smooth and stable pathway for Chinese students into the United States, which in turn creates the possibility for all of the students (and faculty) in those institutions to confront and grapple with the realities of globalization in a daily, personal way.

Whether the process is rough and challenging or smooth and methodical, these programs open up the possibilities for IHEs to embody their objective of globalization. Students should, in theory, graduate with credentials that will qualify them to enter the workforce in the US or China, and have educational and social experiences that prepare them for globalized workplaces in either context. As Culver and colleagues (2012) observed, the primary student gains for at least some students in European exchanges are personal rather than professional. While this potential positive impact exists for every individual student that moves through a joint-degree program, it is also important to recognize that it is common for Chinese students in the US, especially where campuses are unprepared to offer academic or social support, to exist primarily in enclaves, in part in order to support each other through *guanxi* networks (Fraiberg, Wang, and You 2017). Further, the current political climate has left many students feeling that their international degree positions them in an in-between space where their credentials are not desired by either the US or China (Feng 2020). Being cognizant of, and working to break down, these barriers to create truly immersive cross-cultural experiences is incumbent not on the students themselves but on the institutions that admit them and profit on their presence, financially and in self-promotion. This is ethical not only on behalf of the individual students but also for creating a new generation of graduates who are active protagonists for continued globalization and counterisolationist ideologies.

CONCLUSION

Joint-degree programs are far from a panacea for nationalist and isolationist policies; however, they do provide one pathway for combating the negative effects of such ideologies. The challenges identified in this study have been consistent across programs and institutions over time, although the context of these challenges has evolved, in particular through the COVID-19 pandemic. While finances are typically the primary driving factor for IHEs to institute such programs, the deep partnerships and institutional relationships forged in the process result in a greater potential resiliency for joint-degree programs to continue in the face of increased nationalism. The last decade has witnessed growth in the inception of joint-degree programs, suggesting that this trend has had success in surviving the increasingly contentious political climate between the US and China. While the COVID-19 pandemic may have a negative impact on the inception and growth of joint-degree programs in the near future, our findings speak to the resiliency of such programs to persist. With a methodical and informed approach that includes the guidance of language specialists, there is great potential for joint-degree programs to continue to grow and enhance the international educational landscape in this era of nationalism.

APPENDIX 11.A

Semi-Structured Interview Questions

Background information

How many years have you been working at your institution? What is your role there?

What type of Chinese-US partnership do you have at your institution?

When did you first hear about the US-Chinese partnership at your institution? How did you become involved in it?

What is the goal of the partnership as you understand it?

Setup of the program

When did the exchange / joint-degree program begin? How many students did it involve at first?

Do you know who made the first contact / how the program originated?

How has the program changed or expanded since then? How many students are involved currently?

Administration

Who is responsible for administering the program?

Who is able to make decisions about the program / give approval for changes?

Are those people compensated specifically for this work?

Language testing

How do students prove English proficiency? i.e., do you require language testing such as the TOEFL or IELTS, or in-house testing?

What is the policy for students who do not meet the language proficiency requirements?

Are there any other prerequisites or requirements for students entering the program?

Overseas courses

Have any of your institution's classes been "moved" to the Chinese partner university?

Who teaches those courses? Who oversees those courses?

Are they equivalent to courses at your institution? How is equivalency assured?

Orientation

Do the students in this program attend new student orientations, or international student orientations, or is there a special orientation for them?

Are there any efforts or programs to integrate these students into the campus community?

Concerns/problems

What concerns do you have about the administration of the program?

What (other) practical problems have you run into with the program?

How have those issues been resolved?

Support

Have you noticed any impact from this program on your campus generally?

Has this program changed/expanded the support provided for multilingual students on your campus? For example, has this program resulted in new courses, new faculty hires, or impacted the writing center or other support services?

Future

If you could give advice to someone embarking on a program like this, what would it be?

What do you think will happen with the program in the future?

What changes (if any) would you like to see to the program?

NOTE

1. Many attributes for specific programs were not listed or readily available, and as such, the breakdown of program characteristics does not equal the total number.

REFERENCES

Asgaray, N., and M. A. Robbert. 2010. "A Cost-Benefit Analysis of an International Dual Degree Programme." *Journal of Higher Education Policy and Management* 32 (3), 317–25.

Critchfield, H. 2019. "ASU Joins 15 Other Universities in Closing Confucius Institute." *Phoenix New Times*, August 23, 2019. https://www.phoenixnewtimes.com/news/asu-joins-15-other-universities-in-closing-confucius-institute-11348296.

Culver, S., K. Puri, G. Spinelli, K. DePauw, and J. Dooley. 2012. "Collaborative Dual-Degree Programs and Value Added for Students: Lessons Learned through the Evaluate E-project." *Journal of Studies in International Education* 16 (1), 40–61.

DeJoy, N., and B. Q. Smith. 2017. *Collaborations and Innovations: Supporting Multilingual Writers across Campus Units*. Ann Arbor: University of Michigan Press.

Donahue, C. 2018. "Writing Program Administration in an Internationalizing Future." In Rose and Weiser, *Internationalization of US Writing Programs*, 21–43.

Ehlers-Zavala, F. P., J. C. Didier, and N. Berry. 2017. "Preparing Graduates for a Global World: The Transformative Power of a Public-Private Joint Venture in the Internationalization of a Large US Public University." In DeJoy and Smith, *Collaborations and Innovations*, 17–38.

Feng, Z. 2020. "Being a Chinese Student in the US: 'Neither the US nor China Wants Us.'" *BBC News*, August 4, 2020. https://www.bbc.com/news/world-us-canada-53573289.

Fraiberg, S., X. Wang, and X. You. 2017. *Inventing the World Grant University: Chinese International Students' Mobilities, Literacies, and Identities*. Boulder: University Press of Colorado.

Gass, S., and P. Walters. 2017. "Challenges and Opportunities in Preparing English Language Learners for the University Environment." In DeJoy and Smith, *Collaborations and Innovations*, 58–74.

Gueorguiev, D. D., X. Lü, K. Ratigan, M. Rithmire, and R. Truex. 2020. "How to Teach China This Fall." *ChinaFile*, August 20, 2020. https://www.chinafile.com/reporting-opinion/viewpoint/how-teach-china-fall.

Haan, J. E. 2018. "Developing Faculty for the Multilingual Writing Classroom." In Rose and Weiser, *Internationalization of US Writing Programs*, 216–33.

Hou, Y. C., M. Ince, S. Tsai, W. Wang, V. Hung, C. Lin Jiang, and K. H. J. Chen. 2016. "Quality Assurance of Joint Degree Programs from the Perspective of Quality Assurance Agencies: Experience in East Asia." *Higher Education Research & Development* 35 (3): 473–87.

Jones, J. M. 2020. "Fewer in U.S. Regard China Favorably or as Leading Economy." *Gallup*, March 2, 2020. https://news.gallup.com/poll/287108/fewer-regard-china-favorably-leading-economy.aspx.

Jordan, J., and E. Jensen. 2017. "Writing Programs, Student Support, and Privatizing International Recruitment." In DeJoy and Smith, *Collaborations and Innovations*, 39–57.

Knight, J. 2009. "Double and Joint-Degree Programs." *International Higher Education*, no. 55, 55–56.

Martins, D. 2015a. "Transnational Writing Program Administration: An Introduction." In Martins, *Transnational Writing Program Administration*, 1–20.

Martins, D. 2015b. *Transnational Writing Program Administration*. Logan: Utah State University Press.

Meier, J., Y. Choi, and E. Cushman. 2017. "Creating Inclusive Classrooms and Teaching Communities." In DeJoy and Smith, *Collaborations and Innovations: Supporting Multilingual Writers Across Campus Units*, 95–118.

Michael, S. O., and L. Balraj. 2003. "Higher Education Institutional Collaborations: An Analysis of Models of Joint Degree Programs." *Journal of Higher Education Policy and Management* 25 (2): 131–45.

Obst, D., and M. Kuder. 2012. "International Joint and Double-Degree Programs." *International Higher Education*, no. 66, 5-7.

Open Doors. 2020. *Open Doors 2020 Report on International Educational Exchange*. Institute of International Education. https://opendoorsdata.org/annual-release/.

Pelaez-Morales, C. 2017. "Internationalization from the Bottom Up: Writing Faculty's Response to the Presence of Multilingual Writers." In Rose and Weiser, *Internationalization of US Writing Programs*, 234–54.

Redden, E. 2019. "China Issues Warning to U.S. Bound Students." *Inside Higher Ed*, June 4, 2019. https://www.insidehighered.com/news/2019/06/04/chinese-officials-warn-students-visa-problems-if-they-come-us.

Rose, S. K., and I. Weiser. 2018. *The Internationalization of US Writing Programs*. Logan: Utah State University Press.

Shapiro, S., and M. Siczek. 2017. "Strategic Content: How Globally Oriented Writing Courses Can Bridge Pedagogical and Political Spaces." In DeJoy and Smith, *Collaborations and Innovations*, 167–86.

Tardy, C. 2015. "Discourses of Internationalization and Diversity in US Universities and Writing Programs." In Martins, *Transnational Writing Program Administration*, 243–64.

Tessler, H., M. Choi, and G. Kao. 2020. "The Anxiety of Being Asian American: Hate Crimes and Negative Biases during the COVID-19 Pandemic." *American Journal of Criminal Justice*, no. 45, 636–46. https://doi.org/10.1007/s12103-020-09541-5.

Wang, V, and A. Qin. 2020. "As Coronavirus Fades in China, Nationalism and Xenophobia Flare." *New York Times*, April 16, 2020.

Weber, A. S, K. Golkowska, I. Miier, R. Sharkey, M. A. Rishel, and A. Watts. 2015. "The First-Year Writing Seminar Program at Weill Cornell Medical College-Qatar: Balancing Tradition, Culture, and Innovation in Transnational Writing Instruction." In Martins, *Transnational Writing Program Administration*, 72–92.

Weiser, I., and S. K. Rose. 2018. "Introduction: Internationalized Writing Programs in the Twenty-First Century United States: Implications and Opportunities." In Rose and Weiser, *Internationalization of US Writing Programs*, 3–20.

Wetzel, D. Z., and D. W. Reynolds. 2015. "Adaptation across Space and Time: Revealing Pedagogical Assumptions." In Martins, *Transnational Writing Program Administration*, 93–116.

"What We Do." 2018. Ministry of Education, People's Republic of China. http://en.moe.gov.cn/about_MOE/what_we_do.

Yang, D. T. 2016. *The Pursuit of the Chinese Dream in America*. Lanham, MD: Lexington Books.

Yang, L. 2020. "Coronavirus News: NYPD Report Shows Bias Crimes against Asian Americans on the Rise." *ABC News*, May 5, 2020. https://abc7ny.com/bias-crimes-coronavirus-chinatown-covid-19/6151239/.

Yoon-Hendricks, A. 2018. "Visa Restrictions for Chinese Students Alarm Academia." *New York Times*, July 25, 2018. https://www.nytimes.com/2018/07/25/us/politics/visa-restrictions-chinese-students.html.

You, Xiaoye. 2016. *Cosmopolitan English and Transliteracy*. Carbondale: Southern Illinois University Press.

AFTERWORD

Kate Vieira

I am so grateful for this volume's existence. I am grateful for its collaborative energy and for its moral vision, for its creation of knowledge that intervenes in the world. It's an honor to offer some brief closing thoughts.

These chapters turn our attention to some of the most pressing problems in "writing education across borders" today: racism, economic inequities, isolationism, walls. Each chapter does so not only by engaging in rigorous critical analysis of a particular phenomenon but also—and this part is important, especially right now—by undergirding these analyses with a broader theoretical and political vision of how things could be better. Put another way, this volume represents work that is simultaneously scientific and creative, clear-sighted and idealistic. The chapters are researched with rigor. And they are shot through with hope. In this way, this volume gives us—gives *me*—a foundation from which to dream.

For example: Keith Gilyard's incisive and pedagogically urgent rhetorical analyses of white-nationalist logics. Amy Wan's archival revelations of how racialized migration policies have shaped language policing in higher ed. Tony Scott's qualitative analysis of the relationship between the material conditions of adjunct professors and how writing gets taught. Rebecca Lorimer Leonard's social scientific tracking of how assimilationist language ideologies can fragment the experiences of racialized writers, and how in community one can also write one's way whole. These authors bring robust methodological traditions to bear on the crucial issues of how people learn, live, and write in unjust circumstances. With hard-won precision, these chapters outline how we can collectively do better.

Researched with rigor. Shot through with hope.

Consider, too, the nuance with which the scholars in this volume attend to *both* the larger structural violence of racism and colonization *and* the everyday rhetorical practices through which people resist it. In this way, Florianne Jimenez Perzan analyzes the "corrected" essays of students in American schools in the colonial Philippines to show *both* how "literacy adheres to vectors of inequality," a stunning insight, *and* how students find ways to speak their and their community's truths. In this way, Sara Alvarez keeps a sharp eye *both* on racializing and racist migration policies *and* how the undocumented activist with whom she works dynamically writes across genres, institutions, languages, and migration histories to shape a political movement.

Researched with rigor. Shot through with hope.

Speaking of hope, I am grateful for the chapters in this book that do the heavy lifting of examining international pedagogical initiatives that seek to combat the isolationism Martins describes in his introduction. These programs were designed to humanize migration experiences (Miron), unravel US isolationist tendencies (Aksakalova and Chatterji), develop cosmopolitan perspectives (Hanson), and respond institutionally to xenophobia (Schreiber and Bluemel). What beautiful and urgent pedagogical goals. *This* is what education is about. Of course, these authors point out the many ways in which these initiatives are imperfect. But what a gift to follow their analyses to learn how these programs could rise to their antiracist and anti-isolationist potential. As Miron's chapter emphasizes, lives are at stake.

Researched with rigor. Shot through with hope.

I am glad to be in the company of the chapters of this book, researched with rigor, shot through with hope, which at its very best is what I believe academic work does. To be honest, I am also simply glad to be in company. It is October 2020 as of this writing. These months have been long and lonely. As winter sets in here in Wisconsin, as the pandemic continues to rage, it appears they will be longer and lonelier still.

Which brings me to one final thought on community. Literate meaning is made dialogically, which means that you, readers of this book, are engaged in the process of knowledge creation alongside the writers of it. Thank you, writers and readers, for meeting here. Thank you for your belief that the work of knowledge creation is just that—creation—a creation that we must will into being together, with all the force and rumble of our diverse perspectives and backgrounds and dreams.

Collectively these chapters ask: What is the role of writing at a moment of trauma, in which racial and class inequities are exacerbated? How can scholars and educators address the punishing material realities in which human bodies—racialized bodies, moving bodies, bodies that need food to survive, bodies that are medically vulnerable—are implicated? And what is the potential of new collaborations in this context?

Collectively, we are charged with answering.

INDEX

Page numbers followed by *f* indicate figures. Page numbers followed by *t* indicate tables.

academic writing, 79, 82, 109, 115, 123, 124, 190; white gaze of, 112
accreditation, 195, 204–7
activism, 28, 117, 144; political, 124; undocumented, 114–15, 216
administration, 73, 199, 209, 211; civic, 54; writing, 8, 70
Aksakalova, Olga, 11, 12, 145, 154, 166, 176, 189
Alexander, Jonathan, 131
Allarey, Macaria, 59, 60, 62, 63–64; education and, 51, 61
alt-right, 9, 22
Alvarez, Sara P., 11, 102, 117, 118, 146, 216; community-engaged writing and, 92–93; nationalism/isolationism and, 142
"America First," 4, 5
American Nazi Party (ANP), 29*n3*
Angell Treaty (1880), 46*n1*
anti-American sentiment, 12, 198
anti-Asian sentiment, 9, 32
anti-immigration, 113, 141
antiracism, 6, 7, 216; global university and, 44–46
Appiah, Kwame Anthony, 25, 28
appropriateness, 44, 112, 119
argumentation, 9; "academic," 122; white-gazed, 120
Article 370 (Indian Constitution), repeal of, 164
Asian American Political Alliance, 25
Asian Americans, citizenship and, 38
assessments, 8, 12, 72–73, 195; educational, 112; in-house, 208; language, 204, 207–8
assimilation, 44, 45, 54, 96, 119, 215; chosen/forced, 97–99
Atlanta, 116; race riot in, 23
attitudes: cosmopolitan, 183, 189, 190; practices and, 182
awareness, 190; critical, 90–91, 93, 95, 96, 99, 101; cross-cultural, 209; cultural, 187; language, 94, 95; literacy, 11, 90; metalinguistic, 90; multilingual, 90; translingual, 90
Azavedo, Suhaile, 158, 162

Baldwin, James, 21, 26
Baratta, Phil, 9
Barrows, David, 57, 59, 60
Beck, Ulrich: cosmopolitanism and, 172
behavior, 45, 173, 174; ethical, 145; prejudiced, 165; social, 162; textual, 189
Behner, Frederick G., 51
Bell, Bernard, 23
Bell, Derrick, 27, 28
Benda, Jonathan, 74, 75
Beveridge, Albert: Philippines and, 55–56
bias, 45, 188; nurturing, 160; racial, 46
biography, 181, 186; cross-cultural, 182; educational, 182, 185
Biostatistics, 31
Birth of a Nation, The (movie), 24
Black nationalism, 9, 20, 24, 26–27; ideologies of, 23
Black Panther (movie), 24, 25
Black Panther Party for Self-Defense, 25
Black people, 39, 50, 56; exploitation/disappearance of, 21, 24; white power structure and, 23
Blommaert, Jan, 82
Boggs, Abigail, 34
border-crossing, viii, 82, 129
border issues, 132–33; learning about, 144
Border Patrol, 129, 133, 136, 139, 145, 147*n7*; "Chase and Scatter" technique of, 132; checkpoint of, 137; drug cartels and, 140; infrastructure of, 140
borders, 163; construction of, 154, 156; cultural, 164, 188; geographic, 188; linguistic, 164, 183, 188; national, 6, 25, 108, 157, 172; political, 6; socioeconomic, 154
Brandt, Deborah, 107–8, 109, 122; literacy research and, 10
Brasseur, Lee E., 133
Brewer, Pam Estes, 174

Brexit, 3
Brier, Stephen, 34
Brown Berets, 25
Burke, Kenneth, 22
Byram, Michael, 173, 174, 175

Canagarajah, Suresh, 69, 155, 172
capitalism, 34, 146
Carnegie Corporation, 43
CCCC, 9, 91
Center for Civic Engagement and Service Learning (UMass Amherst), 91
Chatterji, Tuli, 145, 154, 166, 176, 189; case study by, 167
Chiang, Yuet-Sim D., 91
Chinese, 39, 53, 208; dominant image of, 43; LGBTQ, 102
Chinese characters, 106–7
Chinese Exclusion Act (1882), 5, 46
Chinese students, 180, 193–94, 199, 207; influx of, 198; pathways for, 201, 210; in US institutions, 197–98
citizenship, 26, 36, 38, 52, 74, 117; cosmopolitanism and, 173; cultivation of, 32; documentation of, 100; exclusionary function of, 123; global, 31, 155; literacy and, 109, 111, 122; racialized, 112–14; white gaze and, 114, 122
civilization, 22, 50, 54, 56
civil rights movement, 27
class, 51, 53, 64, 154; difference, 4; hierarchy, 10
Clay, Phillip, 100
coding, 94, 201; axial, 93; process, 93, 95f; qualitative data analysis, 93; thematic, 51; values, 93; in vivo, 93
COIL. *See* Collaborative Online International Learning
Cold War, 36, 40
collaboration, 11, 54, 89, 152, 155, 156–57, 160, 189–90, 198, 217; activities supporting, 178–79; Belgium, 179–80, 188; China, 180–81; international, 12, 167–68, 176, 178; Italy, 181–82, 186, 187; multi-partner, 158; public/academic writing, 93; self-perception of, 191; student responses to, 181–89; Thailand, 181
Collaborative Online International Learning (COIL), 12, 153, 155, 158, 159, 162, 164, 167, 176; case study of, 154, 156–57; community-building and, 165–66; ethos of, 167; Global Commons, 152; methodology of, 156; partnership with, 165; as pedagogical tool, 165–66; practitioners of, 166; theory, 156; virtual exchange, 189

colonialism, 8, 50, 53, 54, 56, 63, 96; individualism and, 60; legacy of, 5; settler, 20, 141
colonization, 50, 51, 53, 55, 59, 216
Columbine school shooting, 180
comic book program, 130, 131–33, 135–36
Commission on Higher Education, 35
Committee on Cross-Cultural Education (Social Science Research Council), 43
communication, 80, 117, 180, 188, 209; business, 152; collaborative, 186, 187; cosmopolitanism and, 172–75; cross-border, 164; cross-cultural, 183; direct, 189–90; intercultural, 146, 152, 171–75, 206; language difference and, 185; online, 160; professional, 171, 172–75, 176, 177, 179, 189; strategies for, 185, 189–90; technical, 131, 171, 176, 189; transnational, 184; virtual, 159
community, 72, 216; building, 153, 156, 160, 165; global, 119; glocal, 152; immigrant, 124, 125; multilingual, 119; nationalism and, 165; projects, 91–93; virtual, 157
composition, 10, 27, 51, 60, 63, 68, 82; L2, 196; oral, 55; teaching, 55
Computer-Assisted Language Learning (CALL), 176
Confucius Institutes, 198
connection, 7, 63; personal, 178; separation and, 93–94; transnational, 11–12
conversations, viii, 20, 31, 64, 75, 76, 90, 92, 95, 101, 114, 165, 183, 186, 188; cyclical, 115; informal, 164; interview, 96, 99; online, 187; real-time, 182, 185
Cooper, Marilyn, 26
cosmopolitanism, 7, 10, 11–12, 20, 81, 89, 90, 145, 152, 153, 164, 183, 184, 186, 187, 188, 190, 196, 199–200, 209, 216; attitudes/practices consistent with, 175t; citizenship and, 173; conception of, 82; descriptions of, 175; dialogical, 172; ethics of, 69; fostering, 171; fundamental meaning of, 173; isolationism and, 189; professional communication and, 172–75; programmatic scaling and, 72–76; theoretical framework of, 171; translingualism and, 68
Council of Writing Program Administrators, 70
COVID-19 pandemic, 3, 67, 82–83, 193, 198, 210, 211; budget cuts and, 47n5
creativity, 122, 155, 197
critical language, 90, 93, 96, 102, 118
critical race theory, 9
cross-border studies, 156–57

cultural bubbles, 160
cultural contexts, 159, 180, 189, 209
cultural difference, 12, 89, 172, 174, 178, 179, 185, 187, 189, 195; building on, 183–84
cultural model theory, 172, 178
culture, 166, 167, 179, 182, 187, 188; American, 1–2, 55; Black, 23; differences in, 172; educational, 209; exotic, 40; global, 154; Korean, 118; Latinx/e, 118; learning about, 183; literacy in, 161; national, 172; non-Western, 165; Parsi, 161; target, 178; white, 54
Culver, S. K., 199, 210
curriculum, 8, 23, 72, 73, 74, 110, 166, 195, 196, 205, 207; cosmopolitan, 75; designing, 9, 156, 209; equivalency, 12; evolution of, 75; innovation in, 83; revising, 165; scaling of, 69; secondary/postsecondary, 157; theories/research on, 70

DACA. *See* Deferred Action for Childhood Arrivals
Daily O'Meara, Katherine, 73, 74, 75, 76
Dalrymple, William, 158
Daniel, James Rushing, 9
data, 71, 200, 202, 204, 207; analysis, 89, 94; collection of, 93–95, 94*t*, 109, 114–16, 131, 195; interview, 96, 206; NCES, 76; sciences, 203; survey, 177
Dedeck, Michael, 74
Deferred Action for Childhood Arrivals (DACA), 46*n*2, 106, 110
democracy, 6, 19, 37; cultivation of, 34; higher education and, 35; strengthening, 35, 36
Democratic Party, 19
deportation, 3, 129, 133, 136, 144
Derrida, Jacques, 145
Desert Walk, 137–40, 142
detention centers, 133, 135
development: economic, 37, 40; professional, 12, 73, 75, 151–52, 153, 166, 167; social, 37, 40
Development, Relief and Education for Alien Minors Act (DREAM Act), 107, 114, 124
digital divide, 154
discourse, 46, 60, 70, 79; academic, 160; Black, 50; civic, 129; class, 51; disciplinary, 10; Filipino, 49; immigration, 139, 144, 145; nationalized, 44; political, 19, 23; professional, 71; racialized, 44, 50, 51, 56, 64
discrimination, 33; language, 46; linguistic, 8; race, 43

diversity, 111, 155; cultural, 177, 190; digital, 160; international rhetorics of, 197–98; linguistic, 177, 186–87, 190, 195
double-degree programs, 198
DREAM Act. *See* Development, Relief and Education for Alien Minors Act
drug cartels, fear of, 140, 141, 142
Du Bois, Cora, 37
Du Bois, W. E. B., 23
Duke, David, 23
Duke University, 31–32, 33, 198; DGS at, 45
Duolingo, 208

economic issues, 21, 52, 69, 81, 193; personal/professional, 71
education, 37, 39, 40, 52, 60, 62, 71, 89, 117, 154; bilingual, 112; Catholic, 136; colonial, 9, 49, 50, 54, 56; empire and, 54; ESL, 9; foreign language, 152; formal, 102, 131; global, 196, 207; immigration and, 119; industrial, 56, 57; intercultural, 181; international landscape for, 211; leaders and, 51; literacy, 7, 10, 53, 56, 68; mass, 49, 56–57; place-based, 144; postsecondary, 72; rhetorical, 20; social change and, 61; subpar, 79; systems, 163, 206, 207, 209; translingual, 7; transnational, 200; white-gazed, 108, 122; writing, viii, 7, 8, 9, 11, 50, 53, 69, 72, 75, 76, 81, 109, 110–14, 123, 125, 200. *See also* higher education
"Educational Biographies" project, 181
Eli, 93, 162; articulation of, 101; assimilation and, 98; critical awareness of, 99, 101; literacy and, 95–101, 102
Emergency Quota Act (1921), 46*n1*
empathy, 81, 142, 155, 166, 173
English as a Second Language (ESL), 9, 120, 205, 206, 207, 208; classes, 95–96, 98, 117; students, 97–98
English as an International Language (EIL), viii
English language, 42, 49, 54, 106, 117, 178, 183, 208; academic, 80; British, 186; composing, 119–20; conversational, 55; as foreign language, 176; hegemony of, 155; monolingual conceptualizations of, 122; speaking, 186; standard, 79, 82, 97
English Language Institute (ELI), 41
English Language Learner (ELL), 120
environment, 142; academic, 209; cultural, 159; digital, 160; ethnic, 159; learning, 7, 70; linguistic, 45; professional, 68, 186; social, 159; teaching, 70
equity, 77, 123, 151, 153, 159, 167

ethics, 81, 145, 195
ethnicity, 20, 21, 28, 64, 154, 156, 159; race and, 37
ethnography, 71, 115
experiences: collaboration, 172, 182; cross-cultural, 179, 194, 210; cultural, 188; educational, 182, 210; globalized, 204; immersion, 136–44; literacy, 119, 162; lived, 114; peer-review, 162; social, 210; time-space, 68; travel, 177

Fabricant, Michael, 34
Facebook, 115, 157, 160, 161, 163, 164, 165, 181, 184, 188
fascism, 6, 22, 35
Fee, Mary H., 49, 50, 55
feedback, 55, 120, 162, 166, 179–80, 181, 190
Filipinos, 49, 50, 53, 54, 60, 63; engagement of, 56; fitness of, 55–59
Filipino Teacher's Manual, The, 55, 60
Finkbeiner, Claudia, 181
Flarend, Geneva, 135
Flegenheimer, Matt, 4
flexibility, 166, 199; defined, 173
Flower, Linda, 92
Floyd, George, 4, 46
Ford Foundation, 43
Foreign Language Teaching (FLT), 172, 173
foreign students, 33; described, 36–40; higher education and, 40–44; racialized/othered, 44; space for, 36
fracture, recovery and, 95–101
Fraiberg, Steve: on IHEs, 197
free evening English program (FEEP), 92
Freire, Paulo, 21

Gallagher, Chris, 74
genocide, 157, 161
geography, 167; literacy in, 161; non-Western, 165
geopolitics, 37, 61, 156
GI Bill, higher education and, 34
Gilyard, Keith, 215
Girdharry, Kristi, 74
Global Learning Competency and Digital Ability, 166
Global Learning Core Competency, 156
global university: antiracism and, 44–46; cultivation of, 44
globalization, 4, 6, 171; communication and, 190; objective of, 210; white gaze and, 113
Gowan, Thomas, 57
"Great Divide, The" (Dalrymple), 158

Gries, Laurie, 9
Griffith, D. W., 29n4
guest-worker program, 141
Guth, Sarah, 159

Hanson, Joleen, 11, 12, 145, 146
Hart-Cellar Act (1965), 32
Harvard University, 43
Hasian, Marouf A., Jr., 147n7
Helm, Francesca, 159, 176
Henderson v. Mayor of New York (1875), 46n1
Higgins, Lorraine: community-engaged writing and, 92
higher education, 3, 9, 37, 67–68, 110, 111, 205; Chinese influence on, 198; democracy and, 35; demographics in, 76; expansion of, 9, 34–35, 36; foreign students and, 40–44; homogeneity and, 39; isolationism and, 1, 209; landscape of, 167; nationalist, 40, 44; report on, 36; structure of, 31, 44; support for, 35, 68
Higher Education for American Democracy: A Report of the President's Commission on Higher Education (Commission on Higher Education), 35
history, 27; literacy in, 161; non-Western, 163, 165
Hoang, Haivan, 56, 59
Hope Border Institute, 131, 147n4
Horner, Bruce, 82
Hughes, Langston, 27
humanization, 130, 131, 133, 136–44, 145
human rights, 137, 143

I Wor Kuen, 25
ICC. *See* intercultural communicative competence
identity, 11, 26, 96, 122, 167, 174, 177, 182, 190; Asian, 114, 121; Black, 23; cosmopolitan, 173, 183; cultural, 45, 153; ethnic, 38; expression, 8; family language, 90; Filipino, 58; individual, 90; linguistic, 91, 94; literate, 89, 102; multiple vectors of, 111; racial, 38, 45; white, 21, 26, 52
ideology, 23, 32; colonial, 59; colorblind, 108; counterisolationist, 210; curricular, 201; Filipino elite, 10; isolationist, 8; language, 73, 123; monocultural, 112; monolingual, 97, 112, 162; pedagogical, 201; raciolinguistic, 113; white, 56, 109
IELTS, 208
IHEs. *See* institutions of higher education
ILI. *See* International Language Institute of Massachusetts

immersion programs, 130, 131, 136, 138; lessons from, 141–44
immigrant rights, advocacy for, 115, 117, 125*n1*
immigrant students, 124, 146; literacy experiences of, 119; literacy practices of, 111; multilingual, 123; racialized, 119
immigrants, 98, 100, 109, 124; accompanying, 136–44, 145–46; multilingual, 114; scapegoating of, 21; Spanish-speaking, 118; undocumented, 129
immigration, 25, 100, 111, 114; bans, 3; Chinese, 53; crisis, 143; education and, 119; humanizing, 145; law, 5, 136; literacy and, 109; non-European, 38; reform, 141, 142; undocumented, 11, 140, 144
Immigration Act(s): 1891, 46*n1*; 1907, 46*n1*; 1917, 46*n1*; 1965, 47*n3*
Immigration and Nationality Act (1952), 38
immigration judges, 144, 145
immigration policy, 33, 34, 46*n2*, 47*n3*, 107, 131; complicating, 133; exclusionary, 46*n1*; humanizing, 133; isolationist, 46; national, 45; restrictive, 45
immigration system, complexity of, 133–34, 135
imperialism, viii, 49, 51, 53, 61, 62; white-supremacist, vii
Indian Constitution, Article 370 of, 164
Indigenous peoples, genocidal "education" of, viii
individualism: Anglo-Saxon, 54; colonial rule and, 60; social consciousness and, 59–63; Western, 60
inequality, 50, 61, 62; characterization of, 63; class/race, 54; eradication of, 35; structured, 109
inequity, 63, 69, 90; racial, 33–34; social, 79
injustice, 62, 143, 154
Inoue, Asao B., 9
Institute of International Education, 38
institutions of higher education (IHEs), 193–94, 197, 198, 204–5, 206, 209, 210; globalization of, 201; US/Chinese, 200; websites, 202
Intensive English Program, 92
intercultural communicative competence (ICC), 171–72, 173
International Language Institute of Massachusetts (ILI), 91, 92, 93, 95, 96, 102*n2*, 102*n3*
international students, 32, 37, 39, 43, 194, 195; Chinese, 46*n2*, 47*n6*; conflation of, 33; crisis for, 193; experience of, 44, 45; hostility toward, 31; influx of, 196; less-advantaged, 40; mobility of, 201; non-European, 38; support for, 201
International Virtual Exchange Conference, 151
internationalization, 44, 75, 151, 153, 194, 196
interviews, 96, 143; cross-cultural, 182; data from, 195, 204; follow-up, 115, 204; questions for, 211–12; semi-structured, 200, 201, 205, 211–12
Islamophobia, 163
isolationism, vii, viii, 3, 4, 5, 12, 25, 40, 42, 44, 83, 89, 152, 153, 165, 190, 195, 200, 216; cosmopolitanism and, 189; countering, 6, 157, 210; higher education and, 1, 209; promoting, 172; resistance to, 7, 8

Jim Crow 2.0, 5
Jimenez Perzan, Florianne, 216
Johnson-Reed Act (1924), 46*n1*
joint-degree programs, 196, 197, 202–10; Chinese-American, 12, 194, 195; defining, 198–200; development of, 203, 204; managing, 206; number of, 208–9; regulations on, 205; resiliency for, 211
Jordan, Jay, 195
Jung, Carrie, 110, 111, 116–22; academic writing and, 119, 124; English language/nation and, 120–22; immigrant communities and, 125; language and, 109, 114, 116–17, 120, 121; literacies of, 109, 113, 114; poem by, 106, 107, 115; reflection by, 119–20; Spanish and, 118; transnational students and, 123; writing educators and, 121
justice: linguistic, 45; racial, 8; redistributive, 24; social, 22, 28, 77, 143, 151, 155

King, Martin Luther, Jr., 26
Kino Border Initiative, 141, 143, 145; activism and, 144; binational solidarity and, 146*n2*; desert walk of, 147*n7*; educational materials from, 130; immersion program of, 136, 137; introduction to, 130–31; public pedagogy of, 135, 141, 147*n8*
knowledge, 40; construction of, 153, 161, 215, 216; cultural, 155; deep, 99; experiential, 28; production of, 167; subject-based, 120
Ku Klux Klan, 29*n4*

labor: language, 109; literacy, 108, 109, 122; manual, 57, 58; practices, 70, 200
LaGuardia Community College, 160–65; COIL at, 12, 154–59, 166

landscape, 139, 142, 202; cultural/linguistic, 116; higher education, 167, 211; political, 20, 157, 164; social, 157; sociological, 164
language, 33, 44, 61, 76, 108, 110, 120, 122, 167, 179; academic, 107, 112, 113; critical awareness of, 90–91; cross-border, 11, 89; differences in, 81, 172, 185; educational assessment of, 112; entrenchment of, 56; European, 39, 41; literacy and, 96; moving across, 119; practices, 109, 123; primary, 74; race and, 101; white-gazed, 120
language architecture, 120; concept of, 114; framework, 113; multilingual, 109; term, 125*n*2
Lazere, Donald, 20, 23
learning: embodied, 135, 146*n*1; English-language, 71, 100, 117, 152, 186; global, 153, 154; intercultural, 153; peer-to-peer, 162; postsecondary, 82; service, 92, 145, 179; student, 8, 154
Lee, Eunjeong, 155
legacies: colonial, 9; material, 9; negotiating, 8–10; racial, 9
Leonardo, Jose, 132, 133
Lerner, Neal, 74
Lindbergh, Charles, 4
linguistics, 33, 45, 71, 113
Lippi-Green, Rosina, 173
literacy, 8, 33, 44, 61, 64, 96, 98, 101–2, 120, 123, 145, 146, 162; academic, 97, 108, 109, 119; citizenship and, 109, 111, 122; community-based, 7, 10–11; connecting/fragmenting families and, 99; critical, 90–91, 167; cross-border, 89; cross-cultural, 159; Filipino, 57, 58, 59; fitness/unfitness for, 55–59; as fundamental right, 52; global, 161; health, 131; ideology of, 52–55; immigration and, 109; inequality and, 59; language and, 96; lineage and, 99–101; linguistic, 131; migration and, 100; myth of, 10, 62; nature of, 159; negotiated, 69; politics of, 55; power and, 92, 99; racist enactments of, 100; self-worth and, 100; social change and, 51; social significance of, 91; sociocritical, 90; sociomaterial, 100; transcultural, 153; translingual, 92; transnational, 92; as white property, 50, 52–55
literacy practices, 45, 110, 152, 154, 162, 163; cross-border, 11, 83, 156; multilingual, 11, 109
literacy studies, 52, 89, 91, 107; global turn in, 111, 112; undergraduate, 11

literature, 207; American, 54; British, 54; comparative, 71; English, 71; non-Western, 163; partition, 157, 161
Litman-Navarro, Kevin, 24
Lorimer Leonard, Rebecca, 117, 144, 145, 162, 215
Losh, Elizabeth, 131
Loyola Marymount University, Kino and, 136

Malcolm X, 26
Manifest Destiny, 20
Manila Times, 57, 59, 62, 65*n*4
Manto, Saadat Hasan, 161, 165
Mao Zedong, 185, 186
Marantz, Andrew, 21, 29*n*2
marginalization, 36, 52, 62, 64
Martins, David S., 201, 216
materialism, 42, 81–83
Matsuda, Paul Kei, 33, 41, 73, 74, 75, 76
McCarran-Walter Act (1952), 38
Memorandum of Understanding (MOUs), 205, 206, 207
mestizos, 53, 55, 90
Mexican Americans, citizenship and, 38
Meyerhoff, Eli, 34
Michigan State University, 43
Middle East, students from, 193, 196
Middle State Commission on Higher Education, 204
Migrant: Stories of Hope and Resilience (Kino and Hope), 131, 135, 142; page from, 132*f*, 134*f*
migrants, 132, 137, 138, 143; accompanying, 135; body language of, 135; distress of, 135; drug cartels and, 140; experiences of, 142; fatalities among, 139; immigrants and, 146*n*1; learning about, 130
migration, 36, 110, 116, 130, 131, 138, 141, 155; complicating, 135; humanizing, 135; Latinx, 142; literacy and, 100; political movement and, 216; public pedagogy around, 136; undocumented, 137
Milosz, Czeslaw, 6
Ministry of Education (PRC), 193, 204, 206; MOU with, 205
Miron, Layli Maria, 216; community-engaged writing and, 92–93; public pedagogy and, 102
model minorities, 114, 117, 124
monoculturalism, 33, 124
monolingualism, vii–viii, 1–2, 33, 123, 124, 162, 178, 196
MOUs. *See* Memorandum of Understanding

Muhammad, Elijah, 24, 26, 29*n3*
multiculturalism, 4, 111
multilingual students, 82, 109, 113, 114, 120, 123; writing education and, 110–12
multilingualism, 11, 82, 92, 108, 109, 111, 113, 115, 118, 124, 195–96; racialization of, 114; understanding of, 114
multimodality, 121, 131–33, 135–36, 141, 146*n1*
Mumtaz, Mehr, 131, 136, 137, 140, 142, 147*n8*
Museum of Walking, 142
Muslims, 53; ban on, vii, 3, 46*n2*; Hindus and, 156; Sikhs and, 160

narratives, 25, 26, 27, 98, 136, 142, 158, 165, 197; dominant, 111, 112; family, 157, 160; white-nationalist, 20
Nation of Islam (NOI), 29*n3*
National Center of Education Statistics (NCES), 76
National Council of Teachers of English, 70
National Origins Act (1924), 37, 46*n1*
nationalism, 3, 34, 37, 44, 64, 68, 153, 190, 193, 194, 195, 200, 201; Asian American, 25; countering, 165, 210; defensive, 42, 43; ethnic, 26; focusing on, 63; nonessentialist, 26; progressive, 25; resurgence of, 130, 211. *See also* white nationalism
nationality, 156, 159; law, 5; race and, 5
nativism, 6, 79, 141
naturalization: law, 5, 20; limiting, 5
Naturalization Act (1906), 46*n1*
Nazism, 6, 29*n3*
negotiation, 152, 155; verbal, 185–86
neoliberalism, 67
New Literacies Movement, 152
New York Times, 4, 35, 164
Ngai, Mae M., 38, 43
No More Deaths, 139
Nogales, 129, 130, 136, 137, 141, 147*n8*
Northeastern University, 74, 75, 78; writing programs at, 72

O'Dowd, Robert: COIL and, 152–53
Open Doors, 38, 46*n2*, 197
openness, 166, 172; building on, 183–84
Orwell, George, 20
Other, 39, 145, 146, 159, 161

partition, 12, 154, 156–63; history/literature of, 159, 161, 165
partnerships, 11–12, 83, 209, 210; cross-border, 194, 195, 201, 206; educational, 171, 173, 174, 175, 177, 190, 191; international, 163, 174, 176, 177, 184, 190, 200, 201, 204
pedagogy, 7, 8, 55, 72, 76, 154, 157, 189–90, 196, 199, 200, 216; community-based, 10–11; complicating, 145; cosmopolitan, 159; critical/humanizing, 124; critical language, 90; cross-border, 168; implications for, 165–68; innovative, 83, 197; isolationist, 165; literacy, 153, 167; multilingual, 206; public, 11, 102, 129, 130, 131, 135, 136, 141, 142, 143, 144–46; revising, 75, 165; transborder, 151; transnational, 12, 153; VE, 153; writing, 9, 69, 71
people of color, 20, 52; isolating, 5; marginalization of, 64
Philippine-American War, 61
Philippines, 53, 54, 55, 65*n3*; colonization of, 56; seizure of, 49; writing education in, 50
placement, 12, 74, 79, 195, 207
policies, 46, 200; anti-Chinese, 12, 194–95; colonial, 10; economic, 4, 67–68; education, 196–97, 204, 206; English-only, 42, 196; higher education, 32, 33, 34; language, 32; legacies of, 44; migration, 215, 216; nationalist, 204; racialized, 46*n1*. *See also* immigration policy
politics, 23, 52, 54, 55, 193, 209, 210; of eternity, 6; of inevitability, 6; nationalist, 89
populism, 3, 152
precarity, 69, 81–83
Prendergast, Catherine, 52, 59, 97
Prevention through Deterrence, 129, 137
Professional Communication and Emerging Media (PCEM), 177
proficiency, English-language, 205, 207–8
programs, 74; implications for, 165–68; setup of, 211
Puerto Ricans, 25, 39

quotas, immigration, 32, 36, 38, 47*n3*

race, 10, 42, 44, 51, 53, 54, 56, 57, 64, 96, 154, 156, 159; ethnicity and, 37; history of, 46, 52; language and, 101; nationality and, 5; politics of, 55
racial constructions, 10, 20, 54
racialization, 32, 33, 43, 44, 45, 108, 112–13, 121, 124
racism, viii, 4–5, 7, 8–10, 21, 27, 28, 37, 42, 54, 55, 57, 64, 68, 96, 100, 101, 113, 141, 155, 198, 216; history of, 5, 6, 111; legacies of, 56; permanent, 20; Spanish, 53

RCWS. *See* rhetoric, composition, and writing studies
recovery, 89; fracture and, 95–101; postwar, 37
recruitment: international, 194, 196, 197, 199; standard on, 205–6; third-party, 201
relationships, 7, 8, 101, 179; building, 209; civic, 63; institutional, 210; maintaining, 184–85
religion, 27, 156, 159; literacy in, 161
religious extremism, 152, 155
research, 7, 8, 31, 33, 44, 53, 72, 83, 109, 119, 122; alphabetic-based, 115; archival, 51; college, 120, 130; community, 89, 92–93, 101, 102, 145; creative, 71; critical, 124; data, 114; English-language, 96, 120; L2, 73, 74, 75, 120, 196; monocultural, 109; monolingual, 108, 109; multilingual, 108; multimodal, 115; postsecondary, 68; professional, 110, 115, 123; second-language, 33; self-advocacy and, 121; technical, 176; transnational, 92; white-gazed, 108; writing, 109, 176
responsibility, 6, 7, 35, 36, 46n1, 155, 200, 205; family, 81
rhetoric, 5, 10, 20, 29, 50, 51, 68, 69, 90; anti-Asian, 193; anti-Chinese, 193; colonial, 8; sinophobia, 198
rhetoric, composition, and writing studies (RCWS), 68, 69, 70, 71, 72, 75, 76, 82, 83
rights, 56, 61; individual, 28; migrant, 129
Rockefeller Foundation, 43
Rockwell, George Lincoln, 24, 26, 29n3
Roy, Arundhati, 67, 83
Rubin, Jon, 153, 160

Saldaña, Johnny: qualitative inquiry and, 93
scaling: elements, 70; programmatic, 72–76
Scandinavian students, American experience and, 43
Schmidt, Patricia Ruggiano, 181
schooling, 108, 117, 119, 124
Schreiber, Brooke R., 189
Schueler, Herbert, 41
Schwartz-Weinstein, Zach, 34
Scott, Tony, 215
security, 38, 133, 141, 142, 161
self-advocacy, writing and, 121
self-perception, 184, 190, 191
self-worth, literacy and, 100
Singh, Khushwant, 158, 161, 165
slavery, 5, 20, 158
Smith, M. Brewster, 39, 42, 43

social behavior, cultural difference in, 162
social change, 90, 92; education and, 61; literacy and, 51
social institutions, socializing effects of, 174
social media, 22, 29n2, 160, 184, 185
space: border, 153; curricular/physical/ideological, 45; digital, 154, 158, 160; hostile, 34, 44; professional, 120; sociocultural, 154
space-making, 153, 167
Spanish language, 57, 106, 116, 118; learning, 186
Spanish-American War, 49
Starke-Meyerring, Doreen, 171
Statement on Second Language Writing and Writers (CCCC), 73
stereotypes, 8, 107, 142, 162, 188; ethnolinguistic, 10–11; reinforcing, 172
students: Black, 33, 56; Brown, 33; categories of, 41; global, 194; language-minoritized, 45, 46, 111–12; low-income, 76; nontraditional, 76; racialized, 46, 112–13; transnational, 110, 111; undocumented, 110–12. *See also* Chinese students; foreign students; immigrant students; international students; multilingual students
students of color, 33, 76
superdiversity, 69, 75, 155
surveillance, 133; avoiding, 138, 139

Taft, William Howard, 54
TAPP. *See* Transatlantic and Pacific Project
Tardy, Christine, 194
Taylor, Breonna, 4, 46
Teaching English as a Second Language (TESOL), 91, 172, 173
technology, 12, 71, 156; choices of, 167; stealing, 193
Technology-Mediated Transitional Writing Education (TTWE), 152
telecollaboration, 152, 155t, 176
TESOL. *See* Teaching English as a Second Language
TOEFL, 208
training, 37, 39, 209; English-language, 208; rhetorical, 144, 145; scientific, 53; teacher, 210
Transatlantic and Pacific Project (TAPP), 12, 171, 172; collaborations, 175–82, 182–89, 190
translanguaging, 10, 112
translations, 41–42, 176, 178, 179
translingualism, 10, 33, 81, 82, 89, 90, 92, 112, 152; cosmopolitanism and, 68

Transnational Professional Communication, 176–77, 178
transnationalism, 33, 111; writing programs and, 195–97
Trump, Donald, 3, 4, 63; campaign slogan of, 29n1; fascism and, 22; rhetoric of, 4, 5; white nationalism and, 22–23
tuition, 41, 68; in-state, 110; international, 197
Tuskegee Institute, 56, 57

UK Brexit referendum. *See* Brexit
Understanding Rhetoric (Losh and Alexander), 131
undocumented immigration, 117, 131, 141; humanizing/accompanying/complicating, 130, 136, 143
UNESCO, 36
United Nations Sustainable Development Goals, 151
United States Naturalization Law (1790), 20
US Census, 38, 47n4

values: cultural, 98; reevaluating, 187–89
Victoria College, 76, 78, 79–80
Viera, Kate, 100
violence, 29n2, 140, 180; epistemological, 165; sectarian, 156; structural, 216
virtual exchange (VE), 151, 152, 166, 176, 189
vocabulary, 65n3, 183; building, 80; critical, 20

Wakanda, King of (T'Challa), 9, 24
Wang, Xiqiao, 197
WEAB. *See* Writing Education across Borders
white gaze, 109, 111, 112, 114, 117, 119, 120, 122, 124; globalization and, 113
white language supremacy, legacy of, 44
white nationalism, viii, 5, 8, 19, 20, 21, 22–28, 52; formation of, 23; historicizing/contextualizing/problematizing, 9; political discourse of, 23
white supremacy, 9, 21, 23, 29n4, 43, 44; absence of, 27; endurance of, 27
whiteness, 9, 33, 50, 55, 64; academic language and, 112; European, 53; superiority of, 56
whites, 26, 77; foreign-born, 39; superiority of, 5
World Englishes, 145
World War II, 4, 9, 32, 36, 43; foreign students and, 37; higher education after, 34–35
writers: categories of, 73; immigrant, 124; racialized, 120
writing courses, 80, 111, 176; L2, 73
writing education, 114, 123, 124, 130, 144–46; global turn in, 113
Writing Education across Borders (WEAB), vii, viii, 7, 215
Writing Program Administration (WPA), 195, 196
Writing Program Administration (WPA) Consultant-Evaluator Service, 73
Writing Program Administration (WPA) Outcomes Statement, 73
writing programs, 71, 79, 80, 198; establishment/management of, 197; placing assessments for, 72–73; transnationality and, 195–97; writing within/across, 69–70
writing studies, vii, 10, 68, 197
writing teachers, 83, 123–24, 129, 144, 197; material conditions of, 76; work of, 69

xenophobia, 3, 6, 21, 68, 141, 145, 152, 157, 194, 196, 216

You, Xiaoye, 50, 82, 175; educational partnerships and, 173; on IHEs, 197; study abroad programs and, 164
Yu, Han, 131

ABOUT THE AUTHORS

David S. Martins is an associate professor of rhetoric in the Department of English at Rochester Institute of Technology, where he teaches courses in Written Argument, the Rhetoric of Science, and Science Writing. Formerly the founding director of RIT's University Writing Program, he developed his interests in transnational work during a fellowship with the SUNY Collaborative Online International Learning (COIL) Institute. His digital essay "Transnational Writing Programs and Emerging Models for Writing, Teaching, and Learning" (*Kairos*) explores the changing infrastructures for transnational writing programs. His edited collection, *Transnational Writing Program Administration* (USUP), won the CCCC/NCTE 2017 Outstanding Book Award. In addition to this volume, he recently contributed to *Radiant Figures: Visual Rhetorics in Everyday Administrative Contexts*, edited by Rachel Gramer, Logan Bearden, and Derek Mueller: https://ccdigitalpress.org/radiant-figures.

Brooke R. Schreiber is an assistant professor in the English Department of Baruch College, where she teaches courses in second-language writing, globalization of English, language and social media, and other topics in linguistics. Her research focuses on second-language writing pedagogy, translingualism, combating native-speakerism, and global Englishes in teacher education. Her work has appeared in a variety of journals, including *TESOL Quarterly*, the *Journal of Second Language Writing*, the *ELT Journal*, *Language Learning and Technology*, *Composition Studies*, *Composition Forum*, and *Praxis*. She has also contributed to edited collections such as *Transnational Writing Education: Theory and Practice*, *Reconciling Translingualism and Second Language Writing* and *Language Teacher Education for Global Englishes*. In addition to the current volume, she is coeditor of *Linguistic Justice on Campus: Pedagogy and Advocacy for Multilingual Writers*.

Xiaoye You is liberal arts professor of English and Asian studies at The Pennsylvania State University and founder of the Writing Education across Borders (WEAB) Conference. His first monograph, *Writing in the Devil's Tongue: A History of English Composition in China*, won the 2011 CCCC Outstanding Book Award. His recent book, *Cosmopolitan English and Transliteracy*, arguing for ethical use of English in everyday life and for cultivating global citizens in English literacy education, received the 2018 CCCC Research Impact Award.

Olga Aksakalova is an associate professor of English and coordinator of the Collaborative Online International Learning program at LaGuardia Community College, City University of New York. Her research interests include civic engagement in transnational writing programs; International Virtual Exchange (IVE) program administration; IVE in the humanities; twentieth-century American literature, and autobiography studies.

Sara P. Alvarez is an assistant professor of English at Queens College, City University of New York (CUNY), and Associate Investigator with CUNY's Initiative on Immigration and Education (CUNY-IIE). Her research focuses on the intersections and frictions between language, literacy, and race, specifically as directly impacting immigrant communities.

About the Authors

Brody Bluemel is associate professor of applied linguistics at Delaware State University and serves as department chairperson, director of the MA TESOL/Bilingual Education program and the English Language Institute. His research interests include corpus linguistics, parallel corpora and pedagogy, language learning technology, and dual-language immersion education.

Tuli Chatterji is an associate professor in the Department of English at LaGuardia Community College, City University of New York. Her research interests include postcolonial literature, queer studies, and composition theory and pedagogy. She has led and participated in multiple international virtual exchange pedagogical projects.

Keith Gilyard is Edwin Erle Sparks Professor of English and African American Studies at Penn State. He served as chair of the Conference on College Composition and Communication and president of the National Council of Teachers of English. His books include *True to the Language Game* and, with Adam Banks, *On African-American Rhetoric*.

Joleen Hanson, professor of English at the University of Wisconsin–Stout (Menomonie, WI), teaches courses in transnational professional communication, technical editing, and first-year composition. Her research focuses on factors affecting student engagement in international educational partnerships, uptake of peer feedback in interdisciplinary, intercultural contexts, and language-level features of undergraduate academic writing.

Rebecca Lorimer Leonard is associate professor of English and director of the Writing Program at the University of Massachusetts Amherst, where she teaches undergraduate and graduate courses on language diversity, literacy studies, and research methods.

Layli Maria Miron, PhD, is Associate Director of University Writing at Auburn University. In this role, she supports the operations of the Miller Writing Center, pursuing a longstanding interest in writing centers. If you find yourself in eastern Alabama, she encourages you to stop by for a sweet tea and talk about writing, peer tutoring, and intercultural learning.

Florianne Jimenez Perzan is assistant professor of English and co-director of the Writing Center at the University of Massachusetts Boston, where she specializes in postcolonial/decolonial theory, writing center studies, multilingual writing, and cultural rhetorics. She holds a PhD in English from the University of Massachusetts Amherst.

Tony Scott is associate professor in the Department of Writing Studies, Rhetoric, and Composition at Syracuse University. His publications include *Dangerous Writing: Understanding the Political Economy of Composition* and the coedited collections *Tenured Bosses and Disposable Teachers: Writing Instruction in the Managed University* and *Composition in the Age of Austerity*.

Kate Vieira is professor and Susan J. Cellmer Distinguished Chair in Literacy at the University of Wisconsin–Madison. She is the author of *American by Paper* (2016) and *Writing for Love and Money* (2019), and she coedited *Paz: Escribiendo un Corazón Común* (2019). Her scholarship has been recognized by CCCC, the Literacy Research Association, and the Fulbright Association.

Amy J. Wan is associate professor of English at Queens College and the CUNY Graduate Center. She is author of *Producing Good Citizens: Literacy Training in Anxious Times* (2014). Her current project analyzes institutional change and linguistic justice in the US global university.

www.ingramcontent.com/pod-product-compliance
Lightning Source LLC
Chambersburg PA
CBHW020525080526
44583CB00013B/735